Old Thiess,
a Livonian Werewolf

Old Thiess,
a Livonian Werewolf

*A Classic Case in
Comparative Perspective*

Carlo Ginzburg and Bruce Lincoln

The University of Chicago Press
Chicago and London

The University of Chicago Press, Chicago 60637
The University of Chicago Press, Ltd., London
© 2020 by The University of Chicago
All rights reserved. No part of this book may be used or reproduced in any manner
whatsoever without written permission, except in the case of brief quotations in
critical articles and reviews. For more information, contact the University of Chicago
Press, 1427 East 60th Street, Chicago, IL 60637.
Published 2020
Printed in the United States of America

29 28 27 26 25 24 23 22 21 20   1 2 3 4 5

ISBN-13: 978-0-226-67438-4 (cloth)
ISBN-13: 978-0-226-67441-4 (paper)
ISBN-13: 978-0-226-67455-1 (e-book)
DOI: https://doi.org/10.7208/chicago/9780226674551.001.0001

The University of Chicago Press gratefully acknowledges the generous support of
the Divinity School and the Franke Institute for the Humanities at the University of
Chicago toward the publication of this book.

Library of Congress Cataloging-in-Publication Data

Names: Ginzburg, Carlo, author. | Lincoln, Bruce, author, translator. | Höfler, Otto,
    1901–
Title: Old Thiess, a Livonian werewolf : a classic case in comparative perspective /
    Carlo Ginzburg, Bruce Lincoln.
Description: Chicago ; London : The University of Chicago Press, 2020. | Some text
    translated from German. | Includes bibliographical references and index.
Identifiers: LCCN 2019029998 | ISBN 9780226674384 (cloth) | ISBN 9780226674414
    (paperback) | ISBN 9780226674551 (ebook)
Subjects: LCSH: Old Thiess, active 17th century—Trials, litigation, etc. |
    Werewolves—Livonia—History—17th century. | Werewolves—Livonia—
    Religious aspects. | Trials (Witchcraft)—Livonia.
Classification: LCC GR830.W4 G56 2020 | DDC 398.24/54094798—dc23
LC record available at https://lccn.loc.gov/2019029998

♾ This paper meets the requirements of ANSI/NISO Z39.48-1992 (Permanence
of Paper).

Contents

Figures and Tables

Figures

Tables

Introduction

BRUCE LINCOLN

I

Although werewolves abound in folklore, fiction, film, and rumor, relatively few people have been formally charged with being werewolves, and even fewer have accepted that word as an accurate description of themselves. Most of our information for such realia comes from surviving court records that preserve fewer than three hundred cases.[1] And like most defendants of whatever sort, the majority of accused werewolves initially denied the charges. When tortured, however, they regularly confessed, echoing—and thereby reinforcing—both learned and popular stereotypes. Cumulatively, these records permit a historian to understand what European theologians and jurists of the early modern period believed about werewolves, the power these people had to project those beliefs onto others, and the price some poor souls paid as a result.

The case that concerns us is strikingly different.

II

In October 1691, an elderly Latvian peasant sat patiently as he waited to testify at the trial of a fellow villager accused of stealing from the local church. Before he could do so, however, another witness laughed at the idea of this man swearing a solemn oath, since he was commonly known to be a werewolf. And when the man, known to everyone as "Old Thiess" (a nickname for Mātiss, the Latvian equivalent of Matthew),[2] confirmed it was so, the court turned its attention to him.

Hours of questions and answers followed in a high-stakes struggle between decidedly unequal forces. For their part, the judges, and then the village pastor, pressed Thiess to acknowledge that as a werewolf he had given himself to the devil. This he staunchly denied, while admitting that he could change himself into a wolf and that he had, along with fellow werewolves, stolen livestock in that form. Most surprisingly, he described how his werewolf band entered hell at certain times of the year, not to serve Satan—as the judges insisted—but to fight him, with the well-being of people, herds, and crops dependent on the outcome.

Thiess sought not to deny the specific charge but to correct his accusers' prejudices and instruct them on the true, benevolent, distinctly non-Satanic nature of werewolves, a group he understood far better than they.[3] At times, the judges were shocked by the old man's explanations; at others, they reacted with mixed amusement, curiosity, confusion, and frustration. Unable to obtain a confession or adduce evidence that would confirm the key point of diabolic collusion, they failed to reach a verdict on "so difficult and doubtful a case."[4] Accordingly, they decided to have the case reviewed at a later session of the court, with different judges presiding.[5] Apparently, those judges based their verdict on the trial's transcript, which—fortunately for us—was then preserved in the court's archives.

III

For more than two centuries, that transcript sat in the archives of the High Court of Dorpat (today's Tartu) until Hermann von Bruiningk (1849–1927), Latvia's foremost specialist in the nation's premodern history, made it the centerpiece of his pioneering article "The Werewolf in Livonia."[6] Von Bruiningk, exceptionally adept at archival research, was a man of strong nationalist sentiments and proud of his descent in a line of Baltic German nobles.[7] Writing in 1924, shortly after the Baltic republics gained independence, he wished to rebut longstanding stereotypes that made Livonia (a historical region encompassing parts of today's Latvia and Estonia) the classic home of werewolves, much as Transylvania is associated with vampires.[8] On the basis of a thorough investigation of church and legal records, which uncovered barely a trace of werewolf lore before the middle of the sixteenth century, von Bruiningk argued that demonological theories originating elsewhere in Europe had made their way to the Baltic around that time via the learned writings of Olaus Magnus (Sweden's last Catholic archbishop) and others. Through the lens of these imported theories, the latent (and benign) traces of pre-Christian religiosity were misconstrued as diabolical dangers.

As von Bruiningk wrote,

> In Christian times, when people acknowledged the existence of the heathen gods only in order to identify them with the devil, the heathen cult was represented as the horror of devil worship, the servants of the gods as the devil's servants, and the belief in witches began here, with the idea of people who, with Satan's help, change into wolves out of pure bloodthirstiness.[9]

While werewolf beliefs were an "ancient superstition," well attested in legends and folklore throughout all Europe, von Bruiningk found that court records seriously exaggerated and prejudicially distorted the phenomenon in ways that reflected—and also helped maintain and justify—the asymmetric power relations that played out in the dynamics of accusation, denial, torture, and confession. Even so, he did not believe the image of the werewolf found in court records was something the demonologists had fabricated ex nihilo. Rather, following Wilhelm Hertz's *Der Werwolf*, the most authoritative work on the subject in his era, he imagined that in the pre-Christian Baltic, as elsewhere in Europe, "Aryan" religiosity included divine beings who mediated the distinction between human and animal, combining the powers and good qualities of both:[10]

We must consider how much more intimate the relation of *Natur-völker* to the natural world, especially the animal world, had to have been than is true in our environment. Indeed, the "distinction of rank" between human and animal, as Hertz has expressed it, properly first comes to consciousness with our race. For millennia, humans waged struggles for existence in which so many animals surpassed them in strength, agility, and cunning, indeed, even in diligence and readiness, that people's perception and imagination inevitably produced the humanization of certain animals. Conversely, it is no shock that animal fables and animal symbols in their highest elaboration stumble into the deification of animals, or that the restless fantasy of humans, not content with the natural world, adds all sorts of fabulous animal forms like griffins, dragons, vampires, etc.[11]

In von Bruiningk's opinion, old beliefs of this sort became "latent" with the coming of Christianity, although surviving traces gave grist to the demonologists' mill.[12] In this situation, Old Thiess's testimony provided a rare window onto the pre-Christian Baltic, a world where werewolves were good. Conversely, the discourse of the court authorities (judges and pastor) let one see how foreign rulers — Germans, Swedes, and Russians — distorted and misconstrued surviving elements of the older religion, while stigmatizing and oppressing the population that preserved them.[13]

IV

Von Bruiningk was interested in what Old Thiess could reveal about Livonian prehistory, not in werewolves per se. Accordingly, he published his article, which included the full transcript of the Thiess trial, in a journal of which he was the editor, which would reach like-minded readers: the *Mitteilungen aus der livländischen Geschichte*, official organ of the Society of History and Ancient Studies in Riga. Within a few years, the piece had stimulated research along similar lines by other scholars in the Baltic,[14] but it also found its way to Otto Höfler (1901–1987), whose National Socialist commitments led him to see the wild violence attributed to werewolves not as a slander to be rebutted but as the manifestation of admirable energies he associated with a primordial past very different from the one von Bruiningk had imagined.

Höfler shared von Bruiningk's and Hertz's sense that werewolf beliefs provided evidence of "Aryan" religion (although he placed the Aryan homeland in northern Europe, rather than central Asia, and thought Germans best preserved the Aryan blood and spirit). Like von Bruiningk, Höfler was quite taken with the idea of a "good" werewolf who fought on behalf of his people, although their ideas of the good differed significantly.

When von Bruiningk's article alerted Höfler to Old Thiess's testimony, Höfler had just completed a *Habilitationsschrift* equally erudite and tendentious, in the field of *Germanistik*, which combined philological, folkloric, and *religionsgeschichtliche* methods and materials. Most broadly, he argued that male cultic associations and secret societies (*Männerbünde*) were an ancient Germanic institution of great importance, exercising such strong religious, social, political, and moral power that the state itself originated in that context.[15]

According to Höfler's reconstruction, groups of this sort cultivated techniques of ecstasy involving both poetic inspiration and warrior frenzy, i.e., intellectual and physical prowess. In addition, they performed seasonal rituals (initiations, carnivalesque masquerades, etc.), celebrating and renewing the solidarity of living warriors with their ancestors. Werewolves figured prominently in the groups' ideology, symbolism, and cultic practice, because "werewolves often pass for the returning dead."[16]

Höfler found this idea in Hertz's book, the same volume that had given von Bruiningk his model of the "Aryan" werewolf as a benevolent being whose nature and powers transcended the distinctions of animal, human, and divine. Höfler, in contrast, picked up on something Hertz theorized as a second, very different type of werewolf that mediates the categories of living and dead. As Hertz put it, in a passage Höfler cited: "Here, a type of werewolf must be recognized that points to another, much eerier body of traditions, i.e., the ghostly werewolf, which is of a type with the vampire. Here, the werewolf is not a transformed living man, but a corpse arising from the grave in the form of a wolf."[17]

Höfler imagined that his *Männerbundler* cultivated solidarity with their dead, donning wolf pelts and engaging in wolfish behaviors as a means to effect that communion. In his view, accounts of raging werewolf bands preserved the memory of such cultic celebrations, often timed to coincide with the harvest or winter solstice. Höfler had already developed these ideas before reading von Bruiningk's article, but, upon doing so, he took Old Thiess's testimony to confirm his theories on virtually all points and, further, to demonstrate that *Männerbünde* were still active as late as the 1690s in backwaters like Livonia. Accordingly, just before publishing his dissertation, he inserted a bit less than half of the trial transcript as an appendix to the volume, accompanied by his commentary.[18]

In his enthusiasm for Thiess, Höfler failed to note that spirits of the dead figure nowhere in the old man's account. No matter. They were omnipresent in the songs, ideology, and practices of the other, more recent *Männerbünde*, with which Höfler was quite familiar and whose subtextual presence haunts his pages—namely, the Nazi SA, of whose Viennese branch Höfler was an early member, and the SS, to whose ideological branch Heinrich Himmler recruited him after reading his book.[19]

V

Its Nazi subtexts notwithstanding, Höfler's volume was read and greatly appreciated by some of the twentieth century's foremost historians of religions, including Georges Dumézil, Stig Wikander, Geo Widengren, and Mircea Eliade, and by the 1960s it had become something of a classic.[20] The authors of the present volume were both exposed to the book relatively early in their careers (Ginzburg in the mid-1960s, Lincoln in the early 1970s), thanks to which they made Old Thiess's acquaintance. Both found the old werewolf fascinating and sympathetic; both were profoundly dissatisfied with Höfler's analysis-cum-appropriation of him, although one of us (Ginzburg) realized this earlier than the other.[21]

Each of us pondered the case for a good many years, while working on other projects. Ultimately, we each sought to resituate and reinterpret Thiess's testimony, although we pursued that end via different approaches. Ginzburg assembled a vast set of *comparanda* based on morphological resemblances that, in his view, showed Thiess to have preserved a Eurasian style of shamanic religiosity from a period far earlier than the "Aryan" age von Bruiningk and Höfler had contemplated. Lincoln, in contrast and in some measure reacting against both Ginzburg and Höfler, used a comparison of Thiess's testimony to the judges' preconceptions and the learned literature they drew on to situate their debate about the nature of the werewolf within the context of the social tensions that characterized early modern Livonia. Notwithstanding our different methods and interpretations, we both agree that the trial transcript holds extraordinary interest, for it is not often one has the privilege of hearing a werewolf struggle to explain his practices, beliefs, and very being.

Even so, we think it a dangerous exaggeration to regard the document as *unique*, for two reasons. First, more specific, because we have found other reports, testimonies, and examples that resemble Thiess's account in some (but never all) ways or relate to it in one fashion or another. We do not always agree about the extent and significance of their similarities, but close analysis of them has consistently helped clarify Thiess's testimony, sometimes by commonality and sometimes by contrast. Second, more general, because we are convinced that were any human datum so unusual as to be truly incomparable — and we believe none is so — it would be so isolated, so wildly unprecedented and anomalous, that there would be no basis for its understanding and interpretation. Better, then, to describe the Thiess trial as extraordinary, exceptional, and/or astonishing, not just for its compelling content but for the questions of method it inevitably provokes: To what can one reasonably compare this incredible text? How should one manage that comparison? And what does one hope to learn from it?

Over the past several years, we have traded thoughts on this topic, and the exchange has helped both of us sharpen our analysis and deepen our understanding, although neither one has changed his mind in dramatic ways. The question of what to make of Old Thiess thus remains open; this volume brings together materials that might help others carry the inquiry further. These include the first English translation of the complete trial transcript (chapter 1); Höfler's discussion of Old Thiess in connection with his *Männerbund* theory, again translated for the first time (chapter 2); the four publications in which Ginzburg gradually placed the old werewolf in the framework of pre-Christian Eurasian shamanism (chapter 3); Lincoln's Hayes-Robinson lecture of 2015, critiquing Ginzburg's reconstruction and focusing on the Livonian context (chapter 4); Ginzburg's Bogotá lecture of 2017, responding to Lincoln's lecture (chapter 5); and a long letter in which Lincoln responds to Ginzburg's Bogotá lecture (chapter 6). The volume concludes with the transcript of a conversation held in the autumn of 2017 to think through the issues and materials in dialogue with each other (chapter 7). The exchange over the years has been pointed at times, but consistently challenging, collegial, and productive. We hope others find the materials as intriguing as we do and that this book stimulates further exploration of the issues we have raised. Old Thiess deserves no less.

Introduction, a Postscript

CARLO GINZBURG

This book can be described as a historical experiment that starts from a single document and explores its possible contexts. As Marcel Mauss famously observed, "A single case analyzed in depth will suffice to provide the basis for an extensive comparison."[1] Today, in an era of big data, a project like this may sound irrelevant. Even more so, since the document we start from is exceptional (although not unique). But exceptional in what sense?

I

Compared to the massive, heterogenous evidence (literary, judicial, medical, and so on) about werewolves dating from Greek and Roman antiquity, the 1691 trial of Old Thiess, a Latvian peasant, is exceptional both as a document and in its content, being thus doubly anomalous.[2] But, as Thomas Kuhn argued in his famous book *The Structure of Scientific Revolutions*, anomalies can identify the limitations of a well-established scientific paradigm, paving the way to the construction of a new paradigm.[3] Even if the implications of our experiment would turn out to be minimal, its legitimacy should not be questioned.

It has been objected, however, that the category of "werewolves" is it-self misleading, since it arbitrarily conflates local phenomena that differ in their particulars.[4] In principle, such an objection looks dubious, since every word historians use has more-than-local dimensions. It must be admitted, however, that although Thiess's voice is filtered by a notary and possibly by a translator, the discourse that figures in the transcript of his trial involves some *emic*—and not just *etic*—categories, to echo the distinction familiar to linguists and anthropologists between actors' and observers' categories.[5] How can we approach Thiess's singular voice?

A preliminary remark is needed: the distinction between etic and emic categories opens a series of Chinese boxes, not a simple dichot-omy. In a passage of his *Otia imperialia*, Gervase of Tilbury (1155–1234) wrote: "In England we have often seen men change into wolves ac-cording to the phases of the moon. The Gauls call men of this kind *gerulfi*, while the English name for them is *werewolf*, *were* being the English equivalent of *vir* ['man']."[6]

Gervase of Tilbury's medieval Latin lists the vernacular nouns in which the actors' categories were (perhaps) articulated. A large part of the evidence related to werewolves displays this double distance. To quote an example that is closer in both time and space to the trial of Old Thiess: in the 1670s, the German physician Rosinus Lentilius spoke scornfully of Latvian peasants, calling them "cunning people, treacherous and most deceitful" (*vafra gens, versipellis et dolosissima*). Clearly, Lenti-lius was playing on the ambiguity of *versipellis*, a Latin term that can mean "cunning people" but more literally denotes a shapeshifter or werewolf, as in a famous passage of Pliny's *Natural History* (VIII, chapter 37 [22]).[7] To take that word as evidence for a continuity of beliefs about werewolves from antiquity to seventeenth-century Latvian peasants would obviously be absurd—even if such continuity may have existed in Lentilius's mind. But sometimes even a piece of evidence written in Latin can lead us closer to the most unexpected features of Old Thiess's trial. In his *Encomion urbis Rigae Livoniae emporii celeberrimi* (1615), Heinrich von Ulenbrock commented on the beliefs about werewolves shared by Latvian peasants:

> Oh vanity of vanities! Oh deplorable illusion! Have the peasants of Li-vonia been once maddened by such ungodliness, I wonder, that they

succumb to the same insanity today, in the light of the Gospel, and that they even dare to invoke a most precious title for their diabolical cabal [sect]? For they consider themselves to be in friendship and familiarity with God, and they call themselves the friends of God.[8]

The convergence between von Ulenbrock's remark and Thiess's claim that werewolves like himself were "hounds of God" seems to open up, it has been argued, "two distinct windows onto the world of a peasant counterculture."[9] Such convergence was perhaps not limited to Livonia.

II

In the early seventeenth century, an intensive witch-hunt took place in the Pays de Labourd, the French part of the Basque region. A few years later, Pierre de Lancre, who had been actively involved in those trials as a judge (he was royal counselor at the Parliament of Bordeaux) published a treatise based on his own experience: *Tableau de l'inconstance des mauvais anges et demons, où il est amplement traicté des sorciers et de la sorcellerie* (Paris, 1613). De Lancre spoke at length of werewolves and their diabolical transformations; but he also mentioned that, strangely enough, some werewolves claimed to be the enemies of witches. As an example of this bizarre claim, he referred to a case described by the Italian bishop Simone Maioli in his massive work *Dies caniculares*.[10] The event had taken place in Riga—or possibly Reggio, guessed de Lancre, who had spent some years in Italy and was fluent in Italian.[11] But de Lancre was wrong. Maioli was tacitly quoting a page from Kaspar Peucer's *Commentarius de praecipuis generibus divinationum*, a "true narrative" about a Livonian peasant who, like the mythical Lycaon, was able to turn himself into a wolf. The peasant had proudly said he was pursuing a witch (*venefica*, literally, "poisoner") who was flying around in the shape of a fire-colored butterfly: "Werewolves boast that they are compelled to keep away witches," commented Peucer, literally echoed by Maioli.[12]

This remark helped de Lancre to make sense of a case he described in detail in his *Tableau*. Jean Grenier, a thirteen-year-old boy, had been put on trial in 1603 as a werewolf and condemned to spend his life in a

Franciscan convent. Due to his young age, he had not been submitted to torture. In 1610, de Lancre, clearly intrigued, decided to have a long conversation with the young man (who died the year after). After a vivid description of Jean Grenier's physical appearance, de Lancre remarked: "Il n'était aucunement hébeté" (He was not in the least an idiot).[13] "He naively confessed to me," de Lancre went on, "that he had been a werewolf, and therefore he had run across the country by order of the Lord of the Forest. He said this freely to everybody, without denying anything, believing that he was exempt from any reproach or guilt, since he wasn't a werewolf anymore."[14]

"In the past," de Lancre explained, "it has been said that this Lord of the Forest hunts down witches and wizards across woods and fields, and takes them out of their coffins when they die, enjoying tormenting and pursuing them even after their death."[15]

The young werewolf, commented de Lancre, "did not invent the name of Lord of the Forest, as he labels the evil spirit."[16] The distance between the actors' and the observers' categories is explicit. De Lancre had no doubts: the Lord of the Forest, the "big, black man" who had given Jean Grenier his wolf's skin, was a demon. But de Lancre also duly recorded the beliefs related to the Lord of the Forest, associating him with the Livonian werewolves as enemies of witches.

III

The resemblances between the two cases—young Jean Grenier and Old Thiess—are striking. Their confessions, in both cases immune from torture, far from being isolated inventions, seem to point to a more ancient layer of beliefs that were later turned into diabolical witchcraft.[17] Are we entitled to consider, as a linguist would do, the Basque country and Livonia as two peripheral areas, vis-à-vis the area in which the witches' sabbath stereotype first emerged? Are we allowed to look at the two cases in a comparative perspective? "A single case analyzed in depth will suffice to provide the basis for an extensive comparison," Mauss wrote. But how extensive? On this issue, our project coalesced: a sometimes polemical, but always friendly dialogue, which we would like to share with our readers.

The Trial

This trial transcript was filed in the Hofger-Archiv Kriminalakte n. 30 v. J. 1692 and was first published by Hermann von Bruiningk, in his article "Der Werwolf in Livland und das letzte im Wendenschen Landgericht und Dörptschen Hofgericht i. J. 1692 deshalb stattgehabte Strafverfahren," *Mitteilungen aus der livländischen Geschichte* 22 (1924–28): 203–20. I am grateful to Stefan Donecker, Kenneth Northcott, Bernard McGinn, and Louise Lincoln for their help with the translation.—B. L.

Transcript from the Hearings at the Provincial Court of Venden (April 28, 1691)

Judicial Acts of the Royal Court of the provincial district of Venden [today's Cēsis] held at Jürgensburg, the 28th of April, 1691

From the above named trial, from the state's complaint against the church thief of Jürgensburg [today's Jaunpils], Pirsen Tönnis, and further concerning an inhabitant of Kaltenbrunn [today's Kniediņi] named Old Thiess

With regard to Lycanthropy and other prohibited and impious acts (*prohibitorum et nefandorum gestorum*).

Presiding judges: Assessor Bengt Johan Ackerstaff, as substitute District Court Judge Assessor Gabriel Berger.

[1] Thereafter, the Kaltenbrunn innkeeper Peter smiled after taking the oath of witnesses. He was asked: Why did he do that?

A: Since he saw that his tenant, Old Thiess, also had to swear.

Q: Why should that man's testimony concerning the church thief not be confirmed by an oath as well as his own?

A: Everyone knows that he goes around with the devil and was a werewolf. How could Old Thiess swear an oath, since he would not lie about such things and he had pursued them for many years?

[2] Old Thiess was charged accordingly, after hearing the other witnesses giving this testimony with reproaches, and he freely admitted that he had previously been a werewolf. However, he had given it up again after a time and truly that was about ten years ago. He further reported that this had already come up in the case at Nitau [today's Nītaure], where Herr Baron Crohnstern, Herr Rosenthal, and Caulich were still judges, regarding the time Skeistan, a peasant from Lemburg [today's Mālpils] who had recently died, broke Thiess's nose when he was carrying back the grain blossoms that Skeistan winnowed in hell in order to take away the growth of the grain. But the aforementioned judges in that case did nothing to him; rather, they only laughed at it and as Skeistan did not appear, they let him go free again.

[3] A broader inquiry was asked about him: Was Thiess always in good health and with his wits about him? Had he not been, and was he not still, somewhat mad? Whereupon, in addition to the others present who knew Thiess well, the substitute Herr District Court Judge Bengt Johan Ackerstaff, on whose estate Thiess had lived and worked for several years, declared that he understood his health never to have failed him, also that he never lied about such things, and when the aforementioned judges did nothing and let him go free in the earlier case, he was idolized by the peasants.

[4] He was asked this: In what place and at what time had Skeistan struck him and with what?

A: In hell, with a broomstick on which a horsetail was tied.

The Herr Presiding Judge testified that at that time Thiess's nose was injured.

[5] Q: How did the witness come to hell and where is that located?

A: The werewolves go thither on foot in wolf form, to the place at the end of the lake called Puer Esser, in a swamp below Lemburg about a half mile from Klingenberg [today's Akenstaka], the estate of the substitute Herr Presiding Judge. There were lordly chambers and commissioned doorkeepers, who stoutly resist those who want to take back the grain blossoms and the grain the sorcerers brought there. The grain blossoms were guarded in a special container and the grain in another.

[6] Q: Which form do they assume when they transform themselves into wolves?

A: They have a wolf pelt, which only they put on. He had it from a peasant of Marienburg [today's Alūksne], who came from Riga, and he turned it over to a peasant from Alla [today's Allaži] a few years ago. But in response to a question, he would not name either of them. And when a special inquiry was made, he changed his story and said they just went into the bush and took off their normal clothes and immediately changed to wolves. They ran about as wolves and seized whatever horses and livestock fell to them, but he had taken no large animals, only lambs, kids, piglets, and the like. But in the area of Segewold [today's Sigulda] there was a farmhand named Tyrummen, now dead, and he was truly extraordinary. The witness was nothing compared to him, as one person is given more power than another by the devil and that man had taken such large animals as presented themselves, including fattened pigs, and he carried these off from the farm. And then he feasted with his company, as twenty or thirty of them often came together along the road, roasted the animals, and devoured a huge amount.

[7] Q: How did they get fire and tools there?

A: They took fire from the farmstead and made spits out of wood. They took a cauldron from the farmstead and singed the hair off the animals. They eat nothing raw.

[8] Q: Did the witness often take part in such meals and find himself at banquets?

A: Yes, and so what?

Q: What happened to the small animals he had taken?

A: These they also consumed.

[9] Q: If they were transformed into wolves, why didn't they eat meat raw, as wolves do?

A: That wasn't the way. Rather, they eat it like men, roasted.

[10] Q: How could they handle things, if according to his testimony they had wolves' heads and paws? With what could they hold knives, prepare the food, or use other tools to accomplish their work?

A: They used no knives, but tore pieces off with their teeth, and with their paws they stuck the pieces on spits that they found, and when they consumed the meat, they had already turned back into men, but they made no use of bread. They took salt with them from the farmstead as they departed.

[11] Q: Did they fully sate themselves and did the devil eat with them?

A: He affirms the first point and denies the second [*Prius affirmat, posterius negat*]. But the sorcerers [*die zaubere*] eat with the devil in hell. The werewolves were not admitted there with them. Nevertheless, they sometimes quickly run in and snatch something, then run back with it as if fleeing. If they are caught, the guards appointed by the devil strike them with long iron goads they call canes [*ruten*] and they hunt them down as if they were dogs, for the devil can't stand them—*Ne eretz* in the Latvian idiom.

[12] Q: If the devil can't bear them, why do they become werewolves and run to hell?

A: It happens for this reason, that they thereby might drag out of hell the things the sorcerers brought there: animals, grain, and other produce. In the previous year, he and the others had delayed and they did not come into hell at the right time when the gates were still open, so they couldn't carry off the grain blossoms and the grain the sorcerers had taken inside, and we had a bad year for grain. But this year, he and the others did the right things at the proper time. The witness himself brought out of hell as much barley, oats, and rye as he could carry. Therefore, this year we have all kinds of grain in abundance, although more oats than barley.

[13] Q: When do such things take place?

A: On St. Lucia's Eve before Christmas.

Q: How often in the year do they go into hell together?

A: Ordinarily thrice: Pentecost Eve, St. John's Eve, and St. Lucia's Eve. The first two are not always exactly on these nights, but when the grain is blossoming. Then and at the time of sowing, the sorcerers carry off the yield [lit. *segen*, the yield obtained by God's grace] and thereafter carry it into hell, so the werewolves work hard to bring it back.

[14] Q: Who was with him in this company the last St. Lucia's Eve?

A: They came from many places, those from Rodenpeisch [today's Ropaži] and Sunszel [today's Suntaži] together. Who knew them all or asked after their names? There were different bands. Before this, Skeistan Rein, son of the abovementioned Skeistan, had been in his band, but now he didn't see him there and he didn't know how that happened.

To a question regarding the men of Jürgensburg [today's Jaunpils], he said: Those of Jürgensburg must belong to another band, for one finds few of them in his band.

[15] Q: How could the witness say that on last St. Lucia's Eve they had already brought back this year's prosperity from hell, which the sorcerers had taken there, since the sowing and blossoming time was now just approaching and thus nothing could yet be harvested?

A: The sorcerers had their own special time and the devil had already sowed long before. Thereafter, the sorcerers took something from that and brought it to hell, and this was the prosperity the werewolves carried back out of hell, and subsequently much growth followed from our seed, just as rich fruit was obtained from the trees, which was also taken from hell, as was good fishing. Already since Christmas there was perfectly verdant grain of all sorts and trees, whose growth similarly came from hell. Since they also brought a lot of fish back from the sorcerers last St. Lucia's Eve, one could hope for better fishing this year. Nevertheless, if the sorcerers also took the grain blossoms and took them to hell, they would have nothing to work with, except what was sown and grew in hell.

[16] Q: Whenever they go to other feasts at that place in hell, do they find such buildings and do the same ones consistently stay there?

A: Yes.

Q: How is it that the other people who dwell nearby can't also see this?

A: It's not on top but under the earth, and the entrance is protected by a gate that no one can find, except someone who belongs inside.

[17] Q: Weren't there women and girls among the werewolves? Also were Germans found among them?

A: Women were certainly among the werewolves, but girls were not. Rather, they were of use to the flying sprites [*Puicken*] or dragons and were sent out to take away the yield of milk and butter. The Germans don't join their company; rather, they have a special hell of their own.

[18]: Q: Where do the werewolves go after death?

A: They are buried like other people and their souls come to heaven, but the devil takes the sorcerers' souls for himself.

Q: Is the witness diligent toward the church, does he listen faithfully to the word of God, does he pray diligently, and does he take the Lord's Supper?

A: No, he does neither the one nor the other.

[19] Q: How can the soul of someone who does not serve God, but the devil, and who does not go to church, seldom to confession, and does not take the Lord's Supper, as the witness admitted of himself, ever come to God?

A: The werewolves do not serve the devil, for they take away from him that which the sorcerers brought him, and for that reason the devil is so hostile to them that he cannot bear them. Rather, he has them driven off with iron goads, as if they were dogs, for the werewolves are God's hounds. But the sorcerers serve the devil and do everything according to his will, therefore their souls belong to him. Everything the werewolves do profits people best, for if they didn't exist and the devil made off with the prosperity, robbed or stole it, all the world's prosperity would depart, and (the witness) confirmed this with an oath, adding that in the preceding year, the Russian werewolves came earlier and recovered the prosperity of their land. Therefore they had had good growth in their land, while that of this land failed, for they had come too late on this side. But this year they came before the Russians and thus it was a fruitful year and good for flax. And why should God not accept his soul, even if he didn't go to church or take the Lord's Supper, for in his youth he was not properly instructed in this.

[20] Q: Was not evil done, as he admits, by the theft of his neighbor's animals, but also to the image of God in which he as a man had been shaped, by replacing his own proper form with that of a wolf? He broke the oath he had sworn to his savior Christ as part of his holy baptism, in which he had renounced the devil, all his creatures and works. Having forgotten God's way, he committed other highly forbidden sins of similar sort, consistently turning to abomination and scandal, not to God's house where he formerly could come to knowledge and service of God through preaching and Christian instruction. Instead, he preferred to run to hell. But did not the Herr Pastor still nurture the farmhands and diligently exhort them to come to prayer and to church and to let themselves be instructed?

A: He had done little harm to livestock; others did much more. It was true that the pastor nurtured the farmhands, whom he instructed and who prayed with him. The witness also prayed according to what the pastor had recited to him, but having once fallen into ways from which he could not extricate himself, he could not still learn new things at his age.

[21] Q: How old is he and where was he born?

A: When the Swedes captured Riga [1621], he already knew how to plow and harrow. He was by birth a Kurländer.

[22] Q: If he still was in hell last St. Lucia's Eve, why did he previously maintain that he had long before already handed over his wolf-vocation to a peasant from Alla?

A: He had not spoken the truth in that, but now he wanted to renounce that, as he had no more strength and was old.

[23] Q: What advantage did he gain from becoming a werewolf, since in most obvious ways he was a poor man and thoroughly powerless?

A: None. Rather, a scoundrel from Marienburg did this to him by a drink of something he brought and thus from that time on he had to conduct himself like the other werewolves.

[24] Q: Did they receive any sign from the devil through which he could know them?

A: No, but the devil branded the sorcerers and was generous with them, and fed them with dead horses' heads, lizards, snakes, and similar vermin.

[25] Q: Since he is now so old and feeble that he must expect his death any day, does he want to die as a werewolf?

A: No. Before his death, he wants to impart it to another, to whom he alone can convey it.

[26] Q: In what way will he impart this to another?

A: He will do as happened to him and one is permitted only once to drink and to breathe into the tankard three times, and to say the words "It will be for you as it was for me" (*Es werde dir so wie mir*), and if the recipient receives and accepts the tankard, the witness will then be freed from it.

[27] Q: Did he not think that such a thing was also a sin and a delusion from the devil? Can he impart it to anyone unless that man, like him, knows nothing about God and himself chooses to accept it?

A: He can freely impart it to no one except a man who chooses to accept it and wants to have it. But many have already spoken to him about it, since he is old and feeble, so that he might cede it to them.

[28] Q: Who are the ones who spoke to him thus?

A: They were far from here, some around the Herr Judge's estate, some below Sunszel and he knew not to tell their names.

[29] Q: If the witness and others transformed into wolves and had the form of wolves, weren't they attacked by dogs or shot at by guards, especially since, as the witness says, there are big, fierce dogs in hell?

A: They could easily escape the dogs and the guards might well have shot at them, if they could get near them. The hellhounds did nothing to them.

Q: According to his account of this fellow Tyrummen, the peasant from Segewold, they went into farmsteads and carried off some fattened pigs. But the servants were surely not without dogs. Didn't they attack them and weren't they bitten?

A: The dogs were then always on guard and that being the case, the werewolves would run away from them so fast that the dogs couldn't catch them. But Tyrummen had truly been a bad fellow and he had done such great wrongs to the people that God therefore let him die young.

To the question where then does his soul abide, he said that this is unknown to him, whether God or the devil took it.

[30] Q: Where do the grain, trees, and whatever else they snatch from the devil blossom and what do they undertake with it?

A: They throw it in the air and from that, prosperity comes back over the whole land, over the rich and poor.

[31] Q: Hereafter he was spoken to sternly and reproached that this was only a devilish deceit and illusion. One could observe, among other things, that if the people of such a type had lost all their cattle and fattened pigs, wouldn't they track them and find signs of them, particularly the fattened pigs and where they were roasted and consumed?

A: They didn't steal close by; rather, at a distance, and who could track them?

[32] Q: How can such a thing be possible, that one of them could carry off fattened pigs and large horned animals, acting like a wolf, and in this form how could they carry it twenty, thirty miles or more through the woods and untilled fields, indeed going all the way from Estonia to this place here, as the witness testified, whereas he could have taken so much more here? Isn't this just a false flight of the imagination, a devilish deceit and delusion?

A: He maintained that it is truthful and Tyrummen, the fellow from Segewold, often stayed out for a full week. Then the witness and his society waited in the middle of the woods and if he hauled in a fattened pig, they consumed it together, but during the time they were in the woods, they lived on rabbits and other wild animals they caught. Now the witness has no more strength to run so far and trap or catch something, but he could have as much fish as he would like. And if nothing else should happen, then he would have special prosperity thereby.

[33] Q: Was it not his intention, before his death, to convert to

God, to let himself be instructed regarding His nature and will, to renounce such devilish excesses, to repent his sins and thereby save his soul from eternal damnation and the pains of hell?

A: Hereupon, he would not answer properly. He said, who knows where his soul would remain? He was now very old, what more could he grasp of such things? Finally, under pressing exhortations, he declared that he would desist and turn himself to God.

[34] Q: Where, then, did he learn to prophesy, since many people came to him and asked him what would happen to them?

A: He could not prophesy; rather, he was a horse doctor, and if other sinners had done harm to someone's horses, he counteracted that and removed it from them. Toward that end he used a few words, only about three, and he administered bread or salt to them, which he had blessed with these words.

[35] Q: What did he know about the sinners who do harm to horses?

A: They were the same witches or servants of the devil, who do nothing but evil.

[36] Q: What, then, were the words he used in this way?

A: Sun and moon go over the sea, bring back the soul that the devil brought to hell and give the animal back the life and health that was taken from it—and that helps other animals beside horses.

[37] Q: From whom did he learn such things?

A: From the same fellow of Marienburg who made him into a werewolf.

[38] Q: Is this fellow still alive?

A: Ah, it has been more than twenty years ago and the fellow was then already very old.

[39] Q: At that time where did the witness dwell and how did he come in contact with the fellow from Marienburg?

A: Originally below Klingenberg; later he was at Bahling. He first encountered a peasant of Rodenpeisch along the way and later they went together to a tavern in Bull [about three and a half miles away]. Then he taught it to him.

[40] Q: Since he previously said it cannot be taught to anyone who

asks it for himself, why did the witness seek to learn and obtain such knowledge from the fellow from Marienburg?

A: Previously he had not asked for anything, but the fellow from Marienburg gave him a drink in the tavern in the way whose effect was already described. Then he took joy in this and accepted it and was calm. But he hadn't thought it would involve so much evil.

[41] At this, he was strenuously advised, since he now knew that it did involve evil, why then did he not long since abandon it, reveal such things to the pastor and seek Christian means for his conversion, rather than still planning to impart such things to another?

A: He certainly should have done that, but he hadn't thought of it. But now it would accomplish nothing; rather, let everything fall out as it was. Things might go for him as he wished.

[42] He was further reproached with his evil obstinacy, as he still did not desire and would not grasp the means to accomplish his conversion and reconciliation with God.

A: Finally, after long exhortation and introduction of God's wrath and eternal damnation, in which it struck him that although he had not turned to God through proper repentance, a gracious God might still be gracious to him and save him from this.

[43] As he had first taken a wife just a few years before and in order to establish this union it was necessary to address the local Herr Pastor, and there was a palpable rumor of the devilish deeds he had done, did not the Herr Pastor of Lemburg set him straight on that account and warn him away from that, also instruct him regarding the temporal and eternal punishments such things would involve? And since he was able to make that union, had he had proper standing in the church at the time, or celebrated the Lord's Supper?

A: The Herr Pastor had instructed and warned him enough; he had also vowed to desist from such things and to turn himself to God and the Lord's Supper, but he hadn't kept it and things remained as they had been before.

[44] Q: Had he then made so strong a pact with the devil that he cannot withdraw from it?

A: The devil has nothing to do with him. Rather, he—namely, the witness—was God's hound and he stole from the devil that which the sorcerers brought to him. Therefore, the devil was an enemy to him.

[45] Q: Had he also taught such things to his wife?

A: He instantly denied it.

[46] Q: Did he also help people with the words reported previously, if something bad happened to them or something occurred, or did he use other words and means for that?

A: He helped people, as well as animals, with those words, and he gave them salt or bread in a warm beer when he had blown over it three times and spoken the words over it.

[47] Q: What did he get for that?

A: Some people give him one guilder, some two, and everyone gave as much as he wished. From several he got grain, also pigs and other things.

[48] Q: Was it then always a known cure and had he helped many in such a manner?

A: He affirmed that whatever had already come under his care in such a manner, its genesis was known, but how could he recount all of those he had helped? Three years earlier, he had also served a fellow from Jürgensburg, Gricke Jahnen, stepson of the blessed Herr Pastor, and he helped him recover from a truly bad leg. And from him he received one external of wheat for that. And previously in a different place, his advice was also sought by Andreas Ammon, but he could give him no help as a witness.

[49] Q: What means did he use for this cure?

A: He had gathered plants in the field for it and worked holy salt into it, and he gave the patient a drink of this. He also sprinkled a powder made from this over the bad leg by which the sickness must be overcome—and it would have overcome syphilis. If someone had pain in his hands and feet, he could also remove that, as if speaking a charm over a fire.

[50] Q: What charm did he speak and what words did he use?

A: To staunch bleeding, he used these words: *Sausse warne zaur gaissem skreij, asne ne las,* that is: A dried-up crow flew through the air, there are no blood drops there. And then the blood was staunched straightaway. But for pain of the limbs, one uses a few words or one also pronounces a charm over a fire. Now he did not want to admit more, after which he might remark that such things could be badly done. Rather, he said only that if someone burned or injured himself with hot water, and they sought his counsel, he sprinkled a yellow herb and rubbed it over the spot and from that it got better in three or four days; otherwise it took a long time to heal.

[51] Q: What kind of herb was it? Who showed it to him? And did he use any words on it?

A: To the first: It's called fire-herb, it grows in the hayfields. To the second: There are countless people in the world from whom one can learn something. To the third: No. But he put salt on it, over which consecrated words had previously been spoken.

[52] At this point, he had to show the judges how he did this and he was given bread and salt so they could see the way he handled them. Thereafter, he broke the bread in three pieces, saying there must be no more than three pieces. He put salt around them, spoke the first consecrated words over them three times, bowed, rotated the plate on which they lay so that each of the pieces came against his mouth. Then he blew over them, exhaling, and his hand swept around and once again he repeated that with this he could remove all the illnesses and woes that had been done to anyone by the sinners, the sorcerers.

[53] Thereafter, he was ordered to eat the bread himself that had been manipulated in this fashion, since he maintained that he had eaten nothing the previous evening and he was hungry. He himself initially said that he could eat nothing, yet finally, upon further urging, he took the soft part of the bread, dipped it on command in the salt, and called it a type of consecrated bread, but he also did not want to eat it all. Rather, he stood on ceremony and kept requesting something to drink, but it was withheld from him. He was obliged to throw the remaining salt into the fire with his own hand in the presence of those assembled so that there would be no further superstitious misdeeds of his, whereupon he did so unwillingly.

[54] Q: Since he previously complained about his back hurting, but now he had consumed his purportedly consecrated bread and salt, which he normally gave to help all his patients, would it now have the

same effect as when it was given by him so that he would be freed by it and feel no more pains?

A: It could not help himself, but only others.

[55] Q: Why didn't it help him?

A: He could not reach to his own back, otherwise it might well also help him. Still, he repeated his speech that it had no effect on himself.

[56] Q: Why should it not help him as well as others, if it were not a devilish deception?

[A:] Thereafter he hesitated and remained silent a good while. Finally, he said: Sometimes it also helped himself, and sometimes not.

[57] Q: Why did he invoke sun and moon, rather than God, to whom the sun and moon, also heaven and earth, are subject and without whom nothing can happen? Also, cannot the sun and moon come over the sea and appear to us daily?

A: How could he use something other than the customary words— and there was no further clarification to obtain from him.

[58] Q: Did he use such words by day or night?

A: By day.

[59] Q: Could he also do injury to someone who had inflicted harm on him or on someone else?

A: No, all his deeds were directed only to the good. But whoever did evil to him, things would not go well for him.

[60] The Herr Pastor of this place, Magister Bucholtz, was summoned and asked to attend the proceedings. He sought to urge this self-professed *Seegensprecher*,[1] a sinner caught in the devil's snares, to take to heart his grievous sins, by which he was led astray and in which he persisted for so many years, and to stir his conscience that he might convert and repent by a rightful repentance and he might make an abjuration of these devilish things.

[61] He showed himself willing and (the pastor) addressed Thiess most movingly, as he truly had chosen God in holy baptism to protect himself from such works of the devil and he also renounced all the devil's works. Why did he, on the contrary sin in the same manner, wantonly persisting in the same forbidden evil deeds, as he himself admitted, things forbidden by God, for such a long time without repentance or conversion up to now? Also, did he not know that he thereby

sinned grievously against God, and was he prepared for temporal, as well as eternal punishment and damnation if he did not desist? But if there was sincere repentance and suffering for his sins and deceits, God and the authorities offered forgiveness and grace.

[62] At this, he showed himself truly obstinate and remained insistent that all he had done was no sin against God. Rather, he had done God much service thereby in fulfillment of His will that they recover the prosperity from the devil, which the sorcerers had carried to him, and he thereby did good for the whole land. They also shared the prosperity with one another and this year would turn out well. By their diligence they came before the Russians, so that everyone in this land had profited and a magnificent increase would follow. The sorcerers were God's enemies and had no portion in heaven, but they (i.e., the werewolves) were God's friends and hunting dogs, whom he uses against the devil and the sorcerers, and therefore their souls came to heaven.

[63] The more the Herr Pastor reproached him for his errors and devilish delusion, and struggled to lead him away from them to bring him to the path of wisdom, also to move him to repentance, the more obstinate Thiess showed himself to be and throughout he would not hear that it was evil work that he pursued. He said that he understood this better than the Herr Pastor, who was still young, and he lost his temper at the Herr Pastor's speech, adding that what vexed him so much was that previously no one else had been prosecuted, although he was not the first and would not be the last who had practiced these same things. If it was evil, why had they let others get away with it?

[64] Now the court further urged him to change his mind, alternating kindness and threats, urging him to recognize the many misdeeds he had committed and his grievous crimes, or at least their bad results. Instead, he persisted that he had not done wrong and if such things were sins, would not the judges before whom he previously appeared, who were as wise as the present ones and who understood such things well, have informed him of this and not smiled at it? But if they now would have it that he should not do this anymore, he would give it up henceforward, because he was old and feeble.

[65] At this, the court now resumed questioning the church thief

from Jürgensburg, Pirsen Tönnis, and others regarding the previously mentioned trial of Thiess and what happened to him in a tavern of Kaltenbrunn or Nödinghoff [an alternate name for Kaltenbrunn]. On that occasion, twelve questions were put to him regarding the offenses of Old Thiess, further regarding the day that he (i.e., Thiess) was drinking with Pirsen Tönnis and he agreed to make a net for Ilgasch, a peasant from Nitau, who had put lots of coins in his purse. But when Pirsen Tönnis asked him what he did with that, he answered that he used it for a prosperity blessing for all the grain and livestock and there was salt that needed to be blessed. Gurrian, a peasant of Jürgensburg, had given this to him when he went to Riga, so that he could consecrate it. Initially, Thiess denied it, but then he admitted that when he was absent during his trip to Riga, the old innkeeper Gurrian Steppe had left all sorts of grain with Thiess's wife to be blessed and there were wheat, barley, oats, flax, and salt each separately tied up in a piece of cloth. He had left the salt for him to bless, as he had a sick cow in his farmstead.

[66] Pirsen Tönnis further stated that Thiess told what Gurrian sought to obtain thereby, that his livestock would give him milk and the wolf do him no harm, as Thiess also maintained he could provide that.

[67] Thereafter, the following question was offered: In what way did he do such things?

A: With the following words that he spoke thereby: "Sun and moon go over the sea to this farm and give it much milk." And it would be so. Also, when he charmed the wolves, he said: "Sun and moon, come over the sea and lead the livestock of this one so that no wolf does harm to them." So nothing happened to the livestock, yet this did not profit the werewolves, to whom this did not apply; rather, it left them free and it could not be extended to prohibit anyone.

[68] Q: Did anyone other than the peasant from Jürgensburg seek blessing from him?

A: He would not go so far as to admit that and to the next question—Could he also charm bears so they would do no harm to the grain and livestock?—he answered: No one can command birds of the bush and animals of the forest.

[69] Now, in the midst of the last examination of Thiess regarding

the way the missing remainder of church funds was administered, on a judicial demand, Herr Chief Deputy Clodt had the abovementioned peasant Gurrian brought in to speak regarding the testimony Thiess had given about him, i.e., that he had requested of him a blessing for his seed corn and salt for a sick cow. At first, Gurrian denied it and said he knew nothing about it. But after taking to heart all the circumstances, he changed his testimony and at the same time undermined it, particularly admitting that Thiess himself said such things to his face, that it was true, adding the reason he had lied and that it really meant nothing, also that nothing evil or wicked had been done. Who wouldn't want to have prosperity for the grain and help and advice regarding a sick animal? Hereafter, Gurrian spoke out somewhat candidly, that while Thiess was in his vocation he conferred prosperity. And the salt, so he said, could restore health to a sick animal and he himself would use such means as he had.

[70] Q: Was he previously acquainted with Thiess?

A: Who didn't know him? He was already an old fellow and had lived in the vicinity of this place for some time.

[71] Q: Had he not also sought and obtained the same presumed blessings from Thiess previously?

A: They both denied this instantly.

[72] Q: With whom else did Thiess share the presumed blessings in such measure?

A: How could he know that exactly? But it was commonly said of him that he was a werewolf and the former court also knew it well, but they had done nothing to him about it.

[73] Q: Where do the grain and salt purportedly blessed by Thiess remain?

A: He still has them in his farmstead.

[74] After he had named the place where he secured that, he brought it from there and placed it in separate linen bundles.

[75] Afterward, both the royal court and the Herr Pastor of this place, Magister Buchholz, earnestly and movingly reproached Gurrian, as well as Thiess, with their grievous sins, devilish temptations, superstitions, and idolatry. As Thiess still would not understand, it was necessary for Gurrian, who was himself not the subject of evil rumors,

to state that he was given to sorcery, standing in the presence of the judges and all assembled, especially in front of all the assembled peasants, regarding their delusion that some holiness was in these things. On the contrary, nothing could be decreed with regard to Thiess, so all was in confusion. In the end he [Gurrian] cast one bundle after another with his own hand into a fire that had been laid, following the Herr Pastor's proclamation of the true God, concerning his gracious mercy and forgiveness of the sins he had committed, also telling him henceforth to change and to abstain from the things that were previously highly forbidden. In order to avoid temporal and eternal punishments, he did this with fear and trembling and thereby openly atoned for the acknowledged public scandal. At the following Sunday's preaching, he was obliged to stand at the church post and as sacred conclusion he was legally condemned to be struck with twelve pairs of blows by the high executor. The Herr Pastor also emphasized for the whole community the strong and cruel punishment of such a person for his skills, and he admonished each one of them to desist from such things.

[76] Now in spite of the repeated admonitions as were given to Thiess to name the others who sought the same means from him and what he had been paid, he would be led to no further confession, pleading how could he remember that? He was an old fellow and could hardly think anymore what had happened earlier. Who had given him much, sometimes one, sometimes two, even three shillings or something else, but often nothing at all? That was not mercantile activity, in which one demands money. It was based on one's free will, whether one wanted to give or not.

[77] He was thereafter turned over to custody and this case was sent for deliberation and execution by the high commission in the event that His Royal Majesty's newly appointed Herr District Court Judge, whose ship was expected to arrive from Sweden, might complete and publish a judgment.

[78] Truly, even if one thoroughly considered the proceedings after the session at Venden [today's Cēsis], one could and would still not reach a definitive verdict on so difficult and doubtful a case. Rather, it was deemed important to have it pleaded again before the collegium at

the earliest forthcoming session of the new Herr District Court Judge von Palmberg and presented as a subject to be determined in law, so that therewith they might be able to consider and dispose of the most fully developed point of this crime, the like of which has seldom been presented up to now, even if it has been previously judged.

[79] Since District Court Judge von Palmberg's arrival was delayed more than expected and by His Royal Majesty's most gracious decree, the illustrious, praiseworthy Assessor of the Royal High Court, Herman Georg von Trautvetter, officially taking the place of the absent Herr District Court Judge, was ordered to preside over this royal district court. He took this up, along with other cases, and *perlectis actis et unitis votis* [having read the acts and vows], composed the following judgment.

Verdict Pronounced by the High Court of Dorpat [Tartu] (October 31, 1692)[2]

October 31, 1692, Oreshoff

Judges present: The illustrious, praiseworthy Assessor of the Royal
    High Court, Herman Georg von Trautvetter, in place of the absent
    District Court Judges: Assessor ordinarius Bengt Johan Ackerstaff.
    Assessor ordinarius Gabriel Berger.

Judgment

In the officially published interrogation of an inhabitant of Kalten-brunn named Thiess, with regard to lycanthropy, as also the perpetration of other vexatious and highly forbidden misdeeds, the royal district court decided, following the oral testimony of the accused that was heard by the court and what was expressed and established so well by the assigned court, these things were thereby found definitively to be right:

Accordingly, as the accused has made clear by his own testimony, for many years he showed himself to be a werewolf. He ran about with others, was also in hell, and in such groups he stole livestock from others and helped commit more acts of the same sort. It is not only in this case that one should regard all this as a diabolical delusion, since such an opinion is also accepted before this court. Neither through the court's pronouncements, nor the moving speech by the Herr Pastor of Jürgensburg, did the accused let himself be led away from these deeds, nor did he uphold the vow he previously swore to the local Herr Pastor, nor did he listen to the Holy Word, nor did he present himself to take the Holy Sacrament. Rather, since he pronounced all sorts of prophecies and blessings strongly forbidden by the highest divine and lay authorities, thereby powerfully sinning against himself and the others whom he led into superstition, it is fair to consider this and punish him according to the severity of the law due to his truly weighty and vexatious offenses, to subject him to a well-deserved punishment, and to change him into an object of noteworthy aversion by public flogging. However, in view of his advanced age, only twenty pairs of blows will be administered by the hand of the *Scharfrichter*[3] of Lemburg before a public gathering of the peasantry in the parish, whose Herr Pastor will explain the terms of the sentence to demonstrate the offense of this malefactor to the bystanders to warn others against the same vexatious and punishable conduct and to warn them against superstitions. Thereafter, the accused will be condemned to banishment from the land forever, subject to ratification by the illustrious and most august court of Tartu [*salva tamen illustris et augustissimi dicasterii Dorpatensis leuteratione*]. V.R.W.

    L.S.

                    Hermann Georg von Trautvetter, in place of
                        the absent District Court Judge.
                    Bengt Johan von Ackerstaff, Assessor.
                    Gabriel Berger, Assessor.

Comparison of Old Thiess to Germanic Cult Groups, Folklore, and Persephone Myths

OTTO HÖFLER

Translated by Bruce Lincoln

The text and notes in this chapter are translated from portions of Otto Höfler, *Kultische Geheimbünde der Germanen* (Frankfurt am Main: Moritz Diesterweg, 1934). Section I is from the main text (pp. 21–30 in the original edition); section II is from the appendix (pp. 345–47).

I

By noting the temporal agreement between myth and customs, it is not difficult to refute the views of those who interpret myths as nature allegories. Thus, it has often been maintained that the legend of the "Wild Troop" (*Wilde Heer*) is closely connected to Christmastime because the fiercest storms rage in midwinter and legends of the in-rushing souls of the dead have fastened themselves to this time above all. It is not certain, however, that the twelve days of Christmas are to be regarded as the quintessential time of ghosts and spirits. Were the belief in the gathering of the band of the dead (*Totenschar*) merely connected to the raging of storms, it would be impossible to establish calendric regularity; rather, one would have to imagine Wodan and his troop in all stormy nights.

If, on the other hand, the legend simply told that at Yuletide all graves stand open, or that spirits of the dead streak about, invisible and inaudible, it would be entirely conceivable that free fantasy alone was at work here. But since it is always repeated that at Yuletide the demons storm about with raging noise for twelve nights or storm about on specific evenings, this cannot be drawn from thin air and even less can irregular natural events have given rise to these fixed-date legends. Customary annual practices, however, can have such effects.

The Account of Olaus Magnus

In fact, cultic practices can be identified that are set at a fixed time and display precisely the wild, ecstatic character that our legends of the troop of the dead identified—and this is not attested only by the Germans. Precisely at that "time of ghosts and spirits" (according to medieval cult practices), wild demonic actors appear, whose fearsome doings are faithfully reflected in the ghost and spirit legends of the *Volk*.

At the borders of the German area, we find the remnants of the most ancient customs, by which at Christmastime (or at carnival), impersonators of ghosts and spirits appear, sometimes still in primitive theriomorphic form.[1] In their wild, ecstatic rites, these show an unmistakable kinship with the ghostly troop of the Wild Hunt. Highly instructive in this perspective is the following account, which the Swedish Archbishop Olaus Magnus gave in his 1555 *Historia de gentibus septentrionalibus*:

> Since I discussed the different types of wolves in chapter XV of the present book, I am of the opinion that at the end of this book on wild animals, it would be worth treating the type of wolves that are effectively humans converted into wolves—a type that Pliny (Book 8, chapter 22) confidently asserts are to be regarded as imaginary fabulous beings—yet such, I say, still today are encountered in great abundance in the lands situated in the furthest north. In Prussia, Livonia, and Lithuania, nearly all year long the inhabitants suffer great damage from the rapacity of wolves, because a huge number of their

animals are torn to pieces and eaten if they stray only a small distance from the herd in the woods. However, this loss is not reckoned by them to be so great as those they must suffer from men who have turned into wolves. On the feast of Christ's birth, toward nightfall at a determined place a large number of wolves assemble, who have changed from men that dwell in different places, and on that same night, with astonishing ferocity they rage against the human species and all other living beings who do not have a wild nature so that the inhabitants of this region receive more harm from these than from real and natural wolves. For as is known, they assault the houses of people who dwell in the woods with unbelievable wildness and they even attempt to break down the doors so that they may annihilate whatever people and animals remain there. They invade beer cellars and drink some barrels of beer or mead, then pile the empty mugs in the middle of the cellar, one on top of another, in which practice they differ from natural and genuine wolves. However, the inhabitants of these lands consider the places where the werewolves congregate that night to be somewhat prophetic, for if something bad should happen there, like a cart overturning with a person thrown in the snow, they are utterly persuaded that man will die within the year, as they have experienced over a long time. Between Lithuania, Samogetia, and Kurland is a wall, the remains of a demolished castle. There, at a fixed time of year, several thousands of them assemble and test their agility by jumping over it. Those who cannot cross this wall, as usually happens with the fat ones, they are beaten with whips by their leader. Thereafter, it is strongly asserted that among this troop are found the great men of this land and those from the highest nobility. The manner in which they generally fall into that madness and terrible metamorphosis, which they are never able to avoid at certain fixed times, will be made known in the following chapter.[2]

After a polemic against Pliny, who judged the belief in werewolves an audacious lie, Olaus Magnus continued: "In defense of the writings of Evanthes, Agriopas, and other authors, I will here show by a few examples that such things happen even in this day. Thus, as soon as someone, whether a German or native, is curious and against God's commandment wishes to join the company of those accursed men who are turned into wolves, at certain times of year, for the rest of his life he will gather with his comrades at established places and inflict harm, even death itself on animals and other mortals. This reason for his transformation, which is most contrary to his nature, is that someone skilled in this kind of magic gives him a mug of beer to drink (but only one who wants to join the forbidden society will accept it), over which he has spoken certain words. Later when it seems right to him, he will be able to transmute his human form wholly into that of a wolf, when he gathers with others in some cellar or a hidden wood. Finally, he is free to relinquish this form after some time and once again assume his former condition."

In this account by the Swedish prelate, a large number of the motifs occur together that we have so often encountered in the legend of the troop of the dead—but the ancient source expressly describes these as properties of a demonic human band, not a ghostly troop. So this example from the sixteenth century provides direct evidence and a welcome complement to the traditions preserved in legends of ghosts and spirits. Almost all corresponds to the myths discussed here:[3] The men transformed into wolves streak about at Christmastime—like the "Odin's hounds"[4] of legend or the audacious "Christmas lads" (*Weihnachtsburschen*). They rage against people and animals—an extremely primitive feature that still shines through fairly often in Germanic customs[5] and no less in legend: thus, it is told in Denmark how ghostly dogs pursued a man, and when he succeeded in reaching his house and slamming the door, they shook and scratched at the door,[6] exactly like the Baltic "wolves." Similarly, in contemporary German folk beliefs, people are frequently warned to lock the doors fast at Christmastime against the Wild Hunt.[7] The ghostly "wolves" break into houses and drink—another feature that defies every nature-mythological explanation—from the beer barrels, as is consistently reported of the Germanic troop of the dead up through Norway, about which Olaus Magnus naively remarked: *in quo a nativis ac genuinis lupis discrepant* ("in which practice they differ from natural and genuine wolves"). The band gathers in certain disreputable places and it is crucial to note that it is a band, for the social background of these demonic phenomena—which I take to be their very essence—has, as a rule, been overlooked. The test of dexterity also has a social significance, that is, the leap over the wall.

It is only an apparent contrast if here the troop of the dead appears as werewolves, for werewolves are frequently considered to be the returning dead.[8] As an ancient example of this belief, let me cite from the Assyrian epic recounting Ištar's descent into hell, where Ištar threatens the guardians of the underworld: "I will let the dead escape in the form of living werewolves."[9] As further examples will show, we can therefore conclude that in European myth—and cult—bands of wolves also frequently correspond to the troop of the dead.[10]

Contemporary Counterparts

The Northern European account of Olaus Magnus is confirmed in striking ways by Swiss traditions of the twentieth century, for knowledge of which we are indebted to Leopold Rütimeyer.[11] In the isolated region of Lötschental, even today the youths older than twenty dress up on the Sunday before Shrove Tuesday with animal pelts, sashes with bells, and wooden masks, and they storm about, while women, children, and younger boys are locked up in their houses around midday as loud roaring is heard in the streets. Security forces describe their wildness as "horrific." One gives them meat and cream. But the legend is told of them "that they originate from the 'Schurte-thieves' who allegedly dwelt in 'Dietrich' around the fifteenth century, a small clearing in the woods on the south side of Lötschental. According to legend, Dietrich is the first place in which the people of this valley settled. At that place, there still exist the ruined walls of an old manor. 'Schurte' is the name of a short skirt, and the name 'Schurte-thief' could well come from the short sheep's pelt that even today is worn by the masked figures.[12] Further, it is reported how these 'Schurte-thieves,' equipped with wooden masks, break into the villages by night, stealing grain and other things."[13] Another account of this same band states: "In prehistoric time, a band of robbers dwelt in the thick woods on the south side of Lötschental, who were called the 'educated thieves' because the members had to train themselves against

difficult prey. Only upon fulfillment of this condition were they accepted. Thereafter, these robbers made it a game to attack the villagers
who dwelt in the valley. In doing so, they appeared fearsome: in horrid
rags, sheepskins, hideous masks with resounding cowbells and armed
with heavy clubs, these monsters fell on the quaking inhabitants by
dark of night. From this originated the many stories of daring burglar-
ies, whose traces are still evident today. People used these masks for
several centuries to make themselves unrecognizable and they formed
a robber band, using masks to terrify and steal from their neighbors.
In the 17th century, these raids ceased. People now use these masks
only (!) on Mardi Gras, Carnival Monday and Tuesday, in order to
frighten the people."[14]

The agreement of this account recorded in our own century from
the southernmost edge of Germanic territory with Olaus Magnus's
Baltic account from 1555 could hardly be greater. Only the timing of
the masked frenzy is different: here it is carnival, in the Baltic, Christmastime when the demonic pelt-mummers appear. Thus, both also
coincide with the typical times of the Männerbund celebrations,
which we repeatedly encounter as the chief periods for this cult. All
other traits coincide with an interpretation of the demonic "robbers"
in one way, which we would take as the sign of a deep kinship, even if
ethnographic parallels did not instruct us that here, in fact, a piece of
"primordial ethnography" (to use Rütimeyer's phrase) lies in front of
our eyes.

Other Parallels

At least a pair of accounts might be added here, alongside those that
have been mentioned. First an example that J. J. Hanush published
in 1859: "As Vuk Stephanovič recounted, especially in winters toward
Christmastime, *vlkodlaci* (werewolves) are frequently seen, and in
the Russian and Ruthenian Christmas celebrations, wolf mummers
running through the streets draped in *Wilcuren* (wolf pelts) play an
important role. . . . Thus, to the extent that the wolf mummers leave
no peace to anyone in house, home, or in the streets, in that measure
the old customs prevail in the Christmas chambers. . . ."[15] Wilhelm

Hertz was surely right when he supposed these to be the traces of an old winter festival "where what is now fun and games may well have been done in fearful bloody earnest."[16] Already Hanush pointed to a counterpart of this seasonal werewolf transformation that is found in Herodotus's account of the Neuroi: "The Scythians and the Greeks who dwell in Scythia say that once every year, each of the Neuroi becomes a wolf for several days and then takes back his old form."[17]

According to Hertz, the Serbs and modern Greeks in Mytilene and Asia Minor also particularly fear werewolves around Christmas.[18] Johannes Prätorius also gathered a number of examples in the Fourth Proposition of his *Saturnalia* under the title "At Holy Christmas, some people become werewolves."[19] I am convinced the following north German taboos also find their explanation in this Christmas werewolf terror: "Earlier, no one dared to pronounce the name of the wolf during the twelve days. . . . Also, around this time shepherds would rather call the devil than the wolf, for fear that otherwise he would drive off his sheep,[20] and a peasant dared not speak the name of his magistrate, who was called Wolf; rather, he called him 'Herr Monster'[21] and at this time the animal itself was called 'the Gray.'"[22]

Among legends concerning apparitions during the "twelve days," one has the following notice from an auditor of Melanchthon from the year 1557, who communicated that in one of his lectures, the reformer cited an epistolary account he had recently received from Livonia from a "man most worthy of respect" (*vir dignissimus*) (of whom Melanchthon testified "I know he does not write false things" [*quem scio non falsa scribere*]). A man accused of sorcery in Livonia confessed before his execution that every year for twelve days (!) he turned into a wolf. After the feast of Christ's Nativity (!), a small boy appeared to him, who turned him into a wolf. If he failed to do this, a fearful figure with a whip would come and thus he was transformed into a wolf. Then many other wolves gathered, who ran through the woods and tore livestock to pieces, but they could do no harm to humans. When the figure with the whip appeared, they were shivering (?) in a river. And this happened every year over the course of twelve days, after which he resumed human form.[23]

Clearly, this account describes the same Baltic Christmas customs that we know from Olaus Magnus.[24] However, it is not dependent on the Swedish historian and supplements his information in the most important and valuable way.[25] First, we hear that the ghostly troop of demonic wolves is formed precisely on the "Twelve," i.e., the twelve days after Christmas. Then, as with Olaus Magnus, a leader with a whip is mentioned—surely no offspring of a nature-mythological fantasy, but a figure like those we frequently find in Männerbund initiations. Nothing is said here concerning an initiatory leap over a wall; instead, there is the somewhat unclear phrase *praeeunte illo spectaculo cum flagello pavisse eos in flumine*, which conceivably is to be understood as "while that figure with the whip led, they shivered in a river." It thus appears to be a question of testing one's manhood—an initiatory ritual of the most common sort.

In Silesia, people say, much as in Mecklenburg: "During these nights (the Twelve), werewolves go about. At this time, one cannot generally refer to the wolf by his name; rather, one must call him vermin, insect, or filth, lest the herd of wolves tear one apart."[26] Is not this Silesian superstition—like those from Mecklenburg, Greece, and Asia Minor—a precise illustration of the Baltic practices?

Comparing the descriptions that we have presented, which obviously refer to the same primitive customs, the fact leaps back before our eyes, which I take to be typical, as well as methodologically significant. Whereas the modern, enlightened reporters of the Lötschental masquerade tell us that the youths of that place disguise themselves with pelts and horrid masks and terrify the people, scholars of the sixteenth century reported similar things, but with real metamorphosis, rather than changes of costume. This belief Olaus Magnus shared with Melanchthon's Livonian correspondent, with the Livonian court that sentenced that "werewolf" to death, and—who can doubt it?—with every stratum of the *Volk*.

II

Following the conclusion of this work, through a reference provided by Olof von Feilitzens of Uppsala University, I gained knowledge of a trial transcript that confirmed and completed the preceding research in the most welcome fashion. It provides an unexpected glimpse into the doings of the Baltic wolf-demons, whose band has been identified as particularly ancient in the preceding discussion. The transcript, which directly corroborates and focuses on a number of factors previously treated, is briefly discussed here.

In the year 1691, an old man named Thiess appeared as a witness in a trial held at Jürgensburg in Livonia, when another witness identified him as a notorious werewolf and an exhaustive examination concerning his lycanthropy was undertaken. The acts of the trial were published and discussed by Hermann von Bruiningk.[27] I am reproducing the portion that is most important in the present connection.

[Paragraphs 1–33 of the Thiess transcript follow; see pp. 14–22 in this volume.]

The most noticeable difference between the description of the Baltic werewolves' doings in our trial transcript and the reports of Olaus Magnus and Melanchthon lie in the striking motif of the theft of fertility by "sorcerers" and its recovery by "werewolves" on the night of St. Lucia. Psychologically, it is readily understandable that in the court hearing, Old Thiess took pains to press the werewolves' services to the fields into the foreground, while letting their terroristic raids recede from view.[28] It is obvious and can be demonstrated through numerous parallels that he by no means manufactured his narrative from thin air, but based it on traditions of the *Volk*. One can only ask to what extent he provides evidence of "legend," i.e., fantastic accounts, and to what extent his testimony attests to actually practiced cults and truly demonic practices.

That the spiritual doings take place on the Night of Santa Lucia corresponds to a widespread tradition. Thus, in Norway, due to its regular appearance on this night, the *Wilde Heer* is often called *Lussi-færden* ("those who travel with St. Lucy").[29] The procession of the dead spirits took place on the Night of Santa Lucia, since it was previously the longest night of the year.[30] Often enough, the twelve nights before Christmas are a spiritual period in competition with the "Twelve" after December 24.[31] And like the Night of Santa Lucia, Pentecost and St.

John's Eve are repeatedly named as times for the circuit of the ghostly troop.

The theft of fertility and its recovery from "hell" is obviously a very ancient complex and belongs in the circle of myths — and cults — that treat the disappearance of the powers of vegetation into the "underworld" and their successful return to the earth. This is not the place to go into the huge number of pertinent traditions, among which the myths and cults of the *Balder-, Attis-, Demeter-Persephone-,* and *Adonis-*spheres should be counted. Let us mention only a few details.

The Livonian case differs from these myths in one respect, i.e., it appears to know no personification of the fertility that is abducted to the underworld and brought back to earth after the solstice. Rather, it is "animals, grain, and other produce" (trial transcript, para. 12), fish and fruit (para. 15), flax (para. 19), and the grain blossoms (para. 2) that were brought to "hell" by the "sorcerers" and recovered by the werewolves for Santa Lucia.

The antagonism between the Baltic werewolves and the evil race of witches is also described in folk legends. Perhaps one can admit the possibility of real cultic struggles between the two parties.[32] With regard to that, one can recall that in the Demeter celebrations, mock and real competitions took place around a heap of barley.[33] Also, our own mock combats in winter or spring are often a struggle between the friends and enemies of fertility.[34]

The Night of Santa Lucia, in which the earth is granted new fertility, is considered the longest night of the year and, as such, manifests many other customs as the beginning of a new epoch of returning life.[35] Already, Hammarstedt raised the question whether the *Lussi-bruden* ("brides of Lucy") who wander from house to house on this night in Scandinavia are not descended from the pagan goddess who, liberated, returned to the upper world (*till den övre världen*) to redistribute the food necessary for life's renewal.[36] Such a return from the underworld stands close to the myth of *Persephone, Kore,* and their kindred. In addition, it should be mentioned that alongside Lucia's embodiment as a young woman, she is also frequently represented as a (sometimes clothed!) sheaf of grain.[37] In Greece also, Demeter and the sheaves of the harvest are closely connected.[38] The Baltic custom seems to be a bit more primitive, instead of solemnly lifting a figure representing the grain itself out of "hell" as a dispenser of life, but the return from the underworld still appears in Livonia at the end of the seventeenth century, having been maintained in an amazingly primordial form.

If we are not completely deceived, the descent of fertility to the subterranean realm and its subsequent return were, at one time, not just a mythological concept, but the performance of a dramatic cult. What the old "werewolf" Thiess described concerning "hell"—whose precise location he specified[39]—refers to an actual cult site. Greek parallels identify sacred caves of Kore and Demeter, into which people deposited pigs and pine branches rich in seeds. An etiological myth brought this into relation with the abduction of Kore by Hades. After some time, the remains of what was deposited and breads baked in the shape of dragons and people were solemnly raised up from the grotto.[40] Any remnants were then placed under the seed grain and people expected a blessed and prosperous harvest.[41] Other Greek traditions recount that when Demeter was hidden in dark caves, the fields withered.[42] In the same fashion, people believed in the north that Lucia dwelt in caves and mountain clefts.[43] Beyond accepting that the theft of Kore and her disappearance into the underworld should be compared to such myths, one should understand that the cultic caves of Greece—the ones they thought were guarded by serpents (or dragons? Greek δράκοντες)[44]—actually represented the underworld.[45]

I would thus conclude that the information from the Livonian trial transcript refers to a cult that in its original form stood very close to the Greek ones seeking the magical recovery of fertility from the realm of the dead. Just as Kore was abducted by Hades, so the Baltic sorcerers carried off the land's fertility. And the land will become desolate if the werewolves do not bring it back. For "hell" and its demons to be represented so concretely is hardly unheard of. In Nuremburg, they are even led through the streets! Elsewhere, one should discuss whether the legend of Hermóð, who rode into hell to bring back Baldr, might reflect a cultic drama.

It remains to be mentioned that in this sort of fertility ritual, women frequently play an important role. Perhaps it was the ritual's strong

concern with fertility magic that—according to Thiess's testimony—
brought women into the rank of these Latvian werewolves.[46] The
warrior aspect appears to be totally absent in this Latvian band (in
contrast to its Germanic counterparts!).

In other respects, the information in the transcript agrees with the
older accounts discussed above and provides very welcome confirmation on most points of what they revealed. Thus, the "metamorphosis"
was effected by stretching a wolf pelt over one's body (trial transcript,
para. 6).[47] The werewolves appeared in a group and it seems these were
formed according to their place of residence (trial transcript, para. 14).
We can repeatedly observe exclusiveness of this sort: the extraordinary importance of these demonic beings for the development of society is based upon it.[48] Especially instructive is the pronouncement:
"The Germans don't join their company; rather, they have a special
hell of their own" (trial transcript, para. 17). Indeed, Olaus Magnus expressly stated that Germans—as well as the indigenous population—
participated in these doings.[49] The separation according to groups
corresponds to what we already know about such demonic bands.[50]

The whole account is interwoven with demonic motifs: thus, for
instance, reception into the band through a magical drink—a motif
Olaus Magnus also knew[51]—which represents one of the most important rituals of initiation.[52] Also, the ghostly whip-bearer is well
known to us from older accounts: a figure encountered often enough
in secret societies.[53]

It is remarkable that Thiess, who made no attempt to conceal his
werewolfery (trial transcript, paras. 1, 2, 5, 6, 8, 12, et al.) and who was
"idolized by the peasants" (para. 3), described the location of "hell"
without any circumlocution (para. 5). In connection with this, one
should remember that often enough the places of demonic doings
were quite well known. The mysteriousness of the cult exists not in
concealment of its when and where, but only in the spells of its demonic powers!

That Thiess misled his judges somewhat at many points is clear.[54]
In most cases, however, comparison with other sources shows that
Thiess transmitted old, strongly held folk traditions. Among the most
remarkable, perhaps, is his repeated assertion that the werewolves

were "God's hounds."[55] Already, Jacob Grimm thought the designation of wolves as "God's hunting dogs," which is attested by Hans Sachs, was connected to the Old Norse tradition of Óðin's wolves.[56] In 1691, the same terminology surfaced again, not in some animal fable, but in the mouth of a man "idolized" by the peasants: a respected elder, who himself belonged to the demonic wolf-band. An extremely ancient tradition must be at issue here. With regard to that, I would recall that in 1639, the mournful ghostly riders of Åland were called "Oden's Men."[57] The Livonian testimony of 1691 provides a counterpart to this. Here too it is clear that the relationship to a demonic god is the very heart of a demonic band.

This Livonian band stands alongside the most ancient Germanic and Greek traditions; even so, what Old Thiess described is quite distinct from its Germanic counterparts in its deepest grounding. In spite of all the agreement between its peasant vegetative rites with Germanic (and Greek) traditions, the Latvian band lacked the gift that gave the Germanic male associations their high historic significance, i.e., the impulse they provided for the process of state formation. It is this that led our bands out of the atemporal idyllic sphere of customs concerned with the soil into the world of political history.

Also, the astounding agreement in annual customs and rituals ought not lead us to misunderstand this powerful contrast: the most distinctive gift of the Nordic race—its state-building power—found its place in Männerbünde and this drove them to their richest development.

Comparison of Old Thiess to Friulian *Benandanti*, Russian Werewolves, and Shamanic Others

CARLO GINZBURG

Material in this chapter consists of previously published translations of Ginzburg's writing; individual sources are cited within.

From *The Night Battles: Witchcraft and Agrarian Cults in the Sixteenth and Seventeenth Centuries* (1980)[1]

The trial of Gasparutto and Moduco was the first in a long series involving the *benandanti* (both men and women) who declared that they fought at night with witches and warlocks to secure the fertility of the fields and the abundance of the harvests. This belief (we have hinted at its presumably ritual origins) does not appear to the best of our knowledge, in any of the countless trials for witchcraft or superstitious practices held outside the Friuli. The sole and extraordinary exception is furnished by the trial of a Livonian werewolf which took place at Jürgensburg in 1692—more than a century after the trial of Gasparutto and Moduco, and at the other extremity of Europe.[2]

The accused, a certain Thiess, an old man in his eighties, freely confessed to his judges that he was a werewolf (*wahrwolff*). But his account seriously differs from the concept of lycanthropy which was widespread in northern Germany and the Baltic countries. Thiess related that he once had his nose broken by a peasant of Lemburg named Skeistan, who at that time was already dead. Skeistan was a witch, and with his companions had carried seed grain into Hell to keep the crops from growing. With other werewolves Thiess had also gone down into Hell and had fought with Skeistan. The latter, armed with a broom handle (again, the traditional symbol of witches) wrapped in the tail of a horse had struck the old man on the nose. This was not a casual encounter. Three times each year on the nights of St. Lucia before Christmas, of Pentecost, and of St. John, the werewolves proceeded on foot, in the form of wolves, to a place located "beyond the sea": Hell. There they battled the devil and witches, striking them with long iron rods, and pursuing them like dogs. Werewolves, Thiess exclaimed, "cannot tolerate the devil." The judges, undoubtedly astonished, asked for elucidation. If werewolves could not abide the devil, why did they change themselves into wolves and go down into Hell? Because, Old Thiess explained, by doing so they could bring back up to earth what had been stolen by the witches—livestock, grains, and the other fruits of the earth. If they failed to do so, precisely what had occurred the previous year would be repeated: the werewolves had delayed their descent into Hell, found the gates barred and thus failed to bring back the grains and buds carried off by the witches. For this reason last year's harvest had been very bad. But this year, instead, things had been different, and thanks to the werewolves, the harvest of barley and rye, as well as a rich catch of fish, were assured.

At this point the judges asked where the werewolves went after death. Thiess replied that they were buried like other people, but that their souls went to heaven; as for the souls of witches, the devil claimed them for himself. The judges were visibly shaken. How was it possible, they asked, for the souls of werewolves to ascend to God if it was not God they served but the devil? The old man emphatically rejected this notion: the werewolves were anything but servants of the devil. The devil was their enemy to the point that they, just like dogs— because werewolves were indeed the hounds of God—pursued him, tracked him down, and scourged him with whips of iron. They did all this for the sake of mankind: without their good work the devil would carry off the fruits of the earth and everyone would be deprived as a consequence. The Livonian werewolves were not alone in their fight with the devil over the harvests: German werewolves did so as well, although they did not belong the Livonian company and they journeyed to their own particular Hell; and the same also was true of Russian werewolves who that year and the one before had won prosperous and abundant harvests for their land. As soon as the werewolves managed to snatch away from the devil the seed grain he had stolen, they cast it up into the air so that it might fall back down to earth and be spread over the fields of rich and poor alike.

At this juncture, as might have been foreseen, the judges tried to get Thiess to confess that he had entered into a compact with the devil. The old man reiterated, in vain, with monotonous obstinacy that he and his companions were "the hounds of God" and the enemies of the devil, that they protected men from dangers and guaranteed the prosperity of harvests. Then the parish priest was summoned, who scolded him and called on him to abandon the errors and diabolical lies with which he had tried to cover up his sins. But this too was useless. In a burst of anger Thiess shouted at the priest that he was tired of hearing all this talk about his evil doings: his actions were better than the priests, and moreover he, Thiess, would neither be the first nor the last to commit them. The old man remained steadfast in his convictions and refused to repent; on 10 October 1692 he was condemned to ten lashes for his superstitious beliefs and acts of idolatry.

This was not a case, clearly, of more or less ill-defined similarities, or of the repetition of metahistorical religious archetypes.[3] The beliefs of the old werewolf Thiess substantially resemble those which emerged at the trial of the two Friulian *benandanti*: battles waged by means of sticks and blows, enacted on certain nights to secure the fertility of fields, minutely and concretely described. Even details such as the broom handles with which the Livonian witches were armed recalls the stalks of sorghum or millet used by the witches of the Friuli. In the Friuli the struggle was primarily over the vineyards, in Livonia over barley and rye, but the struggle for fertility was understood as a work that was not merely tolerated but was even protected by God, who

actually guaranteed entrance into paradise for the souls of the participants. There is not much doubt about any of this. Obviously, what we
have here is a single agrarian cult, which, to judge from these remnants
surviving in places as distant from one another as were Livonia and
the Friuli, must have been diffused in an earlier period over a much
vaster area, perhaps the whole of central Europe. On the other hand,
these survivals may be explained either by the peripheral positions of
the Friuli and Livonia with respect to the center of diffusion of these
beliefs, or by the influence, in both cases, of Slavic myths and traditions. The fact that in Germanic areas, as we shall see, there were faint
traces of the myth of nocturnal combats waged over fertility, might
lead us to lean towards the second possibility. Only intensive research
may be able to resolve this problem.

But it is not just the beliefs of Old Thiess that remind us of the
Friulian *benandanti*. The reaction of the Jürgensburg judges resembles,
even in particulars, that of the Udine inquisitors: both rejected, with
mingled shock and indignation, the paradoxical boasts of the *benandanti* to be the champions of "Christ's faith," and of the werewolves to
be "the hounds of God." In both cases the judges tried to identify the
benandanti and the werewolves with the witches who were followers
and worshippers of the devil. There is a difference to be noted, however. Gasparutto and Moduco, to the best of our knowledge, were the
first *benandanti* tried by the Holy Office: the very name "*benandanti*"
was unknown to the inquisitors. Only gradually would the *benandanti* assume the traits of diabolical witches. In that late seventeenth-
century Livonian trial we are witnessing the opposite phenomenon.
The figure and negative attributes of werewolves, the ferocious scourge
of flocks and herds, were well known to the judges of Jürgensburg. But
a totally different picture was painted by Old Thiess: werewolves were
defenders of the harvest and of livestock against the constant threat
from the enemies of the prosperity of mankind and of the fertility
of the land—the devil and the witches. This revival of presumably
ancient beliefs can probably be explained by the fact that at the end
of the seventeenth century Livonian judges had ceased to use judicial torture or even rely on leading questions in the interrogation of
defendants.[4] That the favorable image of werewolves was much older

than the end of the seventeenth century is shown first of all by Thiess's venerable age: presumably he must have acquired these beliefs in his distant youth, which brings us to the early years of the century. But there is an even more compelling bit of evidence. In the mid-sixteenth century Kaspar Peucer, during a digression on werewolves and their extraordinary exploits, inserted into his *Commentarius de praecipuis generibus divinationum* an anecdote about a young man of Riga who had suddenly fallen prostrate to the ground during a banquet. One of the onlookers had immediately recognized him as a werewolf. The next day the youth related that he had fought a witch who had been flying about in the guise of a red-hot butterfly. Werewolves, in fact, Peucer commented, boasted that they kept witches away.[5] This *was* an ancient belief, then. But, just as with the *benandanti* in the Friuli, under pressure from the judges, the original positive qualities of the werewolves began gradually to fade away and become corrupted into the execrable image of the man-wolf, ravager of livestock.

In any case, on the basis of this surprising Livonian counterpart, it seems appropriate to suggest that there is a real, not an analogical connection between *benandanti* and shamans. Such phenomena as trances, journeys into the beyond astride animals or in the form of animals (wolves or, as in the Friuli, butterflies and mice) to recover seed grain or to assure the fertility of the land, and as we will note shortly, participation in processions for the dead (which procure prophetic and visionary powers for the *benandanti*) form a coherent pattern which immediately evokes the rites of the shamans. But to trace the threads which tied these beliefs to the Baltic or Slavic world obviously falls outside the scope of this particular investigation.

From "Germanic Mythology and Nazism: Thoughts on an Old Book by Georges Dumézil," in *Clues, Myths, and the Historical Method* (1989)[6]

The scholarly problem occupying Dumézil had entered a new phase as the result of an encounter between two previously separate currents of research: the first, on the *berserkir*; the second, on male societies or associations (*Männerbünde*). Credit for this development, thanks to which the phenomenon of the *berserkir* could be studied for the first time in a context that provided a key to its interpretation, belonged, as Dumézil observed, to two scholars: Lily Weiser (later Weiser-Aall) and Otto Höfler. The connection between their research is very close (both were students of the Germanist Rudolf Much); but under closer scrutiny, differences are also evident.

In her thoughtful book *Altgermanische Jünglingsweihen und Männerbünde* (1927), Weiser studied "male societies" of a religio-initiatory variety. Typologically they resembled groups already categorized by Heinrich Schurtz in various locations around the world, building in a systematic if somewhat abstract manner on work by Hermann Usener.[7] But while Schurtz, from a rigidly evolutionary perspective, had presented these "male groups" as an essential stage on the path towards the formation of society, Weiser's interest differed, at least initially. After reading Theodor Reik on puberty rites among primitive peoples, she identified the "conflict between two generations" behind the initiation ceremonies. Oedipal tensions charge relationships between fathers and sons with ambivalent feelings, a combination of hate and love; the initiation expresses symbolically, through terrifying rituals, the bridling of youthful energies.[8] These ideas, scarcely impaired by a fairly predictable distinction between the interpretations of the Freudian school and the wealth of data which it produced, reveal the probable nonscientific genesis of Weiser's work (shrewdly noted by W. E. Peuckert),[9] namely, the grandiose, composite youth movement through which the cultural gap created between fathers and sons in the early decades of twentieth-century Germany found expression.[10]

Probably this was the origin of Weiser's view of initiation rites as a part of generational conflict. But this idea was allowed to drop, together with the polemical allusion to the importance of female initiation, generally undervalued by scholars.[11] Research took another course, demonstrating the existence of "male societies" in Germanic antiquity through an array of sources that included Tacitus (*Germania*), the Icelandic sagas, the *Historia Danica* by Saxo Grammaticus, and the fables collected by the brothers Grimm. And from the pages of Saxo and the Icelandic sagas, written between the thirteenth and sixteenth centuries, leaped the *berserkir*, an initiatory group of chosen warriors. In rich and sophisticated analysis, impossible to recapitulate here in detail, Weiser demonstrates that they had been portrayed as human beings, although periodically capable of extraordinary feats when they fell into states of unrestrained fury, and also as mythical beings able to assume animal appearances (wolves, bears). By comparing them with similar Germanic phenomena, Weiser concluded that the enigma could be explained: the *berserkir* "originally personified the troop of the dead" (*Totenheer*), and the authors of the sagas were perfectly aware of the twofold identity.[12] This comparison was based in part on the myths and rites still to be found in Germanic folklore, specifically on "the army of the dead" or "Wild Hunt" (*wilde Jagd*), and in part, following Eugen Mogk, on beliefs in werewolves.[13] Such elements as ecstasy, the ability to be transformed into animals, and the connection with the army of the dead always led back to that warlike divinity whom the *berserkir* followed: Odin.

Otto Höfler took these conclusions (later accepted as a whole by Dumézil) as a starting point in his book *Kultische Geheimbünde der Germanen* (1934), the sole volume to appear in a work intended to be joined by two others, which, although partly written, remained unpublished.[14] Its immediate impact internationally was far deeper than Weiser's and touched areas of research ranging from folklore to Iranian studies. In addition to Dumézil and Weiser, other scholars such as Stig Wikander and Karl Meuli responded to the book favorably (though Meuli ended by distancing himself from Höfler).[15] There was also no lack of criticism, some of it harsh, over Höfler's peculiar criteria of interpretation. I noted that Weiser had integrated literary sources (sagas), evidence attesting to the myth of the Wild Hunt, and descriptions of folkloric rituals to argue that the *berserkir* "originally personified the army of the dead." Höfler went a step further. He interpreted all or virtually all the evidence linked to apparitions of the Wild Hunt as proof of the existence of "male societies" of a religio-initiatory type. In other words, behind the presumed manifestations, there were groups of flesh-and-blood youths who believed that they were personifying the army of the dead. Thanks to Höfler's enormous erudition the amount of evidence collected by Weiser was tremendously expanded, and with disconcerting results. Höfler's explication of the sources in his *Kultische Geheimbünde* in almost every instance presents a challenge to elementary common sense. His method of interpretation, characterized by a sort of ingenuous positivism, was completely paradoxical in a scholar who did not hesitate to rail against postivistic flatness in the name of superior spiritual "realities."[16]

Determining the link between myths and rites has always been a delicate and uncertain process in the work of historians of religion, anthropologists, and folklorists. With nothing less than an interpretative *coup de main*, Höfler obliterated every distinction between myths and rites, explaining documents connected with the former as proof for the existence of the latter. The English Egyptologist Margaret Murray, on the basis of an equally indefensible assumption, though founded on totally different ideological presuppositions, had accepted in part descriptions of the sabbat furnished by accused witches as proof of the existence of a secret cult based on fertility rites. Not surprisingly, Höfler accepted Murray's assumptions in full.[17]

The Witch-Cult in Western Europe (Oxford, 1921), Murray's best-known book, was considered authoritative for decades but is totally discredited today.[18] *Kultische Geheimbünde der Germanen* has experienced a different fate. The existence of secret male societies of a ritual type, accepted by many scholars of Germanic areas, has also been discovered elsewhere, for example in Iran. The objections raised by Höfler's critics have had limited impact, with the exception of Friedrich Ranke's extreme views. According to the latter, all the evidence concerning apparitions of the army of the dead was the fruit of hallucinations pure and simple, and pathological rather than mythico-religious statements.[19] But this rationalistic, reductionist interpretation seems to be as baseless as Höfler's.

I have mentioned that the documentation collected in *Kultische Geheimbünde* was much richer than what had been available to Weiser. Nevertheless, Höfler ignored a number of themes. First, Weiser had compared the ecstasy of Eurasian shamans to the unbridled warlike frenzies (*Raserei*) of the *berserkir*. Secondly, she had also pointed out the presence of feminine divinities at the head of the Wild Hunt and had investigated the relationship between the Germanic Perchta and the Mediterranean Artemis. It was from the first that Weiser presumably traced her cautiously advanced hypothesis that the mythico-ritual complex she was studying actually had pre-Indo-European as well as Indo-European roots; from the second, her allusions connected with fertility themes.[20] Behind the Germanic warrior associations Weiser glimpsed something vaster and more complex which was not exclusively martial nor exclusively Germanic.

Höfler decisively minimized the significance of these possible ramifications. The ecstasy of the Germanic warriors was not an individual phenomenon, but a controlled release of restraints obtained through communion with the dead, "an immense source of social and statal energies." As for female divinities and the connotations that had been attached to fertility, Höfler definitely considered them to be of marginal importance. For him the core of "the ecstatic cult of the Germanic religion of the dead" was the "bond (*re-ligio*) understood as a sacred duty, with the living dead and their guide."[21] The heroic and martial myth of the Germanic army of the dead was not reducible to "general concepts in the positivistic study of religion, namely fertility magic and protective magic." Höfler rejected attempts to link Germanic warrior frenzy and shamanic ecstasy, as well as, in general, the superimposition of "oriental concepts" on Germanic mythology: Wodan-Odin was not a god of licentiousness (*Ausschweifung*), but "the god of the dead, of warriors, of kings and of the state."[22]

The above passages, except for the last two, are from the concluding pages of *Kultische Geheimbünde der Germanen*: the last two appear in a polemical reply to a review by Friedrich von der Leyen. A peculiar accident had befallen Höfler between the two publications: he had discovered, *in extremis*, thanks to a reference by Meuli, the proceedings of a late seventeenth-century trial against an old Livonian werewolf.[23] We recall that Weiser, pursuing a suggestion by Mogk, had already proposed adding werewolves to the evidence connected with male societies. Now, through this document the voice of a follower of a secret male society had reached Höfler without passing through the filter of literary tradition. The commentary which accompanied the republication of the trial records in an appendix revealed an obvious embarrassment: the stories told by the old werewolf were full of fabulous elements and difficult to accept as literal descriptions of rites;

moreover, they were based explicitly on the theme of battles fought periodically against witches and warlocks over the fertility of the harvests; and finally, the documents actually mentioned the participation in these combats of female werewolves. Höfler attempted to extricate himself by saying that the werewolf was a braggart, and a Balt besides. The Germanic warrior groups, instead, were strictly male and not concerned with questions of fertility—to sum up, they were something totally different.[24]

Clearly, Höfler's interpretative somersaults were required to save the basic framework of his research; its ideological matrix is clear and confirmed by the closing words of his book: "The specific vocation of the Nordic race, its creativity in bringing states into being, found its proper fulfillment in the male societies (*Männerbünde*), giving them the possibility of flourishing in the richest manner possible. In the fullness of their power they constitute both a productive element and an aggressive force: fighting, educating, and dominating, they entered the history of the world."[25] Such statements certainly did not have an original ring in the Germany of the period. Albert Krebs had already written in the journal *Partei und Gesellschaft: Nationalsozialistische Briefe* (1928) that the male *Bund* was "the nucleus from which states have their origin."[26] Höfler, unlike Weiser, found the inspiration for his research in that current, typified by Krebs and exemplified by the youth movement merging with Nazism. But having given its stamp to the first phase of Nazism, the *bündisch* current ended up being relegated drastically to the background.[27] This, among other factors, explains the violent attack on Höfler's book, published in 1936 in the journal *Rasse*. The author, Harald Spehr, judged *Kultische Geheimbünde der Germanen* and Martin Ninck's *Wodan und germanischer Schicksalglaube* to be "grave dangers for the contemporary politico-cultural situation." The criticism was not only, not even primarily, based on scholarly considerations: by modeling the Germanic image on that of the Viking warriors (the *berserkir*!) who had cut themselves off from their native soil, the two authors had forgotten that "the Germanic man of the pagan period, especially on German soil, was primarily a peasant and a warrior too, of course." He differed greatly from primitive demonic horsemen, from crazed members of secret societies, from ecstatics.

The distinctive trait in the soul of the Nordic race and of the original Indo-Germanic religion, Spehr concluded, was moderation, *eusebeia*, combined with *sophrosyne*, not *ekstasis*, the sacred orgy that characterizes the racial soul of Asia Minor.[28] Evidently, in the eyes of the *Rasse* reviewer, the exaltation of the martial ferocity of the Germanic male societies conjured up the memory of the SA, which had been purged in a bloodbath two years earlier. Höfler was slightly out of step with the times in regard to that solidly rural image, custodian of traditional virtues, that the Nazi regime wanted to project for itself at that particular moment.

"Freud, the Wolf-Man, and the Werewolves," in *Clues, Myths, and the Historical Method* (1989)[29]

I

Among the clinical cases studied by Sigmund Freud, the most famous may be the one of the wolf-man. Although written up in 1914, it was not published until the end of the war, in 1918, with the title "From the History of an Infantile Neurosis."[30] The critical point in this work is a dream experienced in early infancy by the patient, a young Russian from an upper-middle-class family who was twenty-seven years old in 1914. Here is his account:

> I dreamt that it was night and that I was lying in my bed. (My bed stood with its foot towards the window; in front of the window there was a row of old walnut trees. I know it was winter when I had the dream, and night time). Suddenly the window opened of its own accord, and I was terrified to see that some white wolves were sitting on the big walnut tree in front of the window. There were six or seven of them. The wolves were quite white, and looked more like foxes or sheep-dogs and they had their ears pricked like dogs when they are attending to something. In great terror, evidently of being eaten up by the wolves, I screamed and woke up. My nurse hurried to my bed, to see what had happened to me. It took quite a long while before I was convinced that it had only been a dream; I had had such a clear and

life-like picture of the window opening and the wolves sitting on the tree. At last I grew quieter, felt as though I had escaped from some danger, and went to sleep again.

The only piece of action in the dream was the opening of the window, for the wolves sat quite still and without any movement on the branches of the tree, to the right and left of the trunk, and looked at me. It seemed as though they had riveted their whole attention upon me.—I think this was my first anxiety dream. I was three, four, or at most five years old at the time. From then until my eleventh or twelfth year I was always afraid of seeing something terrible in my dreams.[31]

Through a long and minute analysis Freud discovered, behind this infantile dream reconstructed *a posteriori*, the elaboration of an experience lived by the patient at an even more precocious age, when he might have been a year and a half old: the primal scene of coitus between his parents. I will return to this point later. First a digression is necessary that will permit us to look at certain elements in the case of the wolf-man from an angle that differs from Freud's.

II

In a book written several years ago, I studied, on the basis of about fifty inquisitorial trials, a strange sect encountered in the Friuli between the end of the sixteenth and early seventeenth centuries. Its members were men and women who called themselves *benandanti*, well-farers or good-doers. They asserted that they had been born with the caul, and thus were compelled to go forth in spirit four times yearly to fight witches and warlocks for the success of the harvest, or (alternately) participate in processions for the dead. The inquisitors recognized in their accounts a distorted echo of the witches' sabbat: but only after pressure exerted over several decades did they succeed in extorting from the *benandanti* the admission that they were not in fact the adversaries of witches and warlocks, but themselves witches and warlocks.[32]

The beliefs of the *benandanti*—which differed profoundly from the stereotypes of diabolical witchcraft familiar to inquisitors—were not limited to the Friuli. The myth of the procession of the dead is wide-spread in European folklore, while that of the nocturnal battles over fertility, instead, is much rarer. Originally, I succeeded in uncovering only one parallel connected with fertility rites, in a trial held in Livonia against an old werewolf at the end of the seventeenth century. The man in question, Thiess by name, told the judges that three times yearly he traveled with other werewolves "beyond the sea" to battle witches and warlocks over the fertility of the harvests. The analogy with the *benandanti* is obvious, but difficult to explain. My initial hypothesis, of a substratum of Slavic credences common to the Friuli and Livonia,[33] was confirmed by an essay of Roman Jakobson and Marc Szeftel which I had missed. This work demonstrates that in Slavic folklore exceptional powers, such as the ability to become a werewolf, were attributed to people born with the caul.[34] The shamanistic charac-teristics which I had recognized in the *benandanti* now appear to be shared by other figures in European folklore: Slavic and Baltic were-wolves, Hungarian *táltos*, Dalmatian *kersniki*, Corsican *mazzeri*, and so forth. All these personages claimed to be able to travel periodically (in spirit or in animal form) to the world of the dead. Their destiny was indicated by special characteristics: having been born with their teeth (*táltos*), with the caul (*benandanti*, *kersniki*, werewolves), or during the twelve days between Christmas and Epiphany (werewolves).[35]

III

Let us return to the wolf-man. We learn from Freud's published ac-count that the patient was a Russian, that he had been born with the caul, that he had been born on Christmas day.[36] There is an obvious cultural homogeneity between these facts and the infantile dream fo-cusing on the appearance of the wolves. A series of casual coincidences is really quite improbable. The intermediary between the sphere of folkloric beliefs connected with werewolves and Freud's future patient, who belonged, as I have said, to an upper-middle-class family, un-doubtedly must have been the nurse, the *nianja*, described as a "pious and superstitious" woman.[37] The child was deeply attached to the old nurse (it was she, after all, who comforted him after his anguished dream about the wolves). It was from her that he would have learned what extraordinary (not necessarily negative) powers were conferred by the fact that he had been born with the caul. And it was she who would have told him his first fairy tales, before the English governess read to him Grimm's in a Russian translation. Even the fable of the tailor and the wolves, drawn forth during the patient's analysis, which his grandfather (and, who knows? perhaps his nurse too) had recited, was part of the Russian folklore, and Afanasjev included it in his celebrated collection.[38] But the dream, imbued with fairy-tale echoes of the seven wolves on the tree, also recalls the initiatory dreams with which the vocation of the future *benandanti* or of the future *táltos* manifested itself in infancy or adolescence. The Friulian child, for example, who carried around his neck the caul with which he was born and which had been saved by his mother, was visited by an apparition one night many years later: a man who said to him, "You must come with me because you have something of mine."[39] In the case of the *táltos*, what appeared was an animal, generally a stallion or bull.[40]

In the wolf-man's nightmare we discern a dream of an initiatory character, induced by the surrounding cultural setting or, more precisely, by a part of it. Subjected to opposing cultural pressures (the nurse, the English governess, his parents and teachers), the wolf-man's fate differed from what it might have been two or three centuries earlier. Instead of turning into a werewolf, he became a neurotic on the brink of psychosis.[41]

IV

It is not so surprising that Freud (who, incidentally, was himself born with the caul) should have allowed these elements to elude him in the end: the patient came from a cultural world too different from his own. When it was a matter of interpreting the dreams of his Viennese patients (or, even better, his own) Freud was in full command of the everyday context, capable of deciphering literary and other allusions, some of a hidden, innermost nature. In the present case, instead, he did not perceive that in a fable in Afanasjev's collection ("The Imbecile Wolf") he would have found the answer to the question about the number of wolves (why six or seven?) asked by his patient.[42] But the failure to make the connection between being born with the caul and wolves (werewolves) had more serious consequences from a hermeneutic point of view. Freud, who years before had written a work on dreams in folklore in association with D. E. Oppenheim,[43] did not recognize the element of folklore present in the wolf-man's dream. Thus, the cultural context behind the dream was ignored: what remained was only the individual experience, reconstructed through the network of associations deduced by the analyst.

One could object that this is not enough to warrant an alternative interpretation to Freud's. The cultural implications that being born with the caul possessed in Slavic folklore integrate, but do not abolish, the psychological implications that this fact had assumed in the patient's psyche. Similarly, they integrate but do not confute Freud's interpretation.

> The world, he said, was hidden from him by a veil; and our psychoanalytic training forbids our assuming that these words can have been without significance or have been chosen at haphazard . . . It was not until just before taking leave of the treatment that he remembered having been told that he was born with a caul. He had for that reason always looked on himself as a special child of fortune whom no ill could befall. He did not lose that conviction until he was forced to realize that his gonorrhoeal infection constituted a serious injury to his body. The blow to his narcissisms was too much for him and he collapsed. It may be said that in so doing he was repeating a mechanism that he had already brought into play once before. For his wolf phobia had broken out when he found himself faced by the fact that such a thing as castration was possible; and he clearly classed his gonorrhoea as castration.
>
> Thus the caul was the veil that hid him from the world and hid the world from him. The complaint that he made was in reality a fulfilled wish-fantasy that represented the return to the womb; and was, in fact, a wish-fantasy of flight from the world.[44]

Even the general interpretation of the wolf-man's dream as a re-elaboration of the primal scene would not appear, at first glance, to have been even slightly impaired by what I have observed thus far.

V

But what complicates the question is precisely the term "primal scene" (*Urszene*). Although it was used here probably for the first time in a text intended for publication, it had already appeared in a plural form (*Urszenen*) in a letter from Freud to Fliess dated May 2, 1897, and in an accompanying document.[45] The term reemerged with a different meaning, however, after seventeen years. In 1897, in fact, the "primal scenes" referred not to coitus between parents but to acts of seduction perpetrated on children by adults (frequently parents); a decisive ae-tiological role in the formation of neuroses, especially hysteria, was attributed to these acts. As we know, after having upheld this thesis even publicly in an 1896 lecture, Freud abandoned it suddenly in the summer of the following year, with the beginning of his own auto-analysis. He explained in his famous letter to Fliess of September 211, 1897, that all his certainties had vanished: his patients' accounts about sexual seductions experienced in infancy now appeared to him to be pure and simple fantasies. From this turning point, coinciding with the identification of the Oedipus complex, psychoanalysis was born.[46] The term *Urszenen* had emerged immediately before this dramatic crisis, almost as if to crown the seduction theory, after a series of reflections had taken an unexpected turn in that same decisive year, 1897. In two agitated letters to Fliess (dated respectively January 17 and 24), Freud revealed that his theories on the origins of hysteria had been discovered and formulated centuries before by judges in witch-craft trials. Besides comparing witches to hysterics (as Charcot and his followers had already done), Freud identified himself implicitly with the judges: "Why are [the witches'] confessions under torture so like the communications made by my patients in psychic treatment?" He concluded: "Now I understand the harsh therapy of the witches' judges."[47] This twofold analogy was based on an infantile trauma which associated judge and defendant (and thus, implicitly, therapist and patient): "Once more, the inquisitors prick with needles to discover the devil's stigmata, and in a similar situation the victims think of the same old cruel story in fictionalized form (helped perhaps by disguises of the seducers). Thus, not only the victims but also the executioners recalled in this their earliest youth."[48]

A few months later, these painful reflections led to "the surprise that in all cases, the father, not excluding my own, had to be accused of being perverse—the realization of the unexpected frequency of hysteria, with precisely the same conditions prevailing in each, whereas surely such widespread perversions against children are not very probable"; the abandonment of the seduction theory followed from this.[49] But in January 1897 Freud was still convinced that witches' confessions could be explained by that theory since they were symbolic expressions of actual infantile sexual trauma, revived in the course of the trial. He had ordered a *Malleus Maleficarum*, and he proposed to study it. He was leaning towards the belief that in perversion there "could be the remnant of a primeval sexual cult, which once was—perhaps still is—a religion in the Semitic East (Moloch, Astarte)."[50] The term *Urszenen*, when referring explicitly to ontogenesis (infantile sexual trauma that set off neuroses), thus had obvious phylogenetic implications for Freud in 1897. That ontogenesis recapitulated phylogenesis was for Freud, then and later, as it was for a large part of European culture at the turn of the century, an indisputable dogma.

VI

Let us return now to the case of the wolf-man. As I have said, the term "primal scene" was introduced here not to designate infantile seduction but coitus between parents. Freud pondered at length the reality of this scene. Had it been an actual experience on the patient's part or a retrospective fantasy? "I acknowledge that this is the most ticklish question in the whole domain of psycho-analysis," Freud wrote in a note, adding, "No doubt has troubled me more; no other uncertainty has been more decisive in holding me back from publishing my conclusions." He had a different opinion in a passage added in 1918 before the work went to press: "The answer to this question is not in reality a matter of very great importance." But there is no need to consult the famous essay "Negation" (not yet written at that date)[51] to state that the question was indeed of great significance for Freud. The sentence immediately following confirms it: "These scenes of observing parental intercourse, of being seduced in childhood, and of being threatened with castration are unquestionably an inherited endowment, a phylogenetic inheritance, but they may just as easily be acquired by personal experience."[52] Freud's outspoken polemic against Jung's hasty phylogenetic explanations (to which I shall return in a moment) thus led the former unexpectedly to rehabilitate the theory of infantile seduction which he had rejected in 1897. A few pages earlier, Freud had actually written about the final stages in the analysis of the wolf-man, "The old trauma theory which was after all built up upon impressions gained from psycho-analytic practice, had suddenly come to the front once more."[53] This statement flatly contradicted another made in the same year, 1914, in Freud's "On the History of the Psycho-Analytic Movement," where he stated that the theory of seduction constituted "an obstacle . . . that was almost fatal for the young science."[54]

Such fluctuations demonstrate the inadequacy, even philologically, of the thesis recently proposed by J. Moussaieff Masson that Freud's rejection of the seduction theory in 1897 was definitive—and had impaired, with serious consequences, the claims of psychoanalysis to reality.[55] However, it is not my intention to discuss here what is unquestionably a decisive chapter in Freud's intellectual biography. I should prefer, rather, to respond to the following question: what is the significance of the reappearance, after an interval of seventeen years, of the term "primal scenes" (*Urszenen*)?

VII

The possibility of an insignificant coincidence can be eliminated straight-off. Granted, in the piece devoted to the wolf-man, *Urszene* has a different meaning than in Freud's letter to Fliess of May 2, 1897; but, as we saw, the reappearance of the term meant a reflowering of the seduction theory within which it had been originally formulated. To this consideration, internal to Freud's writings, another of an external character needs to be added. The *Urszene* of 1897 had emerged, in its phylogenetic implications, after reflection on witches' accounts of the sabbat; the primal scene of 1914, after reflection upon a dream—the wolf-man's—which, as I have stressed, has folkloristic implications associated with beliefs in werewolves. Now, *from a historical point of view*, there is a connection between werewolves and the sabbat which has the *benandanti* as an intermediate link: both can be considered figures in a vast, half-obliterated stratum of beliefs imbued with shamanistic overtones that under pressure from judges and inquisitors merged with the image of the sabbat.[56] Freud was unaware of this link; even the folkloristic aspects of the wolf-man's dream had escaped him completely. How, then, can one explain the reappearance, at a distance of so many years, of the same key concept, *Urszene*?

In Freudian terms the reply to the question might go like this: the existence of a traumatic sexual nucleus was *perceived clearly* by Freud in 1897 (apropos the witches' confessions), and *discerned dimly* in 1914 (in regard to the dream of the wolf-man). In both cases the original valence suggested by Freud with the prefix *Ur* is ascribable both to the ontogenetic and the phylogenetic spheres. Thus, the folklore beliefs connected with the sabbat and werewolves were thought to preserve the memory, re-elaborated, of sexual trauma experienced not just by individuals but by the human race in a remote past. Freud would undoubtedly have subscribed to this interpretation. His disagreement with Jung, brought out into the open in a passage added in 1918 to his study of the wolf-man did not hinge on whether phylogenetic heredity existed or not, but on the role that the recollection of this heredity should play in the analytical strategy. According to Freud it was permissible to have recourse to phylogenesis for the purpose of explication, but only after having tested all the possibilities for interpretation offered by ontogenesis. The importance Freud attributed to phylogenesis is also testified to by the theory (or anthropological romance) expounded in *Totem and Taboo*, a text which he refers to, significantly, even in the case of the wolf-man.[57]

However, this interpretation, sketched in summary fashion in Freudian terms, is basically unacceptable, for two reasons. First, it rests (just like Jung's theories on the collective unconscious) on an absolutely undemonstrated hypothesis of Lamarckian character: namely, that the psychological and cultural experiences lived by progenitors are part of our cultural baggage. To be sure, Freud, in his piece on the wolf-man, postulates alongside a "phylogenetic experience," inasmuch as it is a repository of specific contents (not too remote from Jungian archetypes), a presumed hereditary disposition of the individual to relive, "in similar situations," events that had occurred in prehistoric periods.[58] But even this disposition still remains an unverifiable conjecture whose potential for explanation does not differ significantly from that *virtus dormitiva* evoked by Molière's physician. The second of the objections is linked to the fact that the identification of a traumatic sexual nucleus in the beliefs connected with the sabbat, with werewolves, and so forth, becomes translated into an arbitrary simplification. When Róheim, for example, reads a sexual initiation into the oneiric initiation of the *táltos*—shamanistic figures in Hungarian folklore in many respects resembling the *benandanti*—the discrepancy between the obscure, intricate documentation and the orderliness of the analysis is all too evident.[59] This interpretation, like others, catches a side, but one side only, of a much richer mythical complex.

VIII

All this, obviously, leads to Jung. His break with Freud occurred over the question of myth (with personality differences contributing). Disagreements began to reveal themselves, almost imperceptibly, from the very first letters exchanged by the two in November 1909. On the eighth Jung wrote to Freud, who at the time was reading Herodotus and Creuzer's work on symbolism, commenting that here "rich lodes open up for the phylogenetic basis of the theory of neurosis." Freud replied three days later in an exultant mood: "I was delighted to learn that you are going into mythology . . . I hope you will soon come to agree with me that in all likelihood mythology centers on the same nuclear complex as the neuroses."[60] The seeds of irreversible discord were already beginning to take root behind this apparent sharing of interests. We can try to describe it in these terms. For Freud the theory of neurosis includes the myth; for Jung it was just the opposite.

Jung's fuzzy-mindedness and lack of rigor caused the failure of a project that, on this point, was potentially much more fruitful than Freud's. The archetypes identified by Jung were the consequence of a superficial intuition (and superficially ethnocentric); his theory of the collective unconscious aggravated Freud's already unacceptable Lamarckianism. Jung's responses to the problem of myth constitute, in a final analysis, the loss of a wonderful opportunity.

IX

The case of the wolf-man poses forcefully that interweaving of myths and neuroses which so engrossed Freud and Jung, albeit from different points of view. I shall not try to explain the neuroses of the wolf-man by the myth of the werewolves. We cannot ignore, however, that the dream of the wolf-man was impregnated by a much more ancient mythical element, visible also in the dreams (in the ecstasies, in the swoons, in the visions) of the *benandanti*, the *táltos*, werewolves, and witches. In obviously different ways, this mythical content impressed itself, through other channels, on Freud, first in 1897 and later, unknown to him, in 1914—and on this writer. It is not an archetype in a Jungian sense: phylogenetic heredity is not at issue. The go-betweens are historical, identifiable, or plausibly conjecturable: men, women, books, and archival documents that tell of men and women. The mothers of the Friulian *benandanti*; the wolf-man's nurse; Charcot and his disciples, intent on deciphering the contortions of the hysterics in the Salpêtrière through the descriptions of the possessed (and vice versa); the trial against the *benandante* drover Menichino da Latisana, discovered by chance in the Archivio di Stato, Venice. We could ask, in a brutal simplification of the problem, are we the ones who think up myths, or is it myths who think us up?

We know that Lévi-Strauss replied to this question by opting for the second alternative, thereby taking a position that unquestionably lends itself to a number of ambiguous, more or less irrational interpretations. In general, it is easy to object that there is a great difference between individual variants of the myth, and especially between the individual contexts within which the myth comes into being and functions. There is an even greater distance between passively living a myth and the attempt to interpret it critically in the broadest and most comprehensive manner possible. But after drawing all these distinctions, we still find ourselves confronting something that our interpretations succeed only in approaching, but not exhausting. Against the hypertrophic (actually solipsistic) image of the interpretative I, today in fashion, the formula "myths think us up" underscores, provocatively, the perpetual inadequacies of our analytical categories.

From *Ecstasies: Deciphering the Witches' Sabbath* (1989)

I

In 1691 at Jürgensburg in Livonia an eighty-year-old man named Thiess, whom the townsmen considered an idolater, confessed to the judges interrogating him that he was a werewolf.[61] Three times a year, he said, on St. Lucy's night before Christmas, the night of St. John, and of the Pentecost, the werewolves of Livonia go into hell, "at the end of the sea" (he later corrected himself: "underground"), to fight with the devil and the sorcerers. Women also fight with the werewolves: but not young girls. The German werewolves go to a separate hell. Similar to dogs (they are the dogs of God, Thiess said), and armed with iron whips, the werewolves pursue the devil and sorcerers, who are armed with broomsticks wrapped in horsetails. Many years before, Thiess explained, a sorcerer (a peasant named Skeistan, no dead) had broken his nose. At stake in the battles was the fertility of the fields: the sorcerers steal the shoots of the grain, and if they cannot be wrested from them there will be famine. However, that year the Livonian and the Russian werewolves had both won. The harvest of barley and of rye was going to be abundant. There was also going to be enough fish for everyone.

In vain the judges tried to induce the old man to admit that he had made a pact with the devil. Thiess obstinately continued to repeat that the worst enemies of the devil and the sorcerers were werewolves like himself: after death, they would go to paradise. Since he refused to repent he was sentenced to ten whiplashes.[62]

We can imagine the judges' bewilderment at finding themselves confronted by a werewolf who protected the cross instead of attacking the cattle. Several modern scholars have reacted in a similar way. In fact, Old Thiess's stories were not confined to disrupting an ancient stereotype. They also wrought havoc with a relatively recent interpretative schema, which included the werewolves in a wider mythical complex, substantially Germanic, intrinsically bellicose, hinging on the theme of "the army of the dead" (*Totenheer*). Testimonies concerning this mythical complex have been accepted for centuries as proof of the existence of rituals performed by groups of men consumed by demonic fury, convinced they impersonated the army of the dead.[63] Now, Thiess's reference to the battles for fertility, also fought by women, seemed to contradict the first point; the extravagance of details, such as the battle fought against the witches "at the end of the sea" seemed to contradict the second. Hence, the impulse more or less subtly to undermine the testimony. The confessions of the old werewolf were judged to be echoes of real events, mingled with fragments of myths, lies, boasting, or a disorderly jumble of superstitions and rituals; or, again, some mixture of elements from sagas and remote memories of actual life experiences.[64] Confronted by this eccentric and incoherent Baltic variation, an attempt was made to reassert the original purity of the Germanic warrior myth, revolving around the "army of the dead."[65]

II

As early as the fifth century BCE, Herodotus alluded to men capable of periodically transforming themselves into wolves. In Africa, in Asia, on the American continent analogous beliefs have been found, concerning temporary metamorphoses of human beings into leopards, hyenas, tigers, and jaguars.[66] It has been supposed that in these parallel myths, dispersed over so vast a spatial and temporal area, an aggressive archetype profoundly rooted in the human psyche is expressed, transmitted by heredity, in the form of psychological disposition, from the Paleolithic age on down.[67] Obviously, this is a totally undemonstrated hypothesis. But the general perplexity that it provokes is accompanied by other, more specific queries. In the case that we are discussing, for example, the image of werewolves as protectors of fertility blatantly contradicts the putative aggressive nucleus of the myth. What value should be attributed to this isolated, apparently atypical testimony?[68]

The verse and prose romances, the sagas, the penitential books, the theological and demonological treatises, the philosophical and medical dissertations that speak of *loup-garous, werwölfen, lupi mannari*, werewolves, *lobis-homem* and so on, are numerous and well-known. But in the medieval texts—especially in the literary ones— werewolves are portrayed as innocent victims of fate, if not indeed as beneficent figures. Only towards the middle of the fifteenth century is the contradictory aura surrounding these ambiguous being obliterated by the superimposition of a ferocious stereotype—that of the werewolf, devourer of flocks of sheep and infants.[69]

Approximately during this same period the hostile image of the witch crystallized. This is not a mere coincidence. In his *Formicarius*, Johannes Nider speaks of male witches who transform themselves into wolves; in the Valais trials, at the beginning of the fifteenth century, the defendants confessed that they had temporarily assumed the shape of wolves when attacking the cattle. From the very first evidence about the Sabbath, the connection between witches and werewolves therefore appears to be quite intimate. But here too anomalous, perhaps even late confessions, such as that of Thiess, allow us to scratch the surface of the stereotype, bringing a deeper stratum to light.

III

The interpretive difficulties raised by Thiess's confessions disappear as soon as we compare the battles against male and female witches described by him with those fought in their ecstasies by the *benandanti*. As we have seen, this term designated in the Friuli, between the sixteenth and seventeenth centuries, those (primarily women) who maintained that they periodically participated in processions of the dead. But the same name was also given to other individuals (predominantly men) who declared that, armed with bunches of fennel stalks, they periodically fought for the fertility of the fields, against

male and female witches armed with canes of sorghum. The name, the
sign that materially identified both types of *benandanti* (having been
born with a caul); the period (the four Ember days) during which they
performed the feats for which they were destined; the state of lethargy
or catalepsis that preceded them—in both cases, these were identical.
The spirits of the *benandanti* (men or women) left the inanimate body
for a space of time, sometimes in the shape of a mouse or a butterfly,
sometimes astride hares, cats or other animals, to journey in ecstasy
to the procession of the dead or the battle against male and female
witches. In both cases, the journey of the soul was compared by the
benandanti themselves to a temporary death. At the end of the journey there was the encounter with the dead. In the processions they
appeared in a Christianized form as purging souls; in the battles, in an
aggressive and probably more archaic guise as *malandanti*—enemies
of fertility assimilated to male and female witches.[70]

But the battles for fertility are not the only point of contact between the werewolf Thiess and the *benandanti*. In the Slavic world
(from Russia to Serbia) it was believed that anyone born with a caul
was destined to become a werewolf. A contemporary chronicle re-
counts that a magician begged the mother of Prince Vseslav of Polock,
who died in 1101 after having briefly been the King of Kiev, to tie to
the child the membrane in which he had been wrapped at birth, so
that he might always have it on his person. That is why, the chronicler
comments, Vseslav was so ruthlessly bloodthirsty. In *Igor's Tale* he is
portrayed as an actual werewolf. Similar characteristics are attributed
to the protagonist of another *bylina* (probably one of the most ancient): Volch Vseslav'evič, who was able to transform himself not only
into a wolf, but also a falcon and an ant.[71]

The Friulian *benandanti*, at their mothers' wish, wore around their
neck the caul in which they had been born.[72] But their future as peasants did not promise glorious, princely enterprises: only the obscure,
irresistible impulse to fight periodically "in spirit" for the harvest,
astride or in the guise of animals, wielding bundles of fennel against
male and female witches. It is to this sort of battle that Old Thiess
insisted he had gone armed with an iron whip and transformed into a
wolf. True enough, he did not say he had fought them "in spirit"; of ec-

stasy or catalepsis he said not a word (we don't even know whether he had been born with a caul). But his stories must certainly be related to a mythical, not a ritual dimension—not unlike the declaration made by the *benandante* Maria Panzona, who stated that she had gone to paradise and to hell *in soul and body*, accompanied by her uncle in the shape of a butterfly.[73] In both cases we sense the attempt to describe an ecstatic experience perceived as absolutely real.

IV

The trial against Thiess is an extraordinary document; however, it is not unique. Other testimonies confirm partially its contents.

In a treatise entitled *Christlich Bedencken und Erinnerung von Zauberey* ("Christian consideration and memory on magic") which appeared in Heidelberg in 1585, the author, who concealed his real name—Hermann Witekind—under the pseudonym of Augustin Lercheimer, devoted a chapter to the question "whether witches and magicians transformed themselves into cats, dogs, wolves, donkeys, etc." The answer he gave—that it was a matter of diabolical delusion—was not particularly original, although even among the erudite the contrary thesis was widespread: that the transformation of witches and werewolves into animals was an incontrovertible physical phenomenon. The singularity of the *Christlich Bedencken* is to be sought elsewhere. It was based in part on a conversation that Witekind, Livonian by birth and a professor at the University of Riga (subsequently at Heidelberg), had had with a werewolf from his region. (Old Thiess, as we are bound to remember, had also been born in Livonia, the land of the werewolves). In fact, some time before, Witekind had visited the governor of the province, who had arranged for him to meet an incarcerated werewolf. "The man," Witekind remembered, "behaved like a crazy person, he laughed, skipped about, as if he were from a place of pleasure and not a prison." The night before Easter (he told his astonished interlocutor) he had transformed himself into a wolf: after freeing himself from his shackles, he had escaped through the window, heading for an immense river. But why had he returned to prison? they had asked him. "I had to do it, the master wishes it." About this master

(Witekind noted retrospectively) he spoke with great emphasis. "An evil master," they had objected. "If you know how to give me a better one, I will follow him," the man had answered. In the eyes of Professor Witekind, author of books on history and astronomy, the nameless werewolf appeared an incomprehensible being: "he knew about God as a wolf might. To see him and listen to him was painful."[74] Perhaps the werewolf thought that about his own mysterious master, Witekind knew just as much as a professor. Certainly, the prisoner's merry insolence brings to mind the assurance, full of sarcasm, with which the *benandanti* sometimes held their own against inquisitors.[75]

An echo of this conversation can be found in a fleeting reference by Kaspar Peucer to the dialogue between a '*homo sapiens*' (certainly Witekind) and a werewolf, eruditely defined as a "rustic Lycaon" from the mythic King of Arcadia transformed into a wolf by Zeus because of his cannibalism. The reference appears in the expanded reprint of Peucer's *Commentarius de praecipuis generibus divinationum*, which was published in 1560, i.e., five years *before* the *Christlich Bedencken*. This apparent chronological oddity is easily explained: around 1550 Witekind, then a student, had spent some time at Wittenberg, where he had evidently told Peucer about his encounter with the anonymous werewolf.[76] Peucer's Latin text is far removed from the almost ethnographic freshness of the conversation reported, at the distance of so many years, by Witekind. The brashness of that peasant werewolf, a precious index of psychological and cultural estrangement, has vanished into thin air in the *Commentarius*. But despite the pedantic allusion to Lycaon, Peucer's treatise transmits a series of details (only partially reproduced in Witekind's work) which contradict the current image of werewolves. They boast of deterring witches and of fighting them when they have changed themselves into butterflies; they assume (or at least believe they assume) the guise of a wolf during the twelve days between Christmas and Epiphany, compelled so to do by the apparition of a lame child; they are driven in their thousands by a tall man armed with an iron whip towards the bank of an enormous river, which they cross without getting wet, because the man separates its waters with a lash of his whip; they attack cattle but cannot do any harm to human beings.[77] Another professor at the University of

Wittenberg lectured on these topics: Philip Melanchthon (who was Peucer's father-in-law). From one of his listeners we learn that as a source he had quoted a letter received from "Hermannus Livonus," a "man most respectable" and totally reliable.[78] In compiling his *Commentarius* Peucer in all likelihood also had before him the letter written to Melanchthon by the Livonian Hermann Witekind.[79] Through this precious informant, close by birth and language to Baltic folk traditions, we have therefore received a piece of information — the hostility of the werewolves towards witches — which substantially coincides with the confessions of Thiess, attenuating the anomaly. We discern a background of beliefs that are far removed from the negative stereotype of the werewolf.

V

From the Scythians and the Greeks living in Scythia, Herodotus had picked up a rumor (which he repeated without giving it credence) concerning a population that he knew only indirectly: the Neuroi. For a number of days each year they changed into wolves. Who the Neuroi were and where they lived, we do not know with certainty. In the sixteenth century, it was thought that they had lived in a region corresponding to Livonia; today, some scholars consider them a proto-Baltic population.[80] But this supposed ethnic continuity, as yet undemonstrated, does not explain why analogous beliefs in werewolves are found in heterogeneous cultural milieux — Mediterranean, Celtic, Germanic, and Slavic — over a very long span of time.

We might ask ourselves whether these really are analogous beliefs. Certainly, the ability to transform oneself into a wolf if periodically attributed to groups of very different sizes. To entire populations, such as the Neuroi, according to Herodotus; to the inhabitants of a region, like Ossory in Ireland, according to Giraldus Cambrensis; to specific families, such as the Anthi in Arcadia, according to Pliny; to individuals fated to this by the Parcae (identifiable with the *Matres*), as Burchard of Worms wrote at the beginning of the eleventh century, condemning the belief as superstitious. However, this variety is accompanied by a number of recurrent elements. First of all, the transformation is always temporary, though of varying duration; nine years in Arcadia, according to Pausanias and Pliny; seven years, or for a specific period every seven years, in medieval Ireland; twelve days in the Germanic and Baltic countries. Secondly, it is preceded by gestures of a ritual character: the werewolf undresses and hangs his clothes on the branches of an oak (Pliny) or sets them on the ground, urinating all around them (Petronius); then he crosses a pond (in Arcadia, according to Pliny) or a river (in Livonia, according to Witekind).[81]

In this crossing and the attendant gestures a rite of passage has been identified; more precisely, an initiatory ceremony, or the equivalent of the crossing of the infernal river that separates the world of the living from that of the dead.[82] The two interpretations are not mutually contradictory, provided we recognize that death is the passage par excellence and that every ritual of initiation hinges on a symbolic death.[83] It is well known that in the ancient world the wolf was associated with the world of the dead; for example, in the Etruscan tomb at Orvieto, Hades is depicted with the head of a wolf covering his head.[84] Various features lead us to extend this connection beyond the spatial, chronological and cultural confines of the ancient Mediterranean world. The time favored by the werewolves for their forays in the Germanic, Baltic and Slavic countries—the twelve nights between Christmas and Epiphany—corresponds to that in which the souls of the dead went roaming.[85] In ancient Germanic law the proscribed—expelled from the community and considered symbolically dead—were referred to by the term *wargr* or *wargus*, i.e., "wolf."[86] A symbolic death—the ecstasy—can be detected behind the stories of the old werewolf Thiess, so similar to those of the *benandanti* of the Friuli. Animal transformation or the cavalcade astride animals represented the temporary departure of the soul from the inanimate body.[87]

In his *Historia de gentibus septentrionalibus* (1555) Olaus Magnus, Bishop of Uppsala, after having described the bloody attacks on men and beasts perpetrated during the night of Christmas by the werewolves in Prussia, Livonia and Lithuania, added: "they enter into the rooms where beer is stored, empty the barrels of wine and mead, and then they place the empty vessels one on top of the other in the middle of the cellar."[88] In this sort of behavior he saw a characteristic trait distinguishing men transformed into wolves from actual wolves. As to the physical reality of their metamorphosis, he entertained not the slightest doubt, and reconfirmed it against Pliny's authority. A century later, the dissertations on werewolves discussed at the Universities of Leipzig and Wittenberg advanced, on the basis of information collected in the Baltic countries, a thesis that concurred with Witekind's: the metamorphosis was preceded by a profound sleep or ecstasy and hence must always, or almost always, be considered purely imaginary (natural or diabolical, depending on the interpreters).[89] Several modern scholars have chosen to follow the opinion of Olaus Magnus, and have used his account to bolster the interpretation already mentioned in connection with Old Thiess's stories: the alleged werewolves were, in reality, young followers of sectarian associations, formed by enchanters or by individuals disguised as wolves, who identified with the army of the dead in their rituals.[90] This last connection is incontrovertible, but it must be understood in a purely symbolic sense. The incursions of Baltic werewolves into the cellars will have to be set alongside those performed "in spirit" by the *benandanti* of the Friuli, who "climbed astride the barrels, drank with a pipe"—wine, naturally, rather than the beer and mead their colleagues drank in the north. In both we perceive the echo of a myth—the myth of the unquenchable thirst of the dead.[91]

VI

We set out from the thirst of the sorcerers in the Valais, of the *benandanti* of the Friuli, of the dead of the Ariège in order to reconstruct a layer of beliefs which later, in partial and distorted form, merged in the Sabbath. We have returned to the same point, following a different route. Through the evidence about the nocturnal battles fought by werewolves and *benandanti* against male and female witches, we begin to glimpse a symmetrical, primarily male version of the predominantly female ecstatic cult analyzed up to this point.

In the Friuli the goddess who led the cohorts of the dead appears in a single testimony:[92] but both versions were present. The subterranean analogy linking them was underscored by the uniqueness of

the term—*benandanti*—which designated those who behaved ecstat-
ically. This is an almost unique instance (only that of the Rumanian
călusari, as we shall see, is comparable). The evidence about the followers of the nocturnal divinities came from a Celto-Mediterranean
environment, which inscribed the theme of the resurrection of animals from their bones in a much vaster framework. As we shall see,
testimony on the night battles sketches a different geography: more
fragmentary and, at least at first sight, incoherent. The Friuli will then
have to be considered as a sort of border country in which the two,
habitually severed versions of the ecstatic cult were superimposed and
merged (see map).

Hitherto it has been the inquisitors, preachers and bishops who
have guided our research; the analogies that their usually infallible
eyes had detected by following the thread of Diana, "goddess of the
pagans," suggested a preliminary organization of the material. Yet the
ecstatic battles have left very faint traces in canonistic as well as demonological literature.[93] In the only region in which they were confronted
by these beliefs—the Friuli—the inquisitors considered them an incomprehensible local variant of the Sabbath. The impossibility of recourse to the comparative efforts of the persecutors has hindered not
only the interpretation, but the very reconstitution, of the documentary series. The morphological strategy, which momentarily flashed
before us the possibility of a Eurasian substratum beneath the ecstatic
cult of the nocturnal goddess, was the only one available.

Recognizing a formal resemblance is never a clear-cut operation.
The dates on which Thiess and the *benandanti* fought their ecstatic
battles were different, as were the weapons used by either side against
the male and female witches. But behind these superficial divergences
we recognize profound similarity, because both cases involve (a) periodic battles, (b) fought in ecstasy, (c) for the purposes of fertility,
(d) against male and female witches. The bundles of fennel wielded by
the *benandanti* and the iron whip brandished by the werewolves, must
be understood not as different but isomorphic elements. The connection, documented in the sphere of Slavic folklore, between being born
with a caul and becoming werewolves then appears as an anticipated

intermediary link of a formal character.[94] In this case it is reinforced by a historical datum: the presence of a Slavic component in the Friuli's ethnic background and culture.

VII

A series of beliefs tracked down in Istria, Slovenia, Croatia, and all along the Dalmatian coast down to Montenegro, analogous to those about the *benandanti* as protectors of the harvest, accords perfectly well with this configuration.[95] As early as the seventeenth century, Monsignor G. F. Tommasini remarked, in a somewhat confused manner, that in Istria people believe

> and cannot escape the fantasy, that there are some men, born under certain constellations, and in particular those who are born closed in a certain membrane (they call these *chresnichi*, and those others *vucodlachi* [i.e., vampires]), who go by night in spirit on the crossroads and also into the houses to inspire fear or do damage, and that they are accustomed to congregating together at some of the most famous crossroads, particularly at the time of the four Ember weeks, and there fight against one another for the abundance or scarcity of all sorts of products . . .[96]

No mention is made of women here. The *kresnik* (or *krestnik*) in Istria and Slovenia, called *krsnik* in Croatia, corresponds in northern Croatian to the *mogut*, in Southern Dalmatia to the *negromanat*, in Bosnia, Herzegovina and above all, Montenegro to the *zduhač*. He is almost invariably a man.[97] Generally, he is marked by some peculiarity connected with his birth. The *kresnik* and the *zduhač* are born with the caul; the *negromanat* has a tail; the *mogut* is the son of a woman who died giving birth to him or has given birth to him after an unusually long pregnancy. They are all destined to fight, sometimes for fixed periods such as the Ember weeks or Christmas night, against sorcerers and vampires, chasing away evil spells or protecting the cross. These combats are savage collisions between animals, boars, dogs, oxen, horses, often of contrasting colors (the witches black, their adversaries white or dappled). The animals are the spirits of the contenders. At times small animals are involved: of the *kresniki* it is said that, while they sleep, their spirit issues from their mouth in the shape of a black fly.

It is also said that the male witches (*strigoi*) are born with a caul: but the envelope in which they are wrapped is black or red, whereas that of the *kresniki* is white. In Istria the midwives sew this envelope around the little *kresniki*, under their armpits; in the island of Krk (Veglia) it is dried and then mixed with food for the future *kresnik* to eat. Then, at the age of seven (more rarely at eighteen or twenty-one), the nocturnal battles commence. But about them the *kresniki* (like the *benandanti*) must preserve secrecy.

At Krk it is said that every people, every stock is protected by a *kresnik* and threatened by a *kudlak* (vampire). Elsewhere the hostile witches are aliens: the Venetians, in Montenegro the Turks or those who come from across the sea. More generally, they are what is most unmitigatedly hostile: the unplacated dead, jealous of the living—the vampire (*vukodlak*), whose terrifying features are confused with those of the witch among the western Slavs.[98] For that matter, in the Friuli male and female witches, men and women of flesh and blood, are obscurely assimilated to the *malandanti*, that is, the vagrant souls of the restless dead.[99]

VIII

In the case of *benandanti* and *kresniki* formal analogies and historical connections converge. But evidence from different sources complicates the picture. In the throng of witches and enchanters who populate Hungarian folklore there stand out, owing to their singularity, a number of figures who have been linked to Oriental, and probably extremely ancient, traditions. The most important is the *táltos*. This name, possibly of Turkish origin, designated the men and women tried for witchcraft as early as the end of the sixteenth century.[100] But the *táltos* strenuously denied the accusations leveled at them. A woman, András Bartha, tried at Debrecen in 1725, declared that she had been named leader of the *táltos* by God himself: because God forms the *táltos* when they are still in their mother's womb, then he takes them under his wing and makes them fly through the sky like birds to fight against male and female witches "for the dominion of the sky,"[101] A number of later testimonies, collected almost down to the present day, confirm and enrich this fundamental juxtaposition. They also modify it: women *táltos* become increasingly rare. The *táltos* are chiefly men, marked since birth by some physical peculiarity, such as being born with teeth, with six fingers on one hand or, more rarely, with the caul.[102] When very young they are silent, melancholy, extremely strong, greedy for milk (then, as adults, for cheese and eggs). At a certain age (usually seven, sometimes thirteen), they have a vision: an older *táltos*, in the shape of an animal—invariably a stallion or bull. A struggle begins between the two: if the youngster succumbs, he remains half a *táltos*; if he prevails, he becomes a full *táltos*. In other localities it is said that the male *táltos* initiate the girls (provided they are virgins) and vice versa. As a rule, the initiation is preceded by a "sleep" that lasts three days; during this time the future *táltos* "hides himself." At times he dreams that he is being chopped to pieces, or he passes extraordinary tests (climbing very tall trees, for example). The *táltos* go into combat periodically (three times a year, or once every seven years, etc.) in the shape of stallions, bulls or flames. Usually, they engage each other, more rarely male and female witches, sometimes enemies of alien origin, for example Turks or Germans, who are likewise transformed into animals or flames, but of a different color. Before changing into an animal, the *táltos* is overcome by a sort of heat and babbles disconnected words, entering into contact with the world of the spirits. Often the battle takes place among the clouds and to the accompaniment of storms; whoever wins ensures abundant harvests for seven years or for the following year for his side. As a result, when there is a drought, the peasants bring money and gifts to the *táltos* so that they may cause rain to fall. For their part, the *táltos* extort milk and cheese from the peasants, threatening to unleash a storm or boasting of their feats: discovering hidden treasures, healing those struck by evil spells, identifying the witches in the village by banging a drum (or, alternately, a sifter). But theirs is a vocation they have not elected: they cannot resist the call. After a while (at the age of fifteen, but often much later) they cease their activities.

From this schematic account the analogy between the *táltos* and *benandanti* clearly emerges. In both cases we find the initiation or the call to work by an older follower, the animal metamorphoses, the struggles for fertility, the ability to discover witches and cure the victims of evil spells, the consciousness of the ineluctability of their extraordinary mission and its justification, sometimes cast in religious terms.[103] Even though they pertain to this analogy, the *kresniki* seem to figure, not only formally but also geographically, as an intermediate term: for example, they are born with a caul like the *benandanti* but, like the *táltos*, they fight in animal form against other *kresniki*, likewise transformed into animals.[104] But the undeniable formal compactness of the series contrasts with the heterogeneity of the phenomena it includes: the Hungarian *táltos* evidently carry us outside the Indo-European linguistic milieu.

IX

Fully part of it, by contrast, are the Ossetians, as the Orientalist Julius Klaproth recognized at the beginning of the nineteenth century, while travelling through the mountains of the northern Caucasus. Klaproth especially studied the language of these very remote descendants from the Scythians of antiquity, the Alans and Roxolans of the Middle Ages, identifying it as having an Iranian origin: but he also took an interest in the religion, which he defined as "a bizarre mixture of Christianity and ancient superstition."[105] He described their intense devotion to the prophet Elijah, whom they consider their supreme protector.[106] Goats are sacrificed to him in caves, and they eat their meat: then they spread the skins under a large tree and worship them, particularly during the prophet's feast day, that he may deign to ward off hail and grant a rich harvest. The Ossetians often visit these caves to intoxicate themselves with the smoke from the *rhododendron caucasicum* which plunges them into sleep: the dreams that ensue are considered to be omens. However, they also have professional soothsayers who live on the sacred cliffs and predict the future in exchange for gifts. "Among them," Klaproth observed,

> there are also some old men and women who, on the eve of St. Sylvester, fall into a sort of ecstasy, remaining motionless on the ground as though asleep. When they awake, they say they've seen the souls of the dead, sometimes in a great swamp, alternatively, astride pigs, dogs, or rams. If they see a soul gathering wheat in the fields and bringing it to the village, they detect the omen of an abundant harvest.[107]

The research conducted towards the end of the nineteenth century by Russian folklorists has confirmed and enriched this evidence. In the period between Christmas and New Year, the Ossetians affirm, some individuals, leaving their body fast asleep, go in spirit to the land of the dead. This land is a great meadow, called *burku* in Digor dialect and *kurys* in the Iron dialect; those who have the ability to visit it are called, respectively, *burkudzäutä* and *kurysdzaütä*. To reach the meadow of the dead they use the most varied mounts: doves, horses, cows, dogs, children, scythes, brooms, benches and bowls. The souls who have undertaken this journey many times already possess the requisite vehicles; the inexperienced steal them from their neighbors. In consequence, with the approach of Christmas, the Ossetians address solemn prayers to Uazilla (i.e., Elijah) to protect children, horses, dogs and household objects from the thieving incursions of "astute and impure people," against whom they invoke the prophet's curse. When they arrive at the great meadow, the inexperienced souls allow themselves to be attracted by the perfume of the flowers and fruits scattered upon it: and so they incautiously pluck a red rose that causes a cough, a white rose that causes a cold, a large red apple that causes a fever, and so on. By contrast, the more experienced souls catch the seeds of the wheat and of other fruits of the earth, pursued by the dead, who try to shoot them with arrows: the hunt ends only on the threshold of the village. The arrows do not cause wounds, but black spots which are incurable; some of the *burkudzäutä* heal by themselves; some from the world of the dead describe their feats to their fellow villagers, who then express their gratitude. The souls who bring back illnesses endure the curses of those who catch the fever or cough.[108]

X

Other neighboring populations appear to have shared analogous beliefs. In 1666, on the twentieth day of the tenth month (according to the Gregorian calendar 28 April), the Turkish geographer and traveller, Evliyâ Celebi, happened to be in a Circassian village. From its inhabitants he learned that that was "the night of the *Kara-Kondjolos* (vampires)." As he later recounted the story, he had left his encampment with eighty people. Suddenly, he had seen the sorcerers of the Abkhaz appear: they crossed the sky astride uprooted trees, terracotta vases, axes, mats, cart wheels, oven shovels, and so on. From the opposite side, hundreds of Circassian sorcerers (*Uyuz*) had immediately risen in flight, with disheveled hair and gnashing teeth, emitting fiery rays from their eyes, nose, ears and mouth. They rode on fishing boats, horse or oxen carcasses, enormous camels, they brandished serpents, dragons, the heads of bears, horses and camels. The battle had lasted six hours. At a certain stage pieces of their mounts had begun to rain down from the sky, frightening the horses. Seven Circassians and seven Abkhaz witches had plunged to the ground, fighting and trying to suck each other's blood. The village's inhabitants had come to the aid of their champions, setting fire to their opponents. At cock crow the contenders had dissolved, becoming invisible. The ground was strewn with corpses, objects and the carcasses of animals. In the past Evliyâ had not believed such stories. Now he was obliged to change his mind: the battle had really taken place, as the thousands of soldiers who had witnessed the scene could confirm. The Circassians swore that they had seen nothing of the kind for forty or fifty years. Usually the combatants were five or ten in number: after engaging each other on the ground, they took flight.[109]

It will be remembered that the Balkan *kresniki* and the Livonian werewolves periodically fought against alien witches. And the aerial cavalries which Evliyâ, in his grandiloquent and fantastic account, attributes to the Abkhaz witches, are more or less identical to those of the Ossetian *burkudzäutä* (and not those of their opponents, as we would expect).[110] However, it is not proven that among the Circassians, the issue of the battle between witches was the abundance of the harvest. For the sake of prudence, let us restrict ourselves to the Ossetian documentation: the resemblances with the phenomena we are investigating leap to the eye. Ecstasy; the flight to the realm of the dead astride an animal (to which are added here children and domestic utensils); the struggle with the dead (elsewhere identified with the witches) to wrest away the seeds of fertility: all this clearly connects the Ossetian *burkudzäutä* to the *benandanti* of the Friuli, the Baltic werewolves like Thiess, to the Balkan *kresniki*, the Hungarian *táltos*. In one case at least the structural analogy even contains superficial coincidences. A young Friulian cowherd, Menichino da Latisana, tried in 1591, recounted that some years before, on a winter night during the Ember weeks, he had dreamt that he was accompanying the *benandanti* (a dream that was destined to be repeated three times every year thereafter):

> And I was afraid and it seemed to me I was in a wide meadow, large and beautiful, and it smelled oily, that is, it gave off a good smell, and it seemed to me that in it were many flowers and roses . . .

There, amidst the perfume of roses—he was unable to see them, everything was enveloped in smoke—he had fought the witches and won, wresting a good harvest from them.

This meadow was the "meadow of Josafat," Menichino said: the meadow of the dead overflowing with roses, which the souls of the *burkudzäutä* visited in ecstasy. Still according to Menichino, it was possible to reach it only in a state of temporary death: "if anyone had turned over our bodies while we were outside . . . we would have died."[111]

XI

The ecstatic experiences of these *burkudzäutä* are echoed in the Ossetian epic of the Narts. Soslan, one of the heroes of this cycle of legends, visits the country of the dead. It is a plain where all the cereals of the world grow and all the animals of the world, domesticated or wild, roam. Along the river are young girls who dance the dance of the Narts. Before them are tables laden with exquisite foods. Soslan barely manages to escape from this place of delights: the devils (who here replace the dead), instigated by his antagonist, Syrdon, pursue him, hurling flaming arrows at him.[112] Thus, in the Caucasus as in the West, the theme of the journey to the world of the dead also nourished the ecstasies of a number of predestined individuals and a series of poetic compositions. Perhaps this is not a coincidence. It has been suggested that the singular parallelisms between the Ossetian epic and the Celtic epic (re-elaborated in the romances of the Arthurian cycle) presuppose precise historical relationships.[113]

But more about all this later. First we must examine more closely the series we have constructed.

XII

The single element which all the components of this series have in common is the capacity to enter into periodic ecstasies. It seems reasonable to postulate an ecstatic experience behind the accounts of Old Thiess (an experience that during the seventeenth century, at any rate, was less and less often attributed to werewolves).[114] During the ecstasy, all the figures whom we have considered fight for the fertility of the fields: only among the *táltos* does this theme enjoy less prominence. All of them, except for the *burkudzäutä*, are predestined for ecstasy by some physical sign (being born with a caul, with teeth, with six fingers on one hand, with a tail); or by some circumstance linked to their birth (the mother dead in childbirth, an exceptionally long pregnancy). Among all of them (here too except for the *burkudzäutä*) the men seem to predominate. For the *benandanti*, *kresniki* and *táltos*, the vocation commences at a variable age, between seven and twenty-eight. To *benandanti* and *táltos* the announcement of vocation is given by another member of the sect, in spirit or animal shape, respectively. The ecstasy is accompanied by egress from the soul in the shape of small animals (mice or flies for *benandanti* and *kresniki*); or by transformation into larger animals (boars, dogs, oxen, horses for *kresniki*; birds, bull, stallions for *táltos*; wolves, or, exceptionally, dogs, donkeys, horses for werewolves[115]); by a journey astride animals (dogs, hares, pigs, cocks for the *benandanti*; dogs, doves, horses, cows for the *burkudzäutä*); by a journey riding children or various objects (benches, mortars, scythes, brooms for the *burkudzäutä*); by a transformation into flame (*táltos*) or smoke (*benandanti*). The ecstatic sleep coincides with calendar dates—sometimes precise, such as the Ember weeks (*benandanti*, *kresniki*) or twelve days (werewolves, *burkudzäutä*); at other times vaguer, such as three times a year or once every seven years (*táltos*).[116] For the *kresniki* and *táltos*, the enemies of the fertility of the fields against whom the battles are fought are the *kresniki* and *táltos* of other communities, or, indeed, other peoples; for the *benandanti*, *kresniki* and werewolves (the latter specify that their opponents are transformed into butterflies), they are the male and female witches; for the *burkudzäutä*, they are the dead.

All this information more or less directly derives from the very protagonists of these ecstatic cults: *benandanti*, werewolves, *kresniki*, *táltos* and *burkudzäutä*. As we have seen, they present themselves as beneficent figures, possessors of an extraordinary power. But in the eyes of the surrounding community this power was inherently ambiguous, apt to be transformed into its opposite. The belief that the *burkudzäutä* could, out of negligence, bring back illnesses instead of prosperity from their nocturnal journeys, highlights a symbolic ambivalence that probably also characterized the diurnal behavior of these figures. The *benandanti* attracted resentment and hostility with their claim that they could identify the witches in the neighborhood; the *táltos* practiced blackmail vis-à-vis the peasants, threatening to unleash storms.

XIII

The series of which we are speaking might be compared to an accumulation of energy distributed in an uneven manner, rather than to an object with well-defined contours. It is indeed true that every component of the series is characterized by the simultaneous presence of several distinctive elements or traits: (a) the periodic battles, (b) fought in ecstasy, (c) for the sake of fertility, (d) against male and female witches (or their stand-ins, the dead).[117] Around this solid nucleus rotate other elements, whose presence is fluctuating, contingent: they are sometimes absent, sometimes present in an attenuated form. Their superimposition and intersection impart to the figures constitutive of the series (*benandanti, táltos,* etc.) a family likeness.[118] Hence the almost irresistible temptation to integrate analogically a record which in other respects seems full of lacunae. In Romania, for example, it is said that *strigoi* are born with the caul (or, alternatively, with a tail); when they become adult, they don it and become invisible. Transformed into animals or astride horses, brooms, or barrels, they move in spirit to the meadow at the end of the world (at the end of the sea, said Old Thiess) where no grass grows. Here they resume human form and fight with cudgels, axes, and sickles. Having warred all night, they become reconciled. Despite the absence of references to the battle for fertility, the approximation to the series that we are discussing seems extremely close.[119]

At other times we glimpse a more complex relationship of morphological proximity. In various parts of Corsica (the Sartenais and the surrounding mountains, the Niolo) it is said that specific persons called *mazzeri* or *lanceri, culpatori, culpamorti, accacciatori, tumbatori,* are in the habit of roaming in spirit during sleep, alone or in groups through the countryside—especially near streams of water, of which they are, however, afraid. They may be either men or women; but the men have greater power. Driven by an irresistible force, they attack animals (wild boars, pigs, but also dogs, etc.), killing them: the men with rifle shots or a cudgel or knife; the women by tearing them to pieces with their teeth. By turning its muzzle, the *mazzeri* momentarily recognize in the killed animal a human face—the face of a fellow villager, sometimes even that of a relative. This person is destined to die within a short time. The *mazzeri* (usually they are imperfectly baptized persons) are the messengers of death: the innocent instruments of fate. Some play their role joyfully; others with resignation; yet others seek forgiveness from the priests for the killings perpetrated in their dreams. However these killings do not exhaust the dream-activities of the *mazzeri*. In certain localities it is believed that once a year, generally during the night of 31 July/1 August, the *mazzeri* of neighboring villages fight each other. These are usually communities separated by geographical obstacles (for example, a hill) or by ethnic differences. In the battles normal weapons are used; only in one village (Soccia) do the contenders employ branches of asphodel, the plant which, according to the ancients, grew in the meadows of the nether world. The community to which the defeated *mazzeri* belong will, in the course of the following year, suffer the greater number of deaths.

This last motif is possibly also traceable in an obscure passage of the confessions of Florida Basili, a *benandante* interrogated in 1599 by the Inquisitor of Aquileia and Concordia:

> I pretended [she said, lying] that I had been born with the caul, that I am compelled to go out every Thursday night, and that we fight the witches on St. Christopher's square, and that wherever the banner dips, there someone dies.[120]

Certainly the *mazzeri*, like the *benandanti*, go out at night "in spirit": and like them, at least in one case, they brandish plants as weapons, though stalks of asphodel, and not bunches of fennel. Instead of male and female witches, their opponents are (as with the *kresniki* and the *táltos*) other *mazzeri*. But rather than being pursued by the dead, like the *burkudzäutä*, the *mazzeri* pursue those who are about to die.

Faced by this partially contradictory tangle, we might be tempted to doubt that the *mazzeri* belong to the series outlined. And yet, it does not seem forced to assimilate the recurrent dreams of the *mazzeri* to ecstatic swoons, and to consider the stake of their dream battles—inflicting on the antagonist the maximum number of dead in the coming year—a formal variant of the combat for the fertility of the fields. The simultaneous presence of the two elements identified as pertinent features of the series would then allow us positively to resolve the classificatory question that we have formulated.

Comparison of Old Thiess to Learned Descriptions and Stereotypes of Livonian Werewolves and to the *Benandanti*

A Seventeenth-Century Werewolf and the Drama of Religious Resistance[1]

BRUCE LINCOLN

I

Before turning to the extraordinary example under consideration in this volume, it seems useful to say a few words about the categories "religion" and "resistance" as they figure in my analysis of Old Thiess's trial. Both terms (and the phenomena they denote) have their intricacies and problems; these are only compounded when the two appear in combination. Let me specify how I understand them.

First, I take resistance to be a defensive strategy, posture, and operation available to subordinate parties in situations of asymmetric power, through which they seek—intentionally or reflexively—to obstruct initiatives that threaten to erode their position and exacerbate the relations of asymmetry. It can also provide a means to evade obligations the dominant party seeks to impose on them and to challenge, disrupt, or confound disparaging constructions advanced by the dominant party to justify the regime of domination. Resistance can and does take a wide variety of forms, including defiance, dissemblance, distraction, evasion, feigned ignorance, foot-dragging, gossip, inefficiency, insolence, insubordination, irony, mimicry, mockery, nostalgia, parodic hypercompliance, reverie, sabotage, subversion, and countless others. Such variety is appropriate to an agonistic strategy designed not to prevail but to survive and persist, ceding as little ground as possible to adversaries who are—or at least seem to be—possessed of superior power.

Calculating whose power is truly superior, however, often proves more complicated than might be expected, for power comes in many forms. Some of these are objective and represent the material resources a group can commit to a struggle: disposable wealth, specialized manpower, technologies of surveillance and repression, etc. Subjective factors also have their importance, however, insofar as these determine the group's willingness to wage a struggle and to make maximum use of whatever objective resources are at their disposal. Under the right circumstances, an inspiring story, firm belief, sentiment of dedication, or ethic of self-sacrifice can—and occasionally does—count for more than demographic, economic, technological, or military advantages. One is reminded of the stories of Christian martyrs or, more recently, of Ho Chi Minh's fierce, proud, and confident prediction of September 1946 at the close of unsuccessful negotiations with the French: "You will kill ten of our men, but we will kill one of yours. And in the end it is you who will tire."

Some theorists might define Uncle Ho's faith as a religion of sorts, his own protestations notwithstanding, and reasonable arguments are available on both sides of the question. Since I take a key feature of religion to be the tendency to invest human entities with more-than-human status (as when a group understands itself as "the elect" or frames its laws as ancestral heritage or divine commandment), the example is instructive. If Ho's confidence were based on the fact that the morale, discipline, and dedication of his troops was superior to that of the French, and later the Americans, then there is nothing religious in his prophecy, since these are all human qualities. If, however, he followed Hegel in imagining that *Geist* realizes itself in history as the irresistible trend toward ever more perfect freedom, and if he saw that *Geist* at work in the struggle for an independent Vietnam, then his faith would seem religious.

Within the dynamic of domination and resistance, religion figures as an independent variable, which is to say it has no necessary relation to either side. Some projects of domination are framed in religious terms, as with the Chinese Mandate of Heaven, the American imperative of manifest destiny, the French *mission civilisatrice*, the Hindu caste system, justifications of slavery grounded in the Biblical story of Noah's sons, or Zionist claims to Palestine—but a great many are not. Similarly, some projects of resistance assume religious form, as in the Native American Ghost Dance, the independent churches of colonial Africa, the Maccabean movement, or the struggle waged by the Nizari Ismailis (aka the "Order of Assassins"). There is no necessity for either side to adopt a religious coloration, although there may be some strategic or tactical benefit in doing so. For wherever and whenever religion enters such struggles, it raises the stakes, since those who understand their interests, values, status and dignity, attachment to certain customs and traditions, or claim on privileged positions or pieces of land to be divinely ordained, mythically chartered, or inscribed in the very structure of the cosmos will struggle more tenaciously, having convinced themselves that they fight not for naked self-interest but for foundational truths and sacred principles.

With that by way of (admittedly inadequate) prologue, let me turn to the example I want to treat, which is drawn from early modern Livonia, a territory that included today's Baltic republics of Estonia and Latvia, and which was among the very last corners of Europe to be converted to Christianity. During the sixteenth and seventeenth centuries, moreover, this was the classic home of werewolves, much like Transylvania's relation to vampires. Witness, for instance, the testimony of Olaus Magnus in his *History of the Peoples of the North* (*Historia de Gentibus Septentrionalibus*, 1555):

> In Prussia, Livonia, and Lithuania, nearly all year long the inhabitants suffer great damage from the rapacity of wolves, because a huge number of their animals are torn to pieces and eaten if they stray only a small distance from the herd in the woods. However, this loss is not reckoned by them to be so great as those they must suffer from men who have turned into wolves. On the feast of Christ's birth, toward nightfall at a determined place a large number of wolves assemble, who have changed from men that dwell in different places, and

on that same night, with astonishing ferocity they rage against the human species and all other living beings who do not have a wild nature so that the inhabitants of this region receive more harm from these than from real and natural wolves. For as is known, they assault the houses of people who dwell in the woods with unbelievable wildness and they even attempt to break down the doors so that they may annihilate whatever people and animals remain there. They invade beer cellars and drink some barrels of beer or mead, then pile the empty mugs in the middle of the cellar, one on top of another, in which practice they differ from natural and genuine wolves.[2]

Similar is the account of Christian Kortholt roughly a century later, in *God's Ape, or Detailed Description of the Shameful Temptations of Satan* (*Simia Dei, Gottes Affe. Das ist: Auszführliche Beschreibung der schändlichen Verführungen des leidigen Satans,* 1677), a text written under the pseudonym Theophilus Sincerus ("Sincere Lover of God"):

It would not be offensive to make use of this opportunity to sketch the common, unfortunately widespread evil of the land, so abundant in the northern lands and bordering realms, especially in Curland and Livonia, whereby witches and sorcerous fiends change themselves into wolves. By night they run about to harm people, animals, and fruit of the fields, and to cause great damage (for this, they are called werewolves or fear-wolves [*Wahr- oder Gefahr- und von etlichen gar Fahr-Wölffe*]). In the morning toward dawn (when one can observe this), they run across fields back to their homes, villages, and dwellings and then they take back their natural human form, carrying out their work and routines like other men, exerting themselves, eating, drinking, speaking, and living as reasonable people tend to do.[3]

II

These stereotyped accounts establish the background for the incident that concerns me. The date is April 1691; the setting, the District Court of Wenden (today's Cēsis, 88 km northeast of Riga),[4] where the trial of an accused thief took an unexpected turn when a witness smiled as he was taking the requisite oath.[5] At this, the judges asked why he smiled and the man said he was amused that his neighbor, Old Thiess (a nickname for Matthias) was waiting to testify. "Everyone knows that he goes around with the devil and was a werewolf," he explained. "How could Old Thiess swear an oath, since he would not lie about such things and he had pursued them for many years?"[6]

With that, the court's attention shifted to Thiess, a man of eighty-some years who freely acknowledged his werewolf past; he recounted how he had earlier told this to another district court (that of Nitau), where the judges laughed and dismissed him without sentence.[7] Hearing this, one of the two presiding judges at Wenden asked whether the old man was in his right mind, whereupon all who knew him—including the other judge, who had been Thiess's employer in years past—vouched for his physical and mental health, his probity, and the accuracy of his account.[8]

The judges then put a series of questions to Old Thiess, trying to establish how he became a werewolf, what he did in that state, the number and identity of his fellow werewolves, his status as a Christian, and the nature of his dealings with the devil. On most points, Thiess's answers conformed to the stereotypes of the passages I cited earlier.[9] Along these lines, he told the judges he had gained the power of lycanthropic transformation when a stranger gave him a charmed drink, after which he was able to put off his human form and assume that of a wolf. Several times each year on ritual occasions, he gathered with a large band of werewolves to steal livestock, dismember the animals, and feast on their meat.[10]

On the most important point, however, Thiess's testimony differed from the judges' expectations. Contrary to their repeated attempt to establish the diabolic nature of his associations and acts, he insisted that werewolves oppose the devil and do battle against the "sorcerers" (*Zauberer*) and "witches" (*Hexen*) who serve him, a point that runs contrary to the stereotypes and most other testimony from early modern Livonia.[11] In response to hostile questions, he acknowledged that the werewolves enter hell each year, but went on to explain that they do so only as "hounds of God" (*Gottes hunde*),[12] who seek to recover the *Seegen*—the blessing that finds expression in abundant crops, live-stock, and general prosperity[13]—that sorcerers had previously stolen. When the werewolves succeeded, the harvest was good; when they failed, there was hardship and famine.[14]

In the face of Thiess's testimony, the judges introduced sophisti-cated theological arguments to show the old man the error of his ways. Did werewolves not defy God, they asked, by abandoning their human form, which the Lord God had created in His own image?[15] And since it was impossible for humans to undo God's creation in this way, did it not follow that their supposed lupine transformation was really "a devilish deceit and delusion"?[16] Then, when these learned arguments failed to persuade the old man on these points, the judges called in reinforcements, as the court transcript reflects:

> The Herr Pastor of this place, Magister Bucholtz, was summoned and asked to attend the proceedings. He sought to urge this self-professed *Seegensprecher*,[17] a sinner caught in the devil's snares, to take to heart his grievous sins, by which he was led astray and in which he persisted for so many years, and to stir his conscience that he might convert and repent by a rightful repentence and he might make an abjuration of these devilish beings.[18]

Going further, the pastor pronounced Thiess a grievous and wan-ton sinner facing harsh punishment in this world and worse in the next should he not confess and repent his sins.[19] Stunningly, Thiess insisted that he understood these things far better than the pastor, who was just a young fellow.[20] Angered at what he considered unjust and ill-founded accusations, he rejected any characterization of his deeds as diabolic or evil.

> He showed himself truly obstinate and remained insistent that all he had done was no sin against God. Rather, he had done God much service thereby in fulfillment of His will that they recover the prosperity from the devil that the sorcerers had carried to him, and he thereby did good for the whole land.[21]

Such defiance placed the judges in a difficult position, as they had neither a confession nor any direct evidence of Thiess's compact with the devil, the normal requisites for conviction. In this situation, they decided they could "not reach a definitive verdict on so difficult and doubtful a case."[22] Accordingly, they asked that the case be considered again at the court's next session, when a new district court judge would preside.[23] On October 31, 1692, a full eighteen months after the trial, the court finally reached a verdict, ruling against Old Thiess, but imposing the relatively light sentence of twenty lashes. Only a few years before, convicted werewolves had been sentenced to death by burning.[24]

III

Since the transcript of Old Thiess's case was first published in 1924, a number of distinguished scholars have devoted attention to it, as it seems to provide the best surviving evidence of a werewolf's self-understanding. Most noteworthy and most influential to date have been the work of Otto Höfler, who associated Thiess with the cult groups of martial males (*Männerbünde*) he took to be characteristic of Aryan northern Europe,[25] and the rival theory of Carlo Ginzburg, who treated Thiess's invasion of hell as an ecstatic journey similar to, and ultimately derived from, those of Eurasian shamans.[26] Subsequently, Mircea Eliade,[27] Hans-Peter Duerr,[28] Gábor Klaniczay,[29] and Éva Pócs[30] have all contributed to the discussion, usually following the lines introduced by either Höfler or Ginzburg (and, in the case of Eliade, trying to combine the two). As much as these authors differed sharply in the political, moral, and religious values they thought they could recognize in this case, almost all agreed on a basic point of method and theory. Viewing Livonian werewolfery as a late survival of something much older, they sought to shed light on a pre-Christian substratum of European religions by comparing details of Thiess's account to other phenomena they thought similar: Old Norse berserkers, Slavic healers and shapeshifters, Italian *benandanti*, witches from the Pyrenees, or Siberian shamans. Conceivably this is possible, although the results of such comparatism remain highly speculative and the history of such endeavors offers repeated lessons in caution.[31] Better, I think, to follow the lead of specialists in Baltic studies who have considered this and other werewolf prosecutions,[32] since close examination of Thiess's trial lets us recognize the dynamics of oppression and resistance in a religious vein.

In order to appreciate this aspect of the trial, it is useful to begin by taking stock of its dramatis personae. The transcript identifies nine individuals as officers of the court and two others as religious authorities who offered their cooperation. In their order of appearance, these are:

Herr Assessor (also referred to as Herr Richter) Bengt Johan Acker-
   staff, substitute judge of the District Court of Wenden, who lives
   in Castle Klingenberg outside Lemburg
Herr Assessor Gabriel Berger, judge of the District Court of Wenden
Herr Baron Crohnstern, judge of the District Court of Nitau
Herr Rosenthal, judge of the District Court of Nitau
Herr Caulich, judge of the District Court of Nitau
Herr Pastor of Lemburg
Herr Pastor of Jürgensburg, Magister Bucholtz
Herr Chief Deputy Clodt
Herr Assessor Martini
The illustrious, praiseworthy Assessor of the Royal High Court, Herr
   Herman Georg von Trautvetter

Note that all these worthies receive the honorific title *Herr* and, with the exception of Bengt Johan Ackerstaff (whose name is Swedish, but whose family had resided in Livonia for centuries, where they were thoroughly Germanized)[33] and Herr Assessor Martini (about whom I have been unable to obtain any information), all have German surnames. They are, transparently, members of the German elite who constituted the upper stratum of Livonian society ever since the Teutonic Knights (specifically, the Livonian Brothers of the Sword) conquered this territory early in the thirteenth century. When Livonia later came under Swedish rule (1629–1721), ethnic Germans continued to own the bulk of the land, just as they controlled most of the wealth and monopolized most of the offices (political and clerical) through which power was exercised over the indigenous peasantry. This lower stratum of the population included the Latvians and Estonians who worked the land their overlords owned. In administrative and common parlance, the two Baltic groups were usually classed together and collectively referred to as *Undeutsche*, literally, "the non-Germans." Old Thiess, the others who were called to testify before the court, and almost everyone they mentioned in their testimony fell into this subordinate group. The transcript identifies them as follows:

The church thief of Jürgensburg, Pirsen Tönnis

An inhabitant of Kaltenbrunn named Old Thiess, "in most obvious ways . . . a poor man and thoroughly powerless"[34]

The Kaltenbrunn innkeeper Peter

Skeistan, a peasant from Lemburg, who broke Thiess's nose

A peasant from Marienburg who gave his wolf pelt to a peasant from Allasch

Skeistan Rein, son of the aforementioned Skeistan

A scoundrel from Marienburg who tricked Thiess into becoming a werewolf

Tyrummen, a peasant from Segewold, a werewolf who was particularly skilled at stealing livestock

A peasant of Rodenpeisch who accompanied Thiess to a tavern

A fellow from Jürgensburg, Gricke Jahnen, stepson of the blessed Herr Pastor, whose leg Thiess healed

Ilgasch, a peasant from Nitau, who obtained a (magical?) net from Thiess

Gurrian, a peasant of Jürgensburg: the old innkeeper Gurrian Steppe, who had his grain blessed by Thiess

All these men came from villages within a very small area in eastern Latvia about nine miles in radius (see figure 1).[35] Most are identified as peasants (*baur*: nine out of thirteen, assuming this description fits the younger Skeistan, whose father is so identified), the others as innkeepers (*krüger*: two out of thirteen), thieves (*dieb*: one out of thirteen), or scoundrels (*schelm*: one out of thirteen). Most of them are given a first name only, usually one that is non-German (Pirsen,

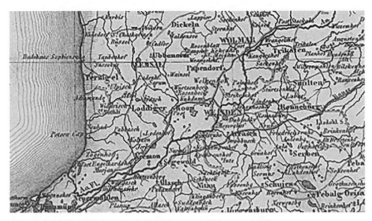

FIGURE 1. Map of the territory in central Livonia named in Thiess's trial. Detail from
R. von L. Ravenstein, *Meyers Hand-Atlas* (Hildburghausen, 1872), 73.
Courtesy of the Public Library of Cincinnati and Hamilton County.

Skeistan, Tyrummen, Gricke, Ilgasch, Gurrian; Peter is an exception).
None of them is accorded the title *Herr*, nor shown courtesy, although
Gricke Jahnen is referred to as a "fellow" (*kerl*, cognate to English
churl), and not a peasant, presumably because he had been adopted
by "the blessed Herr Pastor."

The same social divide is evident in the seventeen other Livonian
werewolf trials for which records survive, in which the court officials
were consistently *Deutsche* and the defendants *Undeutsche*.[36] This was,
in fact, the primary line of cleavage in the early modern Baltic, sepa-
rating the elite from the popular classes, and, as Stefan Donecker and
others have demonstrated, religious difference played an important
role in legitimating and maintaining this sharp hierarchic divide.[37]
Thus, notwithstanding the fact that the last Baltic pagans accepted
Christianity in 1386, a full three hundred years before Thiess's trial, the
Deutsche descendants of the Teutonic Knights justified their dominant
position by stressing their religious difference from the indigenous
population, whose conversion—so they insisted—was superficial,
incomplete, and potentially reversible.

The Non-German peasants were commonly depicted as primitive,
untrustworthy and superstitious folk, in particular their Christian

conviction was regularly doubted, and both Protestant and Catholic observers agreed that many Estonians and Latvians continued to worship pagan gods, even though they had been officially converted to Christianity. They were particularly notorious for their willingness to enter into pacts with the devil and for the magic abilities that they received from such an unholy alliance.[38]

To cite but one example of the way the German elite used werewolf rumors, werewolf trials, and werewolf beliefs to justify their view of the indigenous population as ignorant, superstitious, potentially dangerous, even bestial, and in need of—also grateful for—domination by their class superiors, consider the following passage from Johann Georg Godelmann's *Disputatio de Magis, Veneficis, Maleficis et Lamiis* of 1584:

The devil puts those who believe themselves transformed into wolves to sleep and blinds their external senses. Thus, they fall into the most profound sleep, after which the Old Deceiver presents varied forms of things that trouble their humors and impress themselves on their souls so effectively that they believe themselves to be and to have been wolves. The devil delights in such trickeries and games, so that he torments the unfortunate slaves, ignorant of God, and confirms them in their error and superstition. For there are peasants in Livonia, most unfortunate people, superstitious, barbarous, mere slaves of lords, whom they are compelled to obey in all things, for if they would refuse their commands or neglect to carry out the tasks given to them, they would be chastised with switches and dragged about roughly, like livestock. Whence, it appears that people and nations of this sort are delighted with being ruled, or at least bear it patiently.[39]

Producing a steady stream of *Undeutsche* defendants whom they could successfully prosecute as witches and werewolves permitted the elite to understand and represent themselves as continuing the noble—but interminable—work of advancing civilization, morality, and the True Faith, thereby legitimating their position and power. Institutions of church and state collaborated in providing a moral character to the discriminatory contrast of *Deutsche* and *Undeutsche* by recoding their opposition in religious terms, rather than ethnic, national, or socioeconomic. Witch and werewolf trials thus served as a primary theater in which this recoding was renewed and rendered credible, but after the Swedish king issued a royal decree abolishing the use of torture—in 1686, five years before Thiess's trial—it became more difficult to produce the confessions on which these proceedings depended.[40]

IV

Having already once been acquitted, Thiess faced the court with more confidence than did most of his predecessors.[41] He reasoned that "if such things were sins, would not the judges before whom he previously appeared, who were as wise as the present ones, and who understood such things well, have informed him of this and not smiled at it?"[42] What is more, the outcome of this earlier trial had been much discussed, with consequences for Thiess's standing in the community. As Judge Ackerstaff of the Wenden court observed, after the old man's acquital, "he was idolized by the peasants."[43]

The defense Thiess mounted constitutes an exceptionally revealing example of a resistance that was simultaneously religious, legal, cultural, and political. Thus, after accepting the court's charge of werewolfery, he went on to dispute the judges on all key terms constitutive of that charge, most prominently their constructions of "hell," "devil," and "werewolf." For example, the hell of the court's theologically informed and conventional imaginary was a realm antithetical to God, the church, morality, faith, good Christians and their hopes of salvation. Any contact with a hell of this sort was prima facie evidence that a person was infected with sin and posed a serious danger to others. The judges articulated this most fully when rebuking Thiess as follows (emphasis mine):

> He broke the oath he had sworn to his savior Christ as part of his holy baptism, in which he had renounced the devil, all his creatures and works. Having forgotten God's way, he committed other highly

forbidden sins of similar sort, consistently turning to abomination and scandal, not to God's house where he formerly could come to knowledge and service of God through preaching and Christian instruction. *Instead, he preferred to run to hell.*[44]

Here, Thiess is portrayed as not just a sinner but a backsliding reprobate. Having received care, instruction, and sacraments from a kind and generous church, he abandoned "God's house" (*Gottes hause*) to resume his old ways, which the authorities define as sinful and describe through the metaphor of "running to hell" (*höllen zulauffe*). They held out hope, however, that the old man might avoid eternal torment, if only he would accept their construction of morality, admit his errors and ignorance, acknowledge their authority, and thereby reaffirm not just the proper moral order of the cosmos but also the sociopolitical order of Livonia. The old man declined to cooperate:

> Q: Was it not his intention, before his death, to convert to God, to let himself be instructed regarding His nature and will, to renounce such devilish excesses, to repent his sins and thereby save his soul from eternal damnation and the pains of hell?
>
> A: Hereupon, he would not answer properly. He said, who knows where his soul would remain? He was now very old, what more could he grasp of such things?[45]

In significant measure, Thiess's understanding of "hell" differed from the court's. Evil it was, to be sure, but its evil extended only to the owner of this realm, his guests and servants, even though the place could be accessed by certain others. In his view, the fact that werewolves visited hell each year did not mark them as evil, nor did it condemn them to return after death,[46] since they came there as enemy invaders. Raiding hell was relatively easy, moreover, since it was not distant from their homes, either spatially or metaphysically:

> Q: How did the witness come to hell and where is that located?
>
> A: The werewolves go thither on foot in wolf form, to the place at the end of the lake called Puer Esser, in a swamp below Lemburg

about a half mile from Klingenberg, the estate of the Herr substitute President. There were lordly chambers and commissioned door-keepers, who stoutly resist those who want to take back the grain blossoms and the grain the sorcerers brought there. The grain blossoms were guarded in a special container and the grain in another.[47]

Hell was thus part of the local topography (see figure 1), situated about four miles from Thiess's home in Kaltenbrunn near a lake outside Lemburg, close by the estate of Assessor Bengt Johan Ackerstaff, that is, the judge who heard Thiess's case and had earlier been his employer.[48] For hell to lie close at hand was consistent with Latvian constructions of the otherworld,[49] and it is also possible to imagine there was some confusion between *Hölle* ("hell") and *Höhle* ("cave, cavern") in the exchange between the judges and Thiess, or in the transcript's reproduction of what actually was said. However that might be, by locating the devil's abode in the judge's backyard, the old werewolf managed to insinuate that the infernal associations of the court were closer, stronger, and more enduring than his own. As Thiess further explained, the entrance to this particular hell lay just beneath the earth's surface, hard to find except for those who "belong inside,"[50] like the sorcerers who feast with the devil.[51] Most importantly, perhaps, this hell functions as the storehouse of a great manor, whose lord stockpiles all the grain and seed corn that these sorcerers stole and brought him.[52]

As for the devil, the judges and pastor construed him as the enemy of God and of all righteous Christians, whom he seeks to corrupt and delude. Those who succumb to his snares are branded with his mark[53] and enter a formal pact[54] that leads them to sin and damnation. By deceiving the weak, ignorant, and gullible, the devil leads them away from the religious instruction and moral grounding supplied by the church and robs them of their soul.[55]

Thiess agreed that the devil was a thief of souls, but he understood this differently than did the judges and pastor. Although he nowhere spelled out his views or integrated them in a coherent system, three points emerge from his testimony. First, in response to questions about his own ability to heal sick livestock, Thiess explained how the devil, acting through witches (*Hexen*), could seize the souls of both people and animals, causing illness and death. Thiess's healing practices were designed to recover stolen souls, employing sacred substances and formulas to do so:

> Q: Where, then, did he learn to prophesy, since many people came to him and asked him what would happen to them?
>
> A: He could not prophesy; rather, he was a horse doctor, and if other sinners had done harm to someone's horses, he counteracted that and removed it from them. Toward that end he used a few words, only about three, and he administered bread or salt to them, which he had blessed with these words.
>
> Q: What did he know about the sinners who do harm to horses?
>
> A: They were the same witches or agents of the devil, who do nothing but evil.
>
> Q: What, then, were the words he used in this way?
>
> A: Sun and moon go over the sea, bring back the soul that the devil brought to hell and give back to the animal the life and health that was taken from it—and that helps other animals besides horses.[56]

Thiess also maintained that the devil's servants—a group that included "sorcerers" (*Zauberer*) and "witches" (*Hexe*), but emphatically not werewolves—forfeited their souls to the devil, as a result of which they carried out thefts on his behalf,[57] won the right to banquet with him,[58] and became his after death.[59] Although clergy and court focused on the theft of souls, Thiess voiced greater concern with the devil's thefts of a material nature that the authorities ignored, for he repeatedly charged the devil and his henchmen with stealing crops, seed, animals, and the community's prosperity every winter:[60]

> Q: How could the witness say that on last St. Lucia's Eve [December 13] they had already brought back this year's prosperity from hell, which the sorcerers had taken there, since the sowing and blossoming time was now just approaching [i.e., on April 28, the date of the trial] and thus nothing could yet be harvested?

A: The sorcerers had their own special time and the devil had already sowed long before. Thereafter, the sorcerers took something from that and brought it to hell, and this was the prosperity the werewolves carried back out of hell, and subsequently much growth followed from our seed, just as rich fruit was obtained from the trees, which was also taken from hell, as was good fishing. Already since Christmas there was perfectly verdant grain of all sorts and trees, whose growth similarly came from hell.[61]

The fact that the devil employs servants, has storerooms filled with surplus produce, gives banquets, and lives in dwellings described as *herrlich* identifies him as a noble, and Thiess consistently depicted the source of his wealth as theft from the peasantry. In a trial of 1651, another accused werewolf ventured a bit further, testifying that "the Evil One appeared in person, *in black German clothing*,"[62] and in witchcraft trials such depictions were common. Here, as in the Baltic folklore studied by Ülo Valk, "images of demonic evil acquired a concrete embodiment in the figure of the German landlord."[63]

V

While the authorities aligned werewolves with sin, damnation, hell, and the devil, Thiess disarticulated them from this set and repositioned them in opposition to all evils, which also included sorcerers and witches.[64] In his account, the struggle of werewolves against malevolent forces found its most salient expression in competition over livestock, produce, prosperity, and fertility, in which a three-act drama unfolded each year. Initially, these assets were the rightful possessions of the peasant community, being the material manifestation of the blessed prosperity (*Seegen*) they obtained by God's grace and their own labor. During the winter, sorcerers stole this wealth and carried it beneath the earth's surface, doing so on behalf of the devil, greatest thief of them all.[65] Finally, werewolves raided the devil's storeroom, battled his servants, and took back the stolen goods. In doing so, they did not act as thieves but as agents of restorative justice, returning property, blessings, profits, and the means of production to their rightful owners.

Most often, Thiess described the material stake of this battle in agricultural terms, but he acknowledged that the werewolves also seized animals. Such admissions usually came in response to questions posed by the judges, who focused on livestock more than grain, consistent with their stereotype of werewolves as cattle-rustlers.[66] The following exchange is particularly revealing.[67]

> Q: [When you] were transformed into wolves, why didn't you eat meat raw, as wolves do?
> A: That wasn't the way. Rather, they eat it like men, roasted.
> Q: How could they handle things, if according to his testimony they had wolves' heads and paws? With what could they hold knives, prepare the food, or use other tools to accomplish their work?
> A: They used no knives, but tore pieces off with their teeth, and with their paws they stuck the pieces on spits that they found, and when they consumed the meat, they had already turned back into men, but they made no use of bread. They took salt with them from the farm as they departed.[68]

Here, both parties implicitly theorize "werewolf" as mediating the categorical divide between human and animal, but they do so in markedly different fashions. Thus, the judges maximize the werewolves' bestial nature by imagining they eat their meat raw and run on all fours. In response, Thiess parries as best he can (not without contradiction), describing how the werewolves employ technology (fire and spits) to roast their meat, season it with salt, use their paws as hands, and slip back into human form over the course of their eating.

A sharp contrast existed between the werewolf of the court's imaginary and that of Thiess's narration. In the first instance: a savage beast, ensnared by the devil and lost in sin, driven to commit brutal violence against lesser creatures to satisfy its rapacious appetites. In the second: a fierce and courageous champion of justice, committed to recovering the abundance rightfully belonging to the peasants, which greedy lords and their thieving lackeys regularly steal. Here, as elsewhere, werewolves proper are not at issue; rather, in the discourse of both contesting parties, they figure as a trope for the situation of *Undeut-*

sche Livonians resisting domination, exploitation, and disparagement at the hands of the *Deutsche* elite.

Court officials spoke the interests and perspective of this elite in thinly veiled fashion by construing werewolves as extreme but instructive examples of the paganism, aggression, and bestial violence present as a potential in all *Undeutsche*. The latter group, like subalterns everywhere, had to be more guarded in their attempts to invert the werewolf sign and turn it to their advantage. Only once in the transcript does Thiess explicitly say anything about the elite. The passage is brief and ambiguous, but fascinating.

> Q: Weren't there women and girls among the werewolves? Also were Germans [*Deutsche*] found among them?
>
> A: Women were certainly among the werewolves, but girls were not. Rather, they were of use to the flying sprites or dragons and were sent out to take away the yield of milk and butter. The *Deutsche* don't join their company; rather, they have a special hell of their own.[69]

Neither of the issues raised here was pursued further,[70] and the question of "Germans" (*die Deutsche*) enters almost as an afterthought, which Thiess skillfully deflected. Apparently, the judges were satisfied with his statement that "the *Deutsche* . . . have a special hell of their own" and saw no need to pursue the issue. Yet we might ask what exactly the old man meant. Did he mean to suggest that the *Deutsche* raid a "special" (*sonderliche*) hell that stands apart from the one visited by their *Undeutsche* inferiors? Perhaps, although this would contrast with Thiess's fuller description of Russian werewolves, whom—he said—raided the same hell as his band.[71] Alternatively, did he mean to imply that there is a "special" hell that the *Deutsche* do not raid, but actually own and inhabit? Both interpretations are possible, and to me it seems most likely that Thiess framed his response so that different fractions of his audience could understand it consistent with their interests and inclination. Still, one must note that he never used the verb "to have" when describing the *Undeutsche* werewolves' relation to hell: like most proprietary relations of ownership, this was something reserved for the Germans.[72]

VI

Close analysis of Thiess's trial permits us to recognize a sharp struggle between the *Deutsche* elite and the *Undeutsche* peasantry for control over werewolf discourse, and we can understand that such skirmishes were not just reflections of but also interventions in their larger struggle over the maldistribution of wealth, power, prestige, dignity, and justice. Effectively, Thiess fought to appropriate and rework a tendentious item of discourse through which the *Deutsche* elite demeaned and devalued the *Undeutsche* peasantry. Most of the latter accepted the term, while denying its applicability to them. Thiess, in contrast, accepted the nomenclature, but attempted to redefine it by inverting its moral valence. "Yes, I am a werewolf," he affirmed with pride, "and we werewolves are *good*. We fight the forces of evil and secure our people's welfare." Certain implications in his testimony make an even bolder case, moving beyond the defensive posture of resistance to something approaching insurrection at the level of the symbolic and discursive, for one can hear him saying, albeit *sotto voce*: "We are not the ones in league with the devil. That honor belongs to you!"

As the trial wore on, the judges realized they were making no headway with Thiess, at which point they called on other witnesses to incriminate him. These included a peasant named Gurrian, who—according to others—had sought Thiess's services to heal his cattle, protect them from wolves, and also to bless his grain.[73] Reluctantly, Gurrian admitted this was so, at which point the trial moved toward its finale:

> Both the royal court and the Herr Pastor of this place, Magister Buchholz, earnestly and movingly reproached Gurrian, as well as Thiess, with their grievous sins, devilish temptations, superstitions, and idolatry. As Thiess still would not understand, it was necessary for Gurrian, who was himself not the subject of evil rumors, to state that he was given to sorcery, standing in the presence of the judges and all assembled, especially in front of all the assembled peasants, regarding their delusion that some holiness was in these things. On the contrary, nothing could be decreed with regard to Thiess, so all was

in confusion. In the end Gurrian cast one bundle after another [i.e., the packets of grain and salt that Thiess had blessed for him] with his own hand into a fire that had been laid, following the Herr Pastor's proclamation of the true God, concerning his gracious mercy and forgiveness of the sins he had committed, also telling him henceforth to change and to abstain from the things that were previously highly forbidden. In order to avoid temporal and eternal punishments, he did this with fear and trembling and thereby openly atoned for the acknowledged public scandal. At the following Sunday's preaching, he was obliged to stand at the church post and as sacred conclusion he was legally condemned to be struck with twelve pairs of blows by the high executor. The Herr Pastor also emphasized for the whole community the strong and cruel punishment of such a person for his skills, and he admonished each one of them to desist from such things.[74]

The dénouement is as extraordinary as was the trial. Unable to overcome—indeed, perhaps unable to comprehend—Thiess's skillful, determined, and eminently principled resistance, the agents of state and church turned their attention to the much less culpable Gurrian Steppe. Better schooled than Thiess in the conventional relations of domination and submission, Gurrian assumed the role of the ignorant peasant and repentant sinner that Thiess had declined. As such, he permitted the authorities to maintain their faith in the legitimacy of their power, which they exercised on behalf of God and against the devil. And when his punishment was carried out at the most sacred and most public of times and places—the conclusion of Sunday's service at the church door—poor Gurrian became an object lesson for all the other *Undeutsche* peasants of how they ought behave and what they might expect.

One would like to imagine that things ended differently for Old Thiess, and they did, but only in minor ways. However heroic resistance may be, in most cases it enjoys only limited success, chipping away at the forces of oppression, slowing the advance of superior power, or obstructing the operation of infernal machinery, but only for a while. Thiess was given another chance to confess and again refused, pleading—somewhat contradictorily—that many others had done the same things, but in fact he was old and remembered little.[75]

Having failed to obtain a confession, the Wenden court brought in no verdict, but held Thiess in custody while his case was reviewed by superior courts. On October 10, 1692, a full year and a half after the initial trial, the Royal High Court pronounced him guilty, noting that he had confessed to having been a werewolf, stolen cattle, visited hell, and led others into superstition.[76] Like Gurrian, he was sentenced to public flogging, not just as "a well-deserved punishment" but to serve as an example or, in the parlance of the court, "to change him into an object of noteworthy aversion" that might "warn others against the same vexatious and punishable conduct and warn them to let superstitions flow away from themselves and be banished for eternity."[77] Clearly, the "vexatious and punishable conduct" in question was not limited to werewolfery, but involved the much more serious offense of resistance.

Ginzburg Responds to Lincoln

Conjunctive Anomalies—
A Reflection on Werewolves

I

Why did I choose this topic for our discussion? There are several answers; let's begin with the most obvious. In the more and more globalized world we inhabit, a comparative approach to either history or anthropology is unavoidable.[1] Stories about werewolves spread from Europe to other continents: any approach to this topic will necessarily involve a comparative framework. But comparison should not be taken for granted: we should also reflect on its aims, its assumptions, its methods. I will try to do this, focusing on a specific case study, involving a rather special kind of werewolf.

Behind my choice there is also a personal reason. Fifty years ago I published my first book, *I benandanti*, translated into English as *The Night Battles*.[2] The book explored, on the basis of a series of Inquisition trials, some of them very long and detailed, a previously unknown phenomenon recorded in Friuli, on the northeastern border of Italy, not far from Venice. Men and women, mostly from a peasant background, who called themselves *benandanti* (i.e., people seeking the good) argued in front of the inquisitors that, having been born in a caul (i.e., still wrapped in the amniotic sac), they were compelled to leave their body in spirit four times a year, sometimes transformed into animals, to fight against witches and wizards for the fertility of the crops. As a weapon, the *benandanti* used fennel branches; the witches, sorghum sticks. "And if the *benandanti* win," one of them said, "that year the harvest will be rich."

The inquisitors heard those tales in astonishment: they had never come across anything like that. (My reaction in discovering those documents was not different from the inquisitors' reaction—an analogy on which, some years later, I began to reflect.)[3] The *benandanti* claimed to be counterwitches; the inquisitors, on the contrary, regarded them as real witches who participated in a diabolical cult. Relying on different strategies—leading questions or, occasionally, torture—the inquisitors tried to convince the *benandanti*. After fifty years and many trials, punctuated by endless questions and denials, the *benandanti* ultimately (although not completely) started to confess of being witches, introjecting the hostile image imposed on them by the inquisitors.

What I discovered in the Friulian archives was, I argued, a fragment from a deep layer of peasant culture: the inquisitors' astonished reaction to the *benandanti*'s description of their nocturnal battles with the witches was eloquent enough. But to what extent was the Friulian case, undoubtedly exceptional from a documentary point of view, also related to a unique reality? In my book I advanced the following hypothesis: what happened in Friuli had presumably taken place also in other parts of Europe (as well as, I would say today, perhaps in other continents as well). Peasant beliefs, mostly centered on fertility, possibly rooted in a pre-Christian past, were reinterpreted by the inquisitors as diabolical cults—and then uprooted. A single, also exceptional case seemed to support my hypothesis: a trial which took place in 1691 at Wenden, today's Cēsis, not far from Riga (at that time Livonia, present-day Latvia). The defendant, an old man nicknamed "Old Thiess," was accused of heresy: he countered, objecting that he was a werewolf, and therefore he had gone to hell with other werewolves three times a year, during the night, to recover the grain and fertility that had been taken away by witches. "We are the hounds of God," Thiess said, referring to the werewolves and subverting the usual stereotype, which identified werewolves with devilish beings.

A werewolf saying that he used to fight in spirit, with other were-wolves, against the witches for the fertility of the crops: was I allowed to compare Thiess's isolated, anomalous case with the Friulian *benandanti*? I thought I was—but which kind of comparison was I going to use? Morphological or historical? The former perspective takes into account only formal analogies, disregarding space and time; the latter analyzes the same analogies in a perspective based on space and time, raising the possibility of mutual influences, of a common filiation, and so forth. I first had come across this alternative as a student, when I read Marc Bloch's great book *Les rois thaumaturges* (1924, translated into English as *The Royal Touch*).[4] In the introduction, Bloch opposed two different kinds of comparison: "ethnological" (he did not use the word "morphological") and "historical," based on phenomena related to, respectively, societies that are unconnected or connected to each other in historical times. Following Bloch, in my first book I explicitly chose to limit myself to historical comparison only—a choice which pushed me to suggest that the resemblances between the *benandanti* and Thiess, the Livonian werewolf, pointed at a (completely forgotten) historical connection between Friuli and the Baltic region, possibly implying shared Slavic elements.

II

All this was entirely speculative, and exceedingly vague. A growing feeling of dissatisfaction for this kind of hypothetical history prob-ably reinforced my attraction to morphology—an attraction already nourished by my interest in art history, and most particularly con-noisseurship. (Art-historical attributions usually start from purely formal features.) What I found so challenging in morphology was its ahistorical orientation—its disregard, as I said, for both space and time, which makes it uninteresting, or even distasteful, to most his-torians. But I have long had a personal attraction for the devil's advo-cate: the fictitious character who, according to the early seventeenth-century rules of canonization trials, asked difficult, sometimes aggressive questions about potential saints. I belong to a generation that witnessed the triumph of structuralism: an approach that Claude

Lévi-Strauss repeatedly opposed to history. Structuralism, and more specifically Lévi-Strauss, played for me, for many years, the role of a challenging interlocutor—a devil's advocate of a kind. I regarded morphology not as an alternative to history but as a tool that might have opened up the possibility of overcoming the lack of historical evidence, throwing some light upon the puzzling analogies between the Friulian *benandanti* and the old Livonian werewolf. I suspect that at a subconscious level I was under the influence of the line from Vergil's *Aeneid* that Sigmund Freud put as a motto of his *Interpretation of Dreams*: "flectere si nequeo superos, Acheronta movebo" (*Aen.*, VII, 312), translatable as "If I cannot deflect the will of superior powers, then I shall move the River Acheron" or "If I cannot deflect the will of heaven, then I shall move hell." For me, history was heaven; morphology was hell.

III

Needless to say, I was not comparing myself to Freud; but certainly Freud has been for me, since many years and in many ways, an intellectual model. Not entirely by chance, perhaps, the next step in my research focused on one of the most famous among Freud's case studies: the "wolf-man." At the age of three, four, possibly five, the patient, a Russian, had a dream: six or seven white wolves were sitting on the branches of a tree, intensely staring at him. This was the beginning of a long history of neurosis. In my essay "Freud, the Wolf-Man and the Werewolves" (1986) I focused on a detail from the patient's life, which Freud duly recorded without realizing its relevance. The patient was born in a caul. In Russian folklore, werewolves were supposed to be born in a caul. The dream made by the little Russian child was presumably nourished by the stories of his *nianja* (nanny). It was a dream comparable to the initiatory dreams of the Friulian *benandanti*, who were also born in a caul. "In the wolf-man's nightmare," I wrote, "we discern a dream of an initiatory character, induced by the surrounding cultural setting or, more precisely, by a part of it. Subjected to opposing cultural pressures (the nurse, the English governess, his parents and teachers), the wolf-man's fate differed from what it might have been two or three centuries earlier. Instead of turning into a werewolf, he became a neurotic on the brink of psychosis."[5]

IV

I have discussed the methodological implications of my case study on Freud's case study elsewhere; here I will focus on the werewolves dossier I have been constructing (and reconstructing) so far. The wolf-man, Freud's Russian patient, made me aware of an element that I had initially missed: as I said, in Russian folklore werewolves were supposed, like the Friulian *benandanti*, to be born in a caul. (This detail was not mentioned, I will immediately point out, in the trial against "Old Thiess.") Many years later, after a long research trajectory, I inscribed both the Livonian case and the *benandanti* in a much larger (in fact, Eurasian) perspective, focusing on shamanism and its varieties: one of the elements, I argued, that ultimately entered in the stereotype of the witches' sabbath.[6]

My book *Storia notturna: Una decifrazione del sabba* has been hotly discussed, both as a whole and in detail. In particular, my interpretation of the Livonian trial has been repeatedly criticized; most recently, and most authoritatively, by Bruce Lincoln, professor of history of religion at the University of Chicago.[7] His essay raises some crucial problems about comparison which I would like to address: a further round of a friendly, often polemical debate which has been going on between Bruce Lincoln and me for some years.

Lincoln firmly rejected the possibility of identifying some fragments of ancient beliefs in the speech delivered by "Old Thiess" to the astonished judges of Wenden. After having evoked a number of scholars (including me) who assumed that the Livonian beliefs about werewolves were "a survival of some deep cultural and religious layer," Lincoln commented: "The results of this kind of comparison remained hypothetical at the very best; the history of those large comparative projects is in itself a warning."[8] Lincoln followed a very different path, providing a close reading of the Livonian trial as a "striking example of religious, legal, cultural and political resistance," delivered by Old Thiess, a Livonian peasant, in front of (and against) a group of judges, all of them (with one exception) having German names, which pointed at their belonging to the German elite. (The record of the trial is in German; it is unclear, Lincoln remarked, whether Thiess and the witnesses spoke German.)[9] Therefore, Thiess's reversal of the stereotypes concerning werewolves, far from being rooted in a previous, possibly ancient cultural layer were the result (Lincoln argued) of a bold act of "appropriation and reworking of a tendentious discourse, used by the German elite to debase and degrade the peasants."[10]

In his "Theses on Comparison," coauthored with Cristiano Grottanelli (a recently deceased historian of religions), Bruce Lincoln argued that, after the failure of strong comparative projects, "it is time we entertain a comparatism of weaker and more modest sorts that (a) focus on a relatively small number of *comparanda* that the researcher can study closely; (b) are equally attentive to relations of similarity and those of difference; (c) grant equally dignity and intelligence to all parties considered and (d) are attentive to the social, historical and political contexts and subtexts of religious and literary texts."[11]

But even a restricted comparison immediately invalidates the alleged uniqueness of the Old Thiess case. After having quoted a text describing werewolves and their attacks against livestock, Bruce Lincoln mentions in a footnote a series of works that tell "similar stories." But two of them, as I noted in my book *Storia notturna*, struck a different note.[12] In his *Commentarius de praecipuis generibus divinationum* (*Commentary on the Most Important Kinds of Divination*, 1560), Kaspar Peucer, professor of medicine and mathematics at the University of Wittenberg, referred an episode he had learned of from a Livonian student, Hermann Witekind, who later published a book on witchcraft under a pseudonym (Augustin Lercheimer).[13] A peasant who lived not far from Riga (i.e., in the same region where Old Thiess lived, one century later) suddenly fell asleep. He was identified as a werewolf, since werewolves, before their imaginary metamorphosis into wolves, fell in a swoon.[14] As soon as the peasant woke up, Peucer went on, "he said he had been pursuing a witch who was flying around, turned into a flame butterfly (werewolves boast to be driven to keep witches away)."[15]

From the section on werewolves in Peucer's learned work on divination emerge some "fragments relatively immune from distortion, of the culture that the persecution set out to eradicate."[16] The tiny detail I just mentioned is particularly relevant, because it shows that the unconventional image of werewolves as enemies of the witches, on which Old Thiess insisted, was not without precedent. Individual inventiveness took place in the framework of a preexisting grammar. To explore its features we have to go back to the huge historical dossier centered on werewolves.

V

But first, a warning from Bruce Lincoln's "Theses on Comparison." In one of them the "diffusionist type" is rejected on the following grounds:

> The attempt to show transmission of culture traits always advances— if only subtextually—a tendentious ranking of the peoples involved, constituting temporal primacy ("originality," "invention," "authentic-ity") as the sign of superior status, while conversely treating recep-tion as a mark of relative backwardness, need, and submission.[17]

I wonder whether anybody ever claimed, either directly or in-directly, that the invention of beliefs related to werewolves was the sign of a superior status. But the real point is elsewhere: it concerns the tacit equation of the "diffusionist type" with the "transmission of culture." Diffusion*ism* is a crude, simplistic explanatory model; diffu-sion, as transmission of cultural traits, is a reality. Diffusion*ism* must be rejected, since it takes diffusion for granted; but we should try to understand how the transmission of cultural traits is possible. A long time ago Claude Lévi-Strauss made some dense, challenging remarks on this issue:

> Even if the most ambitious reconstructions of the diffusionist school were to be confirmed, we should still be faced with an essential problem which has nothing to do with history. Why should a cultural trait that has been borrowed or diffused through a long historical period remain intact? Stability is no less mysterious than change. . . . External connections can explain transmission, but only internal

connections can account for persistence. Two entirely different kinds of problems are involved here, and the attempt to explain one in no way prejudges the solution that must be given to the other.[18]

The recent publication of a lecture entitled "A Revolutionary Science: Ethnography" that Lévi-Strauss delivered in 1937 to a group of left-wing militants unveils the hidden, self-critical overtone of his later remark on "the most ambitious reconstructions of the diffusionist school."[19] Lévi-Strauss's early commitment to diffusionism was followed by a rejection, which identified diffusionism with history. I would argue, on the contrary, that the goal of history includes external and internal connections, transmission and persistence. But in order to attain that (admittedly ambitious) goal, historians should listen to the devil's advocate: morphology.

VI

The reasons behind the choice of my case study will now be clear. Werewolves typically confront us with a dilemma: the respective potential of broad versus restricted comparison. The transmission of beliefs about werewolves implies a long chronological trajectory (two and a half millennia) and a widespread diffusion. The central core of it seems pretty stable: in the fifth century BCE, Herodotus, the Greek historian, spoke of a population—the Neuroi—adding, in disbelief, that each of them "once in every year . . . becomes a wolf for a few days and then returns again to his original form" (*Histories*, IV, 105, 1–2). In the novel *Satyricon*, written five hundreds of years later by the Latin writer Petronius (27–66 CE), the identification with a specific population disappeared. The story deals with an ordinary soldier who walks at night into a graveyard with a friend, who, "having pissed all around his clothes, suddenly becomes a wolf."[20] The next day, the soldier's companion learns that a wolf entered the farm and slaughtered the cattle; somebody stabbed the wolf on its neck. Later the companion sees the soldier lying on a bed, and a surgeon taking care of his neck; then he understands, "he was a werewolf" (*intellexi illum versipellem esse*). The Latin word *versipellis* means, literally, somebody who is able to change his own skin, shapeshifting; hence, metaphorically, sly, cunning, crafty. The transformation of the human into a beast is preceded by a ritual sequence: taking off clothes, urinating around them, becoming a wolf. In the meantime (Petronius's character describes in horror), the clothes turn first into stone and later into a pool of blood. Clothes are at the border between the human and the beastly world. In his *Natural History*, Pliny the Elder (23–79 CE) comments on *versipelles*, referring a story told by a Greek writer: a man belonging to a certain family took off his clothes, put them on an oak tree, swam across a marsh, and turned himself into a wolf; after nine years he came back and found his own clothes. Pliny, who referred to the story in disbelief, regarded the last detail as an extreme sign of Greek credulity.[21]

To be born in the amniotic sac—a trait shared by Friulian *benandanti* as well as by Slavic werewolves—meant also to be wrapped in a special kind of cloth. "The amnion," I wrote many years ago, "is an object that belongs to the world of the dead—or that of the non-born. An ambiguous, borderline object that marks borderline figures."[22] *Versipelles* who are able to shift from one skin to another, from one world to another, were some of these. In the transmission of those beliefs, a "primary experience of a corporeal character" played, I argued, a fundamental role.[23] So much about morphology. But as I pointed out, morphology may be seen as an instrument of history, not as an alternative to it. I am strongly in favor of a close-up approach to a single case—Old Thiess, for instance—but we cannot ignore the multiple contexts in which the single case is inscribed. From the frame to the picture, and backward: this trajectory—you may call it, if you wish, microhistory—seems to me particularly promising.

VII

Bruce Lincoln would object that my approach is too hypothetical. Having spent many years reflecting on the issue of proof, I am very sensitive to this kind of criticism.[24] Therefore, instead of insisting on my previous argument, I will try to rely on a different strategy in order to prove it. I will develop the implications of an essay I published some

FIGURE 2. "Composites of the Members of a Family" (Plate XXXI).
From K. Pearson, *The Life, Letters, and Labours of Francis Galton*, vol. 2
(Cambridge: Cambridge University Press, 1914–1930).

years ago dealing with a completely different topic and titled "Family Resemblances and Family Trees: Two Cognitive Metaphors."[25] The first part of my essay deals with "composite photographs," an experiment made around 1880 by Francis Galton, the famous British statistician and polymath. Following a suggestion he had received from a New Zealand correspondent, Galton superimposed a series of transparent negatives of members of the same family and then took a picture of the piling up. The result is a single, compressed, haunting, phantomlike image, shown here in figure 2.

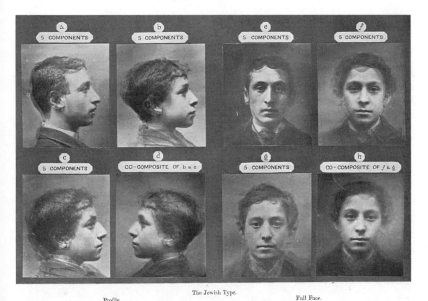

FIGURE 3. "The Jewish Type" (Plate XXXV). From K. Pearson, *The Life, Letters, and Labours of Francis Galton*, vol. 2 (Cambridge: Cambridge University Press, 1914–1930).

A darker center surrounded by a lighter halo: the former corresponds to features that are recurrent in the family, the latter to less frequent or unique traits. A set of family resemblances is displayed in front of us, in a very unusual form. The experiment seems neutral, even innocent; it was not. It was inspired by eugenics, a project aiming at the improvement of the genetic quality of human (in fact, British) population. Galton used photographs to identify types of specific social groups, suggesting that the reproductive capacity of marginal, potentially dangerous minorities, like Jews or criminals, should be controlled (see figures 3 and 4).

The model for good, controlled reproduction was explicit: horse breeding, as shown in figure 5. The racist implications of the project were clear enough. It will be appropriate to recall in this context that the word *raza* (as well as its counterparts in other languages, like Italian *razza*, English *race*, French *race*) derive, as the Italian philologist Gianfranco Contini demonstrated a long time ago, from *haras*, an old French word meaning "horse breeding."

FIGURE 4. "Comparison of Criminal and Normal Populations" (Plate XXIX).
From K. Pearson, *The Life, Letters, and Labours of Francis Galton*, vol. 2 (Cambridge:
Cambridge University Press, 1914–1930).

VIII

The impact of Galton's "composite photographs" that I explored in my
essay was independent (as is often the case) from the ideology that inspired them. Most famously, Ludwig Wittgenstein repeatedly referred,
both explicitly and implicitly, to Galton's "composite photographs":
first, stressing the traits shared by all family members, and later, reflecting on the overall result of the experiment in order to propose a
different, looser definition of "family resemblances." Galton's experiments attracted the attention of Sigmund Freud, Gregory Bateson,
and innumerable others. Galton's visual presentation can be regarded
as a cognitive challenge or a cognitive tool. What attracted me in those
images was the compression of a chronological sequence (different
generations within a family, for instance) into a single image, therefore

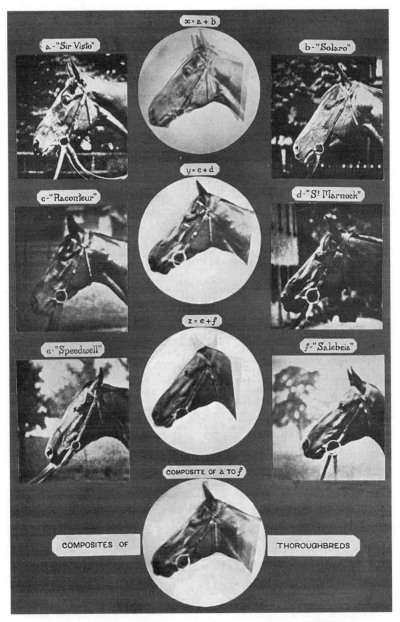

FIGURE 5. "Composites of Thoroughbreds" (Plate XXX). From K. Pearson,
The Life, Letters, and Labours of Francis Galton, vol. 2 (Cambridge: Cambridge
University Press, 1914–1930).

Stemma codicum ex nostra sententia sic fuerit delineandum:

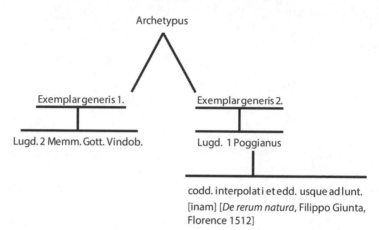

FIGURE 6. Adapted from J. Bernays, "De emendatione Lucretii," *Rheinisches Museum für Philologie*, vol. 5 (1847), 570n.

turning time into space, or (as the linguists would say) diachrony into synchrony. As you may have guessed, I immersed myself once again into my obsessive ruminations about morphology and history. But there was also something else. In my essay I advanced a comparison between Galton's composite photographs and a different kind of visual artifact: genealogical trees. They were for a long time used as diagrams representing family relations, but since the early nineteenth century they have been used by philologists as a metaphor to represent the genealogical relationship existing between different manuscript versions of the same text. This device was first used in 1847 by Jacob Bernays, the great philologist, to describe through a diagram the manuscript transmission of Lucretius's poem *De rerum natura* (figure 6).

Let us look at composite photographs and genealogical trees side by side in figure 7: what elements do they share?

The answer is simple. One word, repeated twice, will be sufficient: reproduction/reproduction. On the left side, you see a sequence related to reproduction in a biological sense: members of the same family, who may belong to different generations. On the right side, reproduction in the material sense: different manuscripts copying the same text. I have been working for many years on this ambivalent

FIGURE 7. "Composites of the Members of a Family" (Plate XXXI). From K. Pearson, *The Life, Letters, and Labours of Francis Galton*, vol. 2 (Cambridge: Cambridge University Press, 1914–1930). (Same as figure 2, above.)

notion — reproduction/reproduction — focusing on Dante.[26] For a long time biological reproduction worked as a metaphor for mechanical reproduction. As an example, I will quote a famous passage by Erasmus, the sixteenth-century humanist, as well as the comment made by Sebastiano Timpanaro in his fundamental book *The Genesis of Lachmann's Method*:

In his *Adagia* [Erasmus] proposed a correction to a proverbial expression used in Aristotle's *Metaphysics* and observed: 'The agreement of the manuscripts will not seem at all astonishing to those who have a modicum of experience in assessing and collating [that is, comparing] manuscripts. For it very often happens that an error of the archetype, so long as it has some specious appearance of the truth, goes on to propagate itself in all the books that form as it were its descendants 'and the children of the children and those who are born later.'[27]

The last line is a quotation from Homer's *Iliad* (20, 308) that Erasmus slightly adapted to the context. The point is clear: an error in the archetype (a word bound to become a fundamental tool, with different meanings, among philologists) will be propagated by its descendants. Cultural transmission took biological transmission as a model, using expressions like "family of manuscripts." In the twentieth century, when biologists started to use expressions like "genetic code," the metaphor was reversed.

IX

One might ask: What has all this to do with the topic I started from, namely, werewolves?

Here is my answer: I will consider the transmission of traditions and beliefs concerning werewolves as something comparable (notwithstanding a fundamental difference I will mention in a moment) to the transmission of a text. Therefore, I will try to approach my topic using the techniques of textual philology, as described by Paul Maas in his *Textual Criticism*: a short, dense book which since its first appearance has become an indispensable reference for anybody working in the field of textual philology. Maas wrote,

> It can be proved that two witnesses (B and C) [witnesses, i.e., manuscripts] belong together as against a third (A) by showing an error common to B and C of such a nature that is highly improbable that B and C committed it independently of each other. Such errors may be called "conjunctive errors" (*errores conjunctivi*).[28]

In which sense should we understand *conjunctive*? Because errors which are not banal prove that families of manuscripts are connected:

either because they are dependent on each other or because they derive from a common ancestor. (*Families, ancestor*: as you may see, in this domain biological metaphors are unavoidable.) This idea, which had already inspired (as Timpanaro has shown) the editorial practice of Poliziano, the fifteenth-century humanist, gave birth to modern textual philology.[29]

At this point I am confronted with a serious difficulty. Textual philology tries to reconstruct a (most often lost) original text, which has usually been corrupted by copyists in its transmission. My aim in analyzing the traditions related to werewolves is completely different. I am not trying to reconstruct an original set of beliefs: I am interested in the ways in which some ancient (possibly lost forever) beliefs have been reworked and modified over centuries and millennia. For this reason I am rephrasing Paul Maas's notion of "conjunctive errors" as "conjunctive anomalies."[30] It must be noted that Maas, after having stressed the distinction between anomaly and singularity (but without clarifying it), referred to anomalies in the following terms:

> As a rule, no writer will aspire to an anomaly for its own sake; an anomaly is a consequence of his desire to say something out of the ordinary for which the normal mode of expression was found to be inadequate.[31]

Maas is describing the activity of an individual writer who makes innovative experiments vis-à-vis literary tradition.[32] I am trying to reconstruct cultural innovations vis-à-vis a common set of beliefs, transmitted by a group, and articulated by specific individuals.[33] But the dates of the recorded evidence do not necessarily coincide with the date of the innovations: as I wrote a long time ago, "very recent testimony might preserve traces of much earlier phenomena."[34] I should have recalled what Giorgio Pasquali, the great philologist, wrote in his book *Storia della tradizione e critica del testo*: *Recentiores non deteriores*, namely, that more recent manuscripts can preserve an uncorrupted version of a passage from an old text.[35] My genealogical tree (figure 8), therefore, will present a series of formal connections, disregarding both chronology and geography (traditionally regarded as the two eyes of history).

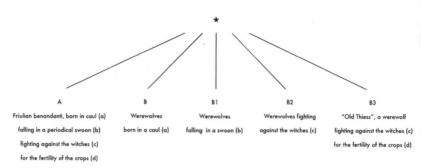

FIGURE 8. Genealogical tree.

The anomalous traits a, b, c, and d are too specific to be ascribed to chance: I consider them "conjunctive anomalies." Therefore, for A and B3, Friulian *benandanti* and the Baltic werewolf Old Thiess, fighting for the fertility of the crops can be regarded as partially overlapping developments from a set of beliefs rooted in a distant, undocumented past. I marked the diagram with an asterisk; is the asterisk pointing to a single event or to a series of independent innovations, followed by a hybrid combination of different traits? We'll never know.

This diagram translates a series of cultural transmissions, related to different times and places, into a synchronic image. Will this diagram be the conclusion of my argument? Only temporarily. From morphology I will have to go back to contexts, to actors, to history.

Lincoln Responds to Ginzburg

Letter of February 8, 2017

Dear Carlo,

I was pleased to read your Bogotá lecture (chapter 5, above), which clarifies some issues and introduces some intriguing problems.

There are many points on which we agree: the necessity of comparison, the dangers of error, and the ethical responsibility of the researcher, to name a few. Beyond that, we admire some of the same authors (Marc Bloch, Ernesto de Martino, and even the unfashionable Sir James George Frazer), while we have focused sharp criticism on others (most notably Georges Dumézil and Otto Höfler). We continue to differ, however, on how to approach the case of Old Thiess, and our differences here have broad implications.

In part, we disagree about what evidence is most relevant for interpreting Thiess's testimony, and we read the transcript of his trial differently, stressing different phrases and passages in it. These differences are rooted, moreover, in a broader disagreement about some basic principles of method that your lecture highlights.

First, there is the relation of morphology and history. Here, I would agree with you that truly strong morphological similarities do not typically arise from chance or coincidence, but beg for explanation. You think a set of historical links usually accounts for such resemblances and it is our task to identify the common origins or points of contact that produced them, even if no direct evidence of such connections survives. To be sure, I would acknowledge that a historical explanation of this sort can be correct. But without supporting evidence beyond the morphological similarities themselves, it must remain a hypothesis, not a conclusion. As such, it needs to be weighed against other possible hypotheses, including those that see no historic connection among the *comparanda* and explain them as independent responses to similar forces, problems, stimuli, and circumstances.

Here, you raise the issue of family resemblances, a phrase that had a different significance for Galton (genetics) than it did for Wittgenstein (classificatory logic). Even within Galton's writings, however, one finds much the same distinction, for not all of his "composite portraits" dealt with families in the literal (i.e., biological) sense. As you will probably recall, Galton invented the method on the suggestion of Sir Edmund Du Cane, His Majesty's Inspector of Prisons, and together they hoped to identify the physiognomic features common to murderers, robbers, and criminals.[1] Along with students he trained, Galton also made composites of victims of certain diseases (tuberculosis, phthisis),[2] "lunatics,"[3] and members of religious-cum-racial groups (Jews).[4] Among the most interesting uses of his method was one for which Galton himself was not responsible, but of which he enthusiastically approved: the composite portrait of "the typical young woman of culture" based on photos of eleven Smith College students. Here, such similarities as the photographs successfully identified and emphasized were grounded in commonalities of gender, class, generation, taste, style, education, and socialization, not history or genetics.[5] As Galton himself recognized, his method could be used to show the resemblances within families, but also those of "any given group."[6]

I'm thus inclined to think that anyone doing comparative research needs to keep two questions in mind: (1) Are the similarities among the *comparanda* numerous, nontrivial, and strong enough to construe these items as a set? (2) If so, what kind of set is it?

This brings us back to the case of Old Thiess. I agree he should

FIGURE 9. Relations among the three bodies of evidence studied comparatively by Ginzburg, *Storia notturna* and "Conjunctive Anomalies."

be compared to the *benandanti*, although I'm less certain about the Russian data you introduce, for reasons I will explain later. The diagram you include in your Bogotá lecture (figure 8 on p. 126, above) provides one useful way to summarize the evidence, but I would take issue with your orienting assumption that the asterisk you place at its apex denotes "a set of beliefs, rooted in a distant, undocumented past."[7] I also think there is some unevenness in your diagram, since it provides geographic and cultural specificity for one of the groups it treats (Friulian *benandanti*), while omitting this for the others. Were I to revise it, I would produce something like figure 9, depicting a triangular relation in which each *comparandum* has one strong similarity—and one only—to each of the other two.[8]

Is this sufficient basis to construe a set? I think not, but clearly you feel otherwise and the arguments I have advanced to date were not enough to persuade you. In my Hayes-Robinson lecture (chapter 4, above), I argued that Thiess is hardly representative of Livonian werewolves in general, but was an anomalous figure, whose anomalies help us understand that in the early modern Baltic, "werewolf" was a discourse, not a role, status, actuality, or historic residue; moreover, it was a discourse whose conventional use was subject to disputation. Most often, it circulated among the German elite, who used it to characterize the indigenous Latvian and Estonian population as less than Christian and less than human, thereby justifying the need to rule these peasants with a strong hand. Emboldened by his knowledge that he would not be tortured, Thiess responded to his judges' accusations by skillfully inverting the discriminatory stereotype that cast werewolves as savage beasts who stole cattle by night, ripped the animals limb from limb, and feasted on them raw. This is, in fact, the constellation that figures most prominently and most frequently in werewolf discourse through-out Europe, and these morphological similarities do reveal certain his-toric connections, since judges, priests, inquisitors, and others drew on many of the same demonological texts.[9] There are also connections of a nonhistorical nature, however, since all these discourses build on aspects of lupine existence that are evident to any observer. As Peter Jackson has recently put it:

> We may continue the analysis by regarding young men's symbolic transformation into wolves as an elaboration of the organized cattle raid. The acquisition of animals from the 'outside' as a source of wealth and prestige requires warlike confrontations with an artificial (i.e. demonized) human enemy. The wolf's semiotic 'fitness' for such a system in terms of its social, economic, and ecological conditions is evident. Not only did the wolf dissimulate the dog as its undomesti-cated counterpart, it was also the quintessential 'enemy of the herd' and thus a looter's perfect token of identification.[10]

Against this stereotype, Thiess stressed that he and his fellow were-wolves were saviors of the seeds, crops, and agricultural prosperity, not destroyers of cattle: forces aligned with God, enemies and not minions of Satan.[11] Thiess's defense was innovative, but not unique, and you are right to see him as having exercised "individual inventiveness . . . in the framework of a preexisting grammar."[12] In support of this, you cited the story preserved by Peucer and Witekind, where a "rustic were-wolf" admitted he had killed and dismembered a nobleman's horse but claimed he did so accidentally, while struggling against a witch who had taken the form of a butterfly and hidden under the horse's belly.[13] Here, the theme of violence against livestock remains central, while the defense of agriculture is absent. Closer to Thiess's testimony is the 1683 trial of Tomas Igund. The most relevant passages of the trial transcript read as follows:

[1] Q: If he is a werewolf, how does he run?

A: For twenty years, he went about in wolf form, but he gave his wolf skin to his father's brother.

[2] Q: How did you do that?

A: When asked, he replied: "Brother, do you want the job that is mine?" and when the man answered "Yes," he handed the job over, and to the question of what should be given to him, he responded "a piece of meat," which the buyer then gave. He gave it to him with the words: "Be happy and serve your master faithfully, as I have done."

[3] Q: Who is his lord, and where do they meet together?

A: Their lord appeared to them at Tukuma on a hill near the Duke's pleasure castle [*hercoga izpriecas pils*; a German gloss is added: *Fürsten lusthause*] as a nobleman, and he lived with his farmer, Šenkinge. They meet each Christmas, Midsummer, and St. John's Day, besides those that would be announced [German gloss: *angesaget würden*] by the overseer [German gloss: *wagger*].[14] Witches also lived beside the same place [in German: *selbigen wohneten auch die hexen bey*], whose job is to steal the blossoms of grain and take them to their lord, but these werewolves take them away from them and restore them to their owners, so that they will suffer no loss.

[4] Q: How should they make their appearance?

A: They had an ointment from their master, which they should rub on themselves and then they pull the wolfskin on very easily, which everyone keeps at home. Then they send a roast to the lord. They helped with the slaughter and gave it to the lord, who drank beer with them in town.

[5] Q: Were sheep also killed?

A: Many.

[6] Q: Where?

A: Everywhere outside the land where the lord lives.

[7] Q: There is prayer at holy dinners—why not hold it for a [pagan] god?

A: He already left the job eight years ago and no longer flies about with the werewolves.

[8] Q: To whom did he do particular evil?

A: To no one. They give more good to folks, because they help and reverse what the witches have done to them [parenthesis in German: *und sie zu rechte brächten,* "and they make things right"].[15]

Aspects of Igund's account are quite close to those given by Thiess, particularly on points where they differ from all others. In light of this, I would be inclined to stage a comparative discussion in three phases:

1. A morphological comparison (with historical implications) of the testimony given by Thiess and Igund, whose similarities justify constituting them as a set and whose spatiotemporal proximity makes a (direct or mediated) connection between them seem plausible, even likely.

2. A morphological contrast (with historical implications) of the set {Thiess + Igund} to the stereotypes regarding Livonian werewolves that figured in all other trials and learned discussions, concluding that the former took shape as a defensive and critical reaction to the latter. Here, historic connection is certain, occurring inter alia in the trials themselves, where the stereotypes found expression in the charges and questions to which the defendants responded. Behind that, one might also imagine a sequence of developments whereby (a) some peasants stole landowners' livestock (from the thirteenth century on, when Teutonic Knights conquered Livonia and established themselves as a ruling elite); (b) landowners (and their ideological apologists) condemned such thieves as less than human and developed a stereotype that disparaged the peasantry in general (by the sixteenth century, when the stereotype appears in learned literature); (c) trials followed, and the confessions extracted through torture confirmed and solidified the stereotype (sixteenth to seventeenth centuries); (d) some peasants contested and inverted the stereotypes, some even daring to do so in the course of trials, particularly when torture had been abolished (late seventeenth century).

3. A morphological comparison (with sociopolitical implications of a transhistorical sort) of {Thiess + Igund}—but not "Livonian werewolves"—to the *benandanti*, explaining their similarities not as evidence for a deep (pre)historic connection, but as the parallel response of independent actors defending themselves against similar charges advanced by similar institutions in similarly asymmetric relations of knowledge and power.

Clearly, you are not convinced and you take the Russian evidence to suggest a deeper historic connection among these (and other) examples. If one examines the Russian material more closely, however, it proves less useful than you would like. There is, in fact, only one text—and a relatively late one, having been produced in 1947—that connects werewolfery and birth in a caul. It reads as follows:

> The son of a princess and a serpent is born with a caul which he wears upon him at the insistence of magicians. His supernatural power and his eagerness to shed blood are predestined and make both his mother and Mother Earth tremble. He grows up and speedily acts as a beast; possessing the gift of second sight, he masters the art of magical transformations and leads the double life of a prince and of a werewolf. He is omnipresent, crafty, and wonder-working; the huntsman's fortune accompanies his predaceous, venturesome chase for power over the animal and human kingdoms. In vain his prospective victims strive to escape. Intimately tied with the forces of the night, he threatens the sun itself. Where he comes running in wolf-shape, there the earth becomes stained with blood, and vampiric ghosts hover over his abode. Glory and suffering are inseparably intermingled in the course of his life as a werewolf—hunter and beast, persecutor and persecuted at the same time.[16]

Like all mythic narratives, this is a work of bricolage that makes use of preexisting materials, which it restructures, embroiders, and expands upon, sometimes subtly and sometimes in more radical fashion. As its authors—Roman Jakobson and Marc Szeftel—acknowledged, they confected this lurid story from three sources:

When we compare the Vseslav legend as reflected in the *Primary Chronicle* [a historic source of the early twelfth century], in the *Slovo* [the "Tale of Igor's Campaign," *Slovo o polku Igoreve*, an epic poem of the late twelfth century], and in the *bylina* [the folk epic devoted to Volx Vseslav'evič, eight variants of which were collected between 1780 and 1938] it appears that each of these three sources presents only fragments of the entire legend and—this is particularly instructive— each source presents a different and distinct selection of these fragments. Only the *Primary Chronicle* offers the caul story, yet omits its cardinal implication, the werewolf motif, and mentions merely a characteristic feature of the werewolf, his bloodthirstiness. A man is born with a caul (thus becoming a werewolf) and "for this reason he is merciless in bloodshed."[17]

The caul thus appears in one source only: the *Primary Chronicle*'s account of Vseslav, Prince of Polotsk (c. 1039–1101). Even there, this detail is less than certain, since the word Jakobson and Szeftel would translate as "caul" has that precise meaning in no other surviving work of Russian literature. Rather, in one form (*jazva*) it normally means "wound, sore, ulcer" and in another form (*jazv'no*), "skin, membrane."[18] The text reads as follows:

> In the year 6552 [1044 CE] . . . Brjacislav died, the son of Izjaslav, grandson of Vladimir, and father of Vseslav, and his son Vseslav came to his throne. The birth of this man came by sorcery. When his mother gave birth to him, there was a *jazva* on his head and the sorcerers told his mother: "Fasten this *jazv'no* on him and he should wear it as long as he lives." Until today, Vseslav wears it on himself and because of this he is merciless in bloodshed.[19]

Some translators have argued that Vseslav was born wounded and this is what made him bloodthirsty. Others, wondering how one could "fasten" or "bind" (*navjazyvat'*) a wound and wear it for the duration of one's life, have favored translation as "caul." Such an interpretation is reasonable enough and is consistent with the text's description of this as a birth characterized by magic (*v'lxvovanija*). Neither here nor in

TABLE 1. Sources for Jakobson and Szeftel's composite "Epos of Vseslav"

Jakobson and Szeftel text	Primary Chronicle	Slovo	Bylina
The son of a princess and a serpent . . .			+
. . . is born with a caul which he wears upon him at the insistence of magicians.	+		
His supernatural power and his eagerness to shed blood are predestined . . .	+		
. . . and make both his mother and Mother Earth tremble.			+
He grows up and speedily acts as a beast; . . .		+	+
. . . possessing the gift of second sight, he masters the art of magical transformations . . .			+
. . . and leads the double life of a prince and of a werewolf.			
He is omnipresent, . . .			
. . . crafty, . . .	+	+	+
. . . and wonder-working.		+	+
The huntsman's fortune accompanies his predaceous, venturesome chase for power over the animal and human kingdoms.			+
In vain his prospective victims strive to escape.			+

any of the other passages where it treats Vseslav, however, does the *Primary Chronicle* describe him as wolfish or bestial, let alone a werewolf.

Neither, for that matter, does the *Slovo*, although that text does make Vseslav both a warrior and a magician, cunning and swift, comparing him to a wolf on three occasions.[20] Jakobson and Szeftel took these references to reflect a tradition of Vseslav as a werewolf, but the passages read more easily as metaphoric descriptions.[21] Regardless of how one understands this, the *Slovo* contains no indication of a miraculous birth, still less a caul.

The source from which Jakobson and Szeftel draw the great bulk of their evidence, as table 1 shows, is the folk epic (*bylina*) celebrating Volx Vseslav'evič. Although the *bylina* makes Volx the son of Vseslav,

Jakobson and Szeftel treated him as a doublet of his father, which provides the basis for their comparison. Other authorities see things differently, however, including Vladimir Propp, who considered the patronym a late addition designed to connect Volx with the traditional history of Kiev by making Vseslav his father.[22] Also, while the *bylina* gives its hero a miraculous birth, it does so in different fashion than the *Primary Chronicle* and assigns Volx a different paternity, making him the son of "a fierce serpent."[23] Apparently, this destined him to be a mighty hunter, as well as a warrior, for his birth threatened all animal species:

> Because of the birth
> of young Volx Vseslav'evič,
> Fish went to the sea's depths,
> Birds flew high to the clouds,
> Aurochs and deer went beyond the mountains,
> Hares and foxes to the thickets,
> Wolves and bears to the fir groves,
> Sables and martens to the islands.[24]

Behind this list, one can perceive a taxonomic structure focused on hunting, as represented in figure 10.

As a youth, Volx was trained in the mystic arts, acquiring the ability

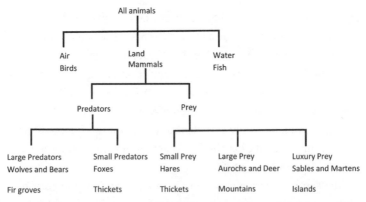

FIGURE 10. Taxonomy implicit in the description of how different species of animals fled at Volx's birth (*Bylina* of Volx Vseslav'evič, ll. 18–25).

to transform himself into various animal species organized along lines that mirror the above taxonomy:

> And when Volx was ten years old,
> He was instructed in mysteries
> The first art he learned
> Was to turn himself into a bright falcon [Air];
> The second art Volx learned
> Was to turn himself into a gray wolf [Large Predator];
> And the third art Volx learned
> Was to turn himself into a bay aurochs [Large Prey],
> A bay aurochs with golden horns.[25]

Here, the relation between human and animal is no metaphor, but real metamorphosis, as signaled by the verb *obvernetsja*, "to turn one's self into, transform." The hero uses this power to assume the form of a wolf on two occasions,[26] but also that of a falcon (three times, when he needs to traverse vast distances),[27] an aurochs (for fast running),[28] an ermine (to burrow and gnaw at the enemies' bowstrings),[29] and even an ant (to pass through an otherwise impenetrable wall).[30] It is thus unduly limited to regard Volx as a werewolf; indeed, the text nowhere names him as such (Russian *volkulak, volkolak,* and *volkodlak*).[31] Rather, he is a sorcerer and shapeshifter, as signaled by the literal sense of his name (*volxv* = "sorcerer, magician").[32]

The three sources from which Jakobson and Szeftel assembled their composite agree in depicting their protagonist—whether named Volx or Vseslav—as a bloody, warlike prince. Beyond that, they part company. One gives him a caul, another makes him a magician skilled at metamorphosis, and the third compares him to wolves, based on his speed, ferocity, and nocturnal habits. The relations among them can be graphed as in figure 11.

In spite of the fact that this title is found in none of their sources (nor truly appropriate to them), Jakobson and Szeftel consistently referred to the composite figure they imagined as the archetype behind all three as a "prince-werewolf," a term they deployed in their opening subtitle and ten times thereafter.[33] Although they understood

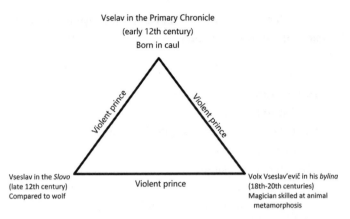

FIGURE 11. Relations among the three sources conflated by Jakobson and Szeftel.

themselves to be using morphological similarities to recover historic connections among the three sources, their desire to reconstruct a shared tradition of deep antiquity led them at points to misperceive, misrepresent, and misinterpret their evidence, imagining a single coherent and cohesive narrative where, in fact, there is none.[34]

Nowhere is this clearer than in their treatment of the caul. To be sure, much Slavic folklore shows that birth in a caul was often understood as a sign of divine favor (protection, good fortune, etc.) and a promise of supernatural powers, including clairvoyance, strength, magic, and animal transformation. The last of these is the most common, and the reasons are clear enough. For just as the caul is a second skin, an alternative exterior form, so the person in question will be able to put on the appearance and assume the nature of other beings. To connect the caul-born Vseslav of the *Primary Chronicle* and the shapeshifting Volx of the *bylina* is thus relatively unproblematic, but this is not enough to support the notion of a "prince-werewolf."

To accomplish that, Jakobson and Szeftel stressed the *Chronicle*'s observation that possession of the caul (if caul it was, and not a wound) made Vseslav "merciless in bloodshed" (*nemilostiv' … na kr'voprolitne*) and they equated this with lycanthropy. In a whirlwind discussion of five pages, they supported this assumption with whatever evidence they could find connecting cauls and werewolves.[35] Even so, these ranking masters of Slavic studies could not cite a single Russian

TABLE 2. Evidence cited by Jakobson and Szeftel to support their claim that Vseslav's birth in a caul identifies him as a werewolf

Results of birth in a caul	Russian	Bulgarian	Serbo-Croatian	Polish	Kashubian	Ukrainian
Protection	+	+				
Good fortune	+		+	+	+	
Wizardry			+	+	+	
Metamorphosis			+	+	+	
Clairvoyance			+	+	+	
Strength			+			
Werewolf			?			?
Vampire			+		+	

example where birth in a caul was believed to mark those who would (or could) become werewolves. What is more, the two examples they adduced from other Slavic groups are both open to question. Thus, the source they cited for Ukrainian beliefs said only that in a certain region (Klechdach), witches and wizards who assumed lupine form could be distinguished from real wolves by the string they wore around their neck (*na szyi sznurek*).[36] Jakobson and Szeftel assumed this string held the caul in which its wearer was born, but nothing in the text says it is so. The other example is similarly weak. For although some Serbo-Croatian sources say the caul-born are fated to become *vukodlaki*,[37] it is impossible to tell whether these are vampires or werewolves, as that word denotes both (and vampires much more often).[38] If one tabulates all the Slavic evidence cited, the picture is far from convincing (table 2).

All this has important consequences for your claim of family resemblances, since the detail on which you based your comparison of "Russian werewolves" to the *benandanti* is anomalous, not typical. The caul is attested in one source only (the *Primary Chronicle*'s account of Vseslav's birth), but that text makes no mention of lycanthropy. Similarly anomalous and atypical is the detail you used to connect Livonian werewolves to the *benandanti*: their struggles to wrest crops and fertility from the devil and his minions, something asserted only by Old Thiess and Igund.

Ultimately, I am inclined to think a comparison between Thiess and the *benandanti* is appropriate, given the strong morphological similarities between them. I would not explain those similarities, however, as the residue of some deep historic connection. Rather, on the principle of Occam's razor, they are best understood as part of a defensive strategy adopted in both Livonia and the Friuli by principled and ingenious peasants who confronted similar discriminatory stereotypes and similar kinds of pressure. It's also productive to compare the Livonian werewolf stereotypes to the Vseslav epos, if only to show how the same qualities characteristic of lupine existence—ferocity, predation, appetite, rapine violence, and conscience-free aggression—were judged negatively in Livonia when attributed to the subordinate population, but positively in Old Russia when attributed to high-ranking warrior-nobles.[39]

This brings me to one last comparison that I offer only in tentative fashion. Reflecting on why Jakobson and Szeftel were so determined to see Vseslav as a "prince-werewolf," it strikes me that their attitude toward this character was considerably more critical than that of their sources. In Vseslav they saw a model of state power that used brutal, bloody force to accomplish results that were glorious, but also deeply disquieting and attributed to some kind of magical power. Writing in 1947, shortly after the end of the war, could these men—both Russian emigrés then working in America—have read Stalin into their Vseslav?

If so, it seems that another triangular figure can be constructed, placing your treatment of the *benandanti* and Thiess alongside Jakobson and Szeftel's treatment of Vseslav and Höfler's treatment of werewolves. In different ways, all of you think you can recover a deep past through your comparative approach to these data. Two of you see something you very much like, although your ideals are quite opposed. Thus, Höfler imagined the violence of lycanthropic *Männerbünde* was responsible for the miracle of state formation, while you imagine an archaic community outside (and in ways, opposed to) the state, marked by shamanic healing, ecstatic flights, and a principled desire to fight for the common good. Szeftel and Jakobson mediate

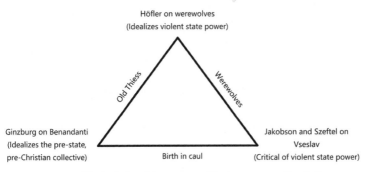

FIGURE 12. Ideological positions advanced in three comparative studies.

these positions, for what they describe resembles Höfler's vision of state power, but like you, they see that as monstrous (figure 12).

One of the great dangers when one tries to move from morphology to history is the tendency, even in the most scrupulous and learned scholars, to fill the gaps in our knowledge by imagining an originary state that not only connects and unites the *comparanda* but also reflects the scholar's deepest fears, desires, and/or ideals. This is surely what happened with Georges Dumézil, as you and I have both argued.[40] If I am not mistaken, much the same thing happened with Roman Jakobson and Marc Szeftel; also, my friend, with you. Having fallen victim to the same temptation myself on numerous occasions, I have come to think the best prophylaxis is to limit the number of examples one treats so that one can examine each one closely, with careful attention to the context in which it occurs; to be attentive even to subtle differences; and to entertain the possibility that the resemblances at issue may be nonfamilial, representing common responses to similar problems and circumstances, rather than resulting from (and bearing witness to) some deep historic connection.

But I am sure you will see things differently and will make your point, as you always do, with force, intelligence, a host of evidence, and good arguments. I very much look forward to hearing what you will have to say.

The Case of Old Thiess

A Comparative Perspective

A Conversation: Saturday, September 30, 2017

Carlo Ginzburg: As I told you, I would prefer to start from something general about comparison, and then we can focus on this case and our different approaches to it. Why, in my view, should we start from the general problem of comparison? Because in principle I agree with your approach, but the reverse is not true. So there is an interesting asymmetry between our respective attitudes.

Bruce Lincoln: Yes.

CG: I think that one could say that the *onus probandi*, the weight of the proof, should be on you. But this is not my attitude, because I am deeply interested in a sort of endless conversation with the devil's advocate.

BL: Yes, you've said this several times and I'm pleased to play that role.

CG: Exactly. So you are the devil's advocate and I am on your side. And what I would like to explore with you is the range of arguments that can be raised against my position. I'm not abandoning my attitude and I would still like to defend it, but I would *also* like to defend the idea that there is this asymmetry.

BL: Yes, and one of the things I appreciate in this conversation is that you defend your position without becoming defensive.

CG: We can perhaps begin with a general remark: comparison has been an issue in the large field of the humanities for a long time, but it became something different in the last few decades. I have an example in mind that is, in my view, controversial, but also challenging.

BL: Please.

CG: That is Franco Moretti's article "The Slaughterhouse of Literature."[1] I don't know if you have seen it.

BL: I don't know it, I'm sorry.

CG: OK. Moretti took as his title a line from Hegel. The "slaughterhouse of literature" is a reference to the fact that there is an incredibly large number of novels and work on novels; it would be impossible to master all of them. So, it's really a slaughterhouse: only a few are selected. Then he observed that we are confronted with this enormous amount of texts, of novels, and so forth in different languages: what can we do in order to overcome this challenge? The solution he suggested, in this and other related essays, was distant (i.e., secondhand) reading. But paradoxically, he also published a brilliant essay on clues, in which he focused on the way clues were dealt with in late nineteenth-century English literature, putting Conan Doyle in a larger perspective.[2] So, on the one hand he was advancing his theory about secondhand reading, and on the other he was writing an essay based on a close-reading approach to a circumscribed corpus of texts. Franco is a dear friend, but I was completely dissatisfied with his idea of secondhand reading and thought it was potentially dangerous; therefore I wrote a critical comment about it in an essay.[3] Yet even in this case, I would like to see whether this answer, which I dislike, is not related to a serious question. So, I ask myself: in principle, in addition to close reading of primary texts, shouldn't we also check *all* references to secondary literature related to the issue we are working on? But if I am not mistaken, except in a few fields of inquiry, this does not happen.

BL: You could go further. It is impossible to carry out that protocol, because it would take more than a lifetime to consult the enormous amount of evidence necessary and available.

CG: Exactly. So, this would imply the end of any advance in knowledge, because . . .

BL: If you have to read everything before you can speak, then you
will never speak.

CG: Yes. Now, this seems to me an interesting point, because we
have two extremes: an ideal that would mean the end of any advance
in knowledge and, on the other hand, a completely unacceptable
"solution" that relies on secondhand reading. Now, I like extremes
because they imply a challenge and we have to deal with a challenge,
but I never thought the middle road leads anywhere. Every road leads
to Rome, except the middle road, as Arnold Schoenberg, apparently,
used to say.

BL: But I do think there's a solution to that issue.

CG: No, no, I agree. We have to look for a solution. But a middle
way does not make sense—it's too vague.

BL: That depends on what you mean by "makes sense." The position that strikes me as the only viable one is first to accept that one
will never master all the evidence one would ideally like to master, and
one then has to make choices about what pieces of the whole are most
likely to be useful. Accordingly, one is obliged to acknowledge that the
work is incomplete and the conclusions provisional, and then invite
the criticism of colleagues—those living and yet to come—who will
read some of the things you failed to read and revise the provisional
construction you offered.

CG: I agree. Let me think if we can take a step further.

BL: Please.

CG: Can we accept as a vague reference the idea that we are living
in an age of globalization?

BL: Surely.

CG: If we accept this, comparison has become even more timely
than it was. But *what kind* of comparison? In my view, microhistory is
one of the possible solutions. If we take microhistory in the analytic
perspective that is connected to the word *micro*, it implies a back and
forth between a case and the larger phenomenon of which it is a case.

BL: Yes—the general category and one specific instantiation.

CG: Yes, but the category is not given. It must be discovered through a close reading of that case. And that is why I immediately reacted positively to your suggestion, because I thought here we have two different readings of the same case and that case certainly has larger implications. So, it makes sense. Again, I'm still hesitating, but this is a minor detail about the presentation: at which moment should we make the larger point about the relevance of this case in terms of the general issue, meaning comparison? I don't know when, but in my view, probably in the subtitle. Maybe "A case in comparison."

BL: Yes.

CG: I'm fond of the two words: "case" and "comparison."

BL: I was wondering whether "comparison" should be in the plural there.

CG: It sounds odd.

BL: I don't know if its oddness is off-putting or provocative. We should ponder this.

CG: Yes. "A case study in comparative approaches" would be . . .

BL: Cumbersome.

CG: "A case in comparisons"? We have to think about this. In any case—you started with a metaphor, which you used several times when you wrote about comparisons, meaning "weak" versus "strong."

BL: Yes.

CG: OK, in my view this is a metaphor, but we may add as a sort of overtone to this *opposition*, meaning prudent versus risky.

BL: Yes.

CG: Actually, when I reread your pieces on comparison,[4] a dictum by a friend of mine, Francesco Orlando, came to my mind. Well, Orlando used to say—he was from Palermo, I have to say this in Italian: "Sul portone di ogni università italiana, ci dovrebbe essere una targa di marmo nero con su scritto in lettere d'oro, 'Chi non *rrr*isica non *rrr*osica.'"

BL: *Non capisco*.

CG: It's a comment in a heavy *palermitano* accent. The proverb is "If you don't take risks, you won't be able to eat anything"—*risica, rosica*. Now, I like that: not taking risks seems to me a major risk in the Italian academic system (with due exceptions).

BL: That's true in any academic economy where jobs are scarce.

CG: Would you say so?

BL: I think so. I see it increasingly in our students. As the job market contracts, the fear of being frozen out of a position because you have said something dangerous increases.

CG: Yes. And so, the idea of taking risks seems to me embedded in the idea of scientific research.

BL: The risk of saying nothing that has real interest or importance is probably the greatest risk of all.

CG: Exactly. So maybe it would be interesting to have a look, from a historical point of view, at some major scientific enterprise based on a large, ambitious comparison. The most obvious example would be Darwin. But let us limit ourselves to the field of humanities, to see the amount of intellectual risk that was implicit or explicit, starting—but I didn't do any research on this—from the idea of reconstructing the Indo-European languages; we obviously have become accustomed to this, but at the beginning it was a very risky enterprise. So, I would say this is the most obvious example of a risky but successful enterprise involving comparison in the field of humanities.

BL: Successful, I think, is a very ambiguous judgment here.

CG: Ah!

BL: Also, to trace the beginning of that is difficult. Conventionally, it's attributed to Sir William Jones, but for several centuries before Jones, there were people who anticipated his work that resulted in the Indo-European hypothesis.[5] Jones gave this its classic formulation and since Jones we have worked with the notion that there is an Indo-European language, that all these are . . .

CG: You are going too fast, in my view.

BL: All right.

CG: Actually, I think your presentation could be much more prudent, because after all, the genealogical argument is not necessarily a part of the reconstruction of a—oh, I was going to say a *family* of languages, which already implies genealogy. But, let's say there was some, let's say *similarity* . . .

BL: To observe that there is a relation among these languages that is deep and cannot possibly be the result of chance . . .

CG: Mmm.

BL: . . . is certain and indisputable. But Jones went further than that.

CG: OK.

BL: Jones posited the existence of a protolanguage from which the others developed and a protohomeland from which the peoples diffused.

CG: So, when I said "successful," I was not thinking about those two additional and . . .

BL: . . . dangerous hypotheses. We can say, however, that there are systemic relations among these languages.

CG: OK. And this was not something that was self-evident. This is something that has been achieved.

BL: Yes.

CG: So, when I said "successful," I was thinking about this. Could one say that this was already a risky hypothesis?

BL: Yes.

CG: OK, so maybe we can imagine other hypotheses that were not self-evident and that we would now accept, because it would be interesting to see the asymmetry between the evidence available and the riskiness of the hypothesis. Sort of a "shot in the dark" that seems to me unavoidable at a certain stage of research. Earlier, I was thinking about possible results, but here I am thinking about the trajectory. And when we are thinking about the trajectory, I think the opposition between "weak" and "strong" comparisons becomes less helpful.

BL: Let me try to rephrase it.

CG: Yes.

BL: I have the impression that along some continuum of varying levels of risk, you prefer a position toward the riskier hypotheses.

CG: Mmm.

BL: You find that more daring and more promising, more adventurous and more fraught with possibility.

CG: Mmm.

BL: In contrast to which, I prefer a position where the ratio between the promised returns and the level of risk is most favorable. I'm less comfortable with risk per se than you are, and I think I'm more prudent in assembling a body of evidence I can manage in detail, so as to keep the risk at an acceptable level, while anticipating sufficient return to make the labor worthwhile. You, I think, are drawn to a position much further out on the spectrum of risk.

CG: Yes. I think I recognize myself in this portrait. Actually, when I was speaking of prudent versus risky, I was thinking about something different. However, let's say that this opposition, which has psychological overtones, is not very interesting. It may be interesting for us, but from a general point of view, it's not interesting. So, I think . . .

BL: But I think it becomes interesting if one starts with the assertion that comparison is inescapable.

CG: OK.

BL: There is no knowledge without comparison.

CG: OK.

BL: Second, comparison always implies some measure of risk and the results are uncertain.

CG: Mmm.

BL: But I would observe that most comparative work has succumbed to risks and gone astray. Most of the scholars we regard as the giants of comparison are now figures of historic interest only, because of how badly mistaken they were in constructing their various theories. The question that arises is: Why is it that comparison, which is necessary, so often leads to failed results? I suspect the seductive attraction of risk is so great that ambitious, intelligent, energetic, and visionary scholars are regularly drawn beyond what they can really master.

CG: Yeah. Now, actually I agree.

BL: I assumed you would.

CG: And I will tell you why. In the text I sent you on "medals and shells," I quoted that witty comment by Wendy Doniger.[6]

BL: Oh, yes.

CG: And she quoted the observation I made in a footnote that my Frazer had read Wittgenstein. Now, what does that mean? We can say that Frazer was so enormously wrong, but if Frazer had never existed, would our cognitive landscape be more rich? Or less?

BL: Oh, less rich; much less.

CG: OK . . .

BL: Frazer went less wrong than most people think.

CG: I agree. In other words, even if a lot of answers are unacceptable to subsequent scholars, the questions remain and were not self-evident. So again, we go back to the notion of risks and certainly Frazer took a lot of risks.

BL: Yes.

CG: What does it mean? I think I would be in favor of a secular version of the theological notion of *felix culpa*.

BL: (*Laughs.*)

CG: You see . . .

BL: If we pursue this . . .

CG: Yes.

BL: How could Frazer be reworked to salvage what's best, while avoiding his pitfalls? How does Wittgenstein help?

CG: Well, Wittgenstein was very provocative in his comments, but I took some distance from Wittgenstein as well. Just now, I'm correcting the proofs for the new edition of my book *Storia notturna*. In the introduction I had quoted a passage from Wittgenstein, in which he said that turning a circle into an ellipse does not imply a sort of genetic relationship. It could be the reverse. And then I said that in the sublunar world we inhabit, human beings are involved in a series of irreversible trajectories, and so Wittgenstein's comparison is misleading. And if we go back to Frazer, it would be interesting to identify one section and see how he worked with his evidence, trying to look for more evidence and trying to dissect the connections he posited and have a closer look at his research trajectory. Why? Because when we are talking about comparison, we should not focus only on the results. And the trajectory from taking risks to results is full of potential bifurcations and one needs to take account of what goes on in between. In other words, there is this moment of shooting in the dark. When we start our research, very often we are completely unfamiliar with the topic. And as I used to say, very often I had the feeling that we start from the answers and have to work for years to construct the questions. This is a sort of counterintuitive description of what research is, but it might even make sense. One could say OK, we start with a piece of evidence and aha! There is this moment, which seems to me crucial:

the idea that this is promising. And then, we commit ourselves, but we may start with a wild hypothesis and we try to collect evidence starting from a hypothesis that we later reject. And so this sort of tortuous trajectory seems to me something which should also be part of our picture about comparisons.

BL: I'm reminded of your earlier observations about the interest of considering *case* and *comparison* together. Research often begins when one stumbles across a datum that, for whatever reason, catches your attention and provokes you to work further on it for reasons you don't yet understand.

CG: Mmm.

BL: If you take the time, and few scholars do, to cross-examine what happens in that moment, it seems to me you have an intuitive sense that this datum is a case of some broader phenomenon. Something here is either typical of a broader category or sufficiently atypical and challenging to a broader category that it warrants being considered in its particularity, i.e., in contrast to an array of other examples that are like it in certain fashions and unlike it in others.

CG: You know, I think you are absolutely right, but in my view the opposition between norm and anomaly is at least as important as that between prudent and risky.

BL: Yes.

CG: In a way, we are getting close to the case we are going to deal with, because this is certainly anomalous from the point of view of the evidence. But I would like to ask you: What attracted you to this case?

BL: I first read the Thiess case in 1974 or thereabout, when I was working on my dissertation. Höfler's work had been recommended to me by my *Doktorvater*, Mircea Eliade, who spoke of the book as brilliant and revelatory. My German was not very good at the time and I worked very hard to make my way through the book. Largely under Eliade's influence, I took the *Männerbund* thesis as established fact and I saw the Thiess case through his eyes, as well as Höfler's.

CG: Yes.

BL: I took Thiess as evidence that *Männerbund* institutions of a werewolf type had not only existed in deep prehistory but were still attested in the early modern period. I thought it was an astounding datum to have survived. A bit later, I was discussing Höfler's work and that of Stig Wikander on Iranian werewolves[7] with Carsten Colpe, who very somberly warned me: "You need to look more deeply at this *Männerbund* thesis and treat it with extreme caution." That not only changed my sense of the Thiess case, it also changed my sense of research. Did you have to read a book in the historic context in which it's written? If so, you had to know a great deal more about the author and the author's commitments than I knew about Höfler. And as I began to exercise the caution that Carsten had rightly urged on me, I became more and more suspicious, more and more scandalized at the way this datum had been treated by a whole set of scholars and had been presented to me by people I trusted. And I began reading *everything* more cautiously, but I did not return to Thiess until much later, when you had written about it and I said "Oh yes, I remember this case, but I've never really explored it for myself and I need to study it more carefully." So for me, it was an object lesson in prudence, suspicion of risk, and caution in the face of seductive hypotheses.

CG: Yes, I see. Very interesting. Now, I think I would make a sort of paradoxical comment. For Höfler, for Eliade, and in a very different way, even opposite, for yourself, this was a case of "normal exceptional." Let me tell you why. Both for Höfler and for Eliade, that piece of evidence was certainly exceptional from the point of view of evidence, but referred to a much larger phenomenon.

BL: Yes.

CG: So, there is this asymmetrical relationship, which is not obvious, because in some cases you have an exceptional piece of evidence that refers to something that is also exceptional in terms of behavior, but this was not the case according to Höfler and Eliade. Now, in your case, this exceptional document turned into a norm of cautiousness vis-à-vis documents.

BL: Yes.

CG: I think that's interesting, because it says something about the way this case had relevance for each of us.

BL: It's a riveting document and it has aroused rather different sorts of enthusiasm, curiosity, and suspicion in a good number of scholars, all of whom intuitively felt that it resonated with some of their pre-existing ideas and commitments.

CG: Absolutely. I think we will come back to this.

BL: Yes.

CG: But let me tell you something. I think this bears not only on the first opposition that emerged in our conversation today, caution versus risk, but also on the relation between this and the second opposition, between norms and anomalies. They are not identical, nor overlapping, but I think there is a quite intriguing relationship between them. Let me tell you why. Even if you insist on saying "No, I would like to remain cautious," you may be confronted and attracted by anomalous documents.

BL: Yes. Anomalies always have the fascination of the unfamiliar.

CG: OK. I think this complicates your cautiousness.

BL: Yes.

CG: OK, so there is this arresting moment when the piece of evidence looks unpredictable. Otherwise, it would be impossible to speak of an anomaly.

BL: Mm-hmm.

CG: So, what does it mean: "unpredictable"? Well, what is predicted has been predicted by other scholars and it's part of common wisdom, which is not the case with an anomaly. So we are entering a kind of untrodden ground, which is the necessary result of an encounter with an anomalous document.

BL: Yes.

CG: I'm trying to convince you that your commitment to prudence still implies a lot of risky behavior. I still believe there is a sort of psychological difference between us and I believe that if at a certain moment we look more closely at this, there will be a divergence between us. But, at that early stage of research, the idea of entering an untrodden ground . . .

BL: . . . is as appealing to me as it is to you.

CG: Yes. And not just appealing, but actually put into practice.

BL: Yes.

CG: OK, and what comes after this already implies an effort toward generalization.

BL: Yes.

CG: And this is maybe the starting point of our divergence. I'm not sure, because I've never reflected on this very closely. Maybe my reaction to this case, to the Thiess trial, isn't that telling, because I was struck, of course, by the anomaly of the trial, but on the other hand, since I'd just finished my book on the *benandanti*, for me it made sense in a perspective that was very different from Höfler's reaction or Eliade's reaction. Comparison to the *benandanti* let me reframe this anomaly, which still remained an anomaly, but whose comprehensibility and import were enhanced by being placed in that broader context.

BL: Why was it you were reading Höfler in that moment? Was it simply an accident of chance? You had finished your dissertation and your research on the *benandanti*.

CG: Yes. I had sent the manuscript to my friend Corrado Vivanti, who was a pupil of Delio Cantimori; he was working at Einaudi. And there was a misunderstanding between us, because I thought the book was finished, but in fact he was waiting for some corrections. So, I still had the manuscript with me and I was working at the Vatican Library. Now, I probably found the trial on the shelves, that volume with von Bruiningk's edition. But I don't remember. Maybe we can look in my book and there will be a clue there. . . .

BL: My recollection is that you cited it from Höfler and not from von Bruiningk.

CG (*after consulting* I benandanti): No, von Bruiningk.

BL (*looking at page*): Ah, yes. So you found von Bruiningk.[8]

CG: Yeah, yeah. But let me check. OK, you see the footnote.

BL: Oh, yes.

CG: So, certainly I came to this starting from . . .

BL: You read Höfler, who led you to von Bruiningk.

CG: Yes.

BL: That's the way most people find it.

CG: But now I am unable to recall what led me to Höfler, but let me check one more thing. (*After leafing through book*) Maybe this entry from Lily Weiser-Aall.[9] She must have mentioned Höfler. I was looking for the date, but there's no date listed. It was probably late 1930s. But I could be wrong. I will check this.

BL: My sense is that the Thiess datum had two great attractions for you. One, it was the first *comparandum* you found that had strong similarities to the *benandanti* and it removed them from isolation, potentially connecting them to a broader universe. Second, you encountered it in Höfler, where it was put to radically different use—politically, morally, socially, intellectually—and, I think, from your position, offensively so.

CG: Yes.

BL: And by putting Thiess in relation to the *benandanti*, rather than to the Norse werewolves, you effected a repositioning and redefinition that was intellectually appealing, while being attractive in more than just intellectual ways.

CG: Yes, certainly that is so, although I had actually already found another comparison beyond the Friuli.

BL: Oh, really?

CG: Yes, I spent one month at the Warburg Institute in 1964. I had recently published a little piece on the Warburg Library when it was in danger of being reabsorbed by the University of London Library, in a journal called *Common Knowledge*. My article was titled "Une machine à penser"—an allusion to Le Corbusier's "une machine à habiter" but also, I thought, a good description of the library. At the end I also mentioned the fact that when the Warburg Library was going to be built, Fritz Saxl suggested, unsuccessfully, Le Corbusier's name.[10] In 1964, this *machine à penser* led me toward a sixteenth-century trial of a Bavarian herdsman, Chonradt Stoeckhlin, who claimed that during the Ember days he was able to join the "nocturnal band" of the dead, as some *benandanti* (especially women) did. Much later this Bavarian case became the topic of a book by Wolfgang Behringer.[11]

BL: Uh-huh.

CG: But this Bavarian *comparandum* was geographically closer to the territory of the *benandanti* in the Friuli and so, less unexpected. The real exception was the Thiess case, which was much further away, and it's true, there was this shock on many levels. And I was able, rightly or wrongly, to put this anomalous case into a context along-side the *benandanti*. Let's imagine a different kind of case, in which the anomaly persists and so we are trying to construct some sort of provisional generalization. And I would emphasize the provisional element, just because we are talking about the trajectory. So, obviously, you might mention a great many cases related to your own experience, in which by *tâtonnements*, you struggle to make sense of something. I often think of myself being in a dark room and trying to understand what is there. I'm trying to argue that even a most prudent scholar, like yourself, must be involved in some provisional generalizations.

BL: Oh, there's no question. The point of departure, I think . . . I fully agree when you adduce morphological similarities of a striking sort between the case of Thiess and that of the *benandanti*.

CG: Mm-hmm.

BL: And when you expand the set further, I still . . . some of the morphological resemblances become weaker, others enter that are novel, but I generally find the morphological aspects of your comparisons convincing: the *kresniki*, the *táltos*, etc. Not each example is equally compelling, but in general there is enough similarity to say that it's worth talking about these *as a group*.

CG: Mmm.

BL: This is because the morphological resemblances are numerous, and they seem noncoincidental. At that point, however, I would reflect on the question: What can possibly account for these morphological resemblances? And in some cases—for instance, I would say that when human beings in widely separate places are all breathing oxygen, that doesn't demand an explanation. It's just natural. But when we get past cases like that and morphological similarities can't be dismissed as the result of nature or mere coincidence, I'm less inclined than you are to look for a historical connection. It seems to me that given your disciplinary orientation, that strikes you as the most likely hypothesis to be pursued. And in this case, it led you to generate a hypothetical picture of a deep prehistory that permitted direct contact, transmission, connection. Although the past with which you seek to explain the similarities does not leave direct records, you maintain it can be inferred through comparative method.

CG: Now, two remarks. First of all, you say "noncoincidental."

BL: Mm-hmm.

CG: I understand what you mean, but maybe there is something more to be said about that. Because this goes back to the issue of anomalies.

BL: Yes.

CG: Because if something is normal—you used the example of breathing . . .

BL: Mm-hmm.

CG: . . . *that* would not be a particularly interesting coincidence.

BL: Mm-hmm.

CG: OK. Actually, there is more to be said about that.

BL: And we can return to it.

CG: Then you said that since I am a historian, I look for historical transmission. But you are a historian as well. . . .

BL: I'm flattered when I'm considered a historian, and I might like to be a historian, but . . .

CG: Your interpretation of the case is put in historical terms.

BL: Yes.

CG: Absolutely! So, let's put it in compressed form. I would say there is something beyond both cases which in principle could explain their similarities.

BL: Yes. So far, so good.

CG: On the other hand, you say: Since there are those resemblances, we have to assume that different people at different times in different societies were reacting to similar pressures. This seems to me a risky answer, notwithstanding the appearances, because it deals with anomalous traits. As an explanation for the coincidence of *anomalous* traits, your hypothesis seems to me unconvincing. Since in this case we are dealing with traits that are not as widespread as breathing, I think the argument about breathing can be used against you.

BL: I think not, but explain why you do.

CG: I would say this. We agree on the fact that the starting point is related to anomalous traits.

BL: Yes.

CG: *Benandanti* fighting for fertility and a werewolf who says he is stealing seeds of . . .

BL: Yes.

CG: In both cases, we could say they are anomalous, but vis-à-vis what? Well, in the case of the *benandanti*, vis-à-vis the vast number of witchcraft trials from the Friuli Inquisition, where there is nothing else like this, and I would add something: the obvious surprise we can read between the lines, meaning the inquisitors were surprised as they tried to make sense of the *benandanti*.

BL: They themselves recognized this as anomalous.

CG: In the case of Thiess, we don't have any evidence in this sense, so . . .

BL: No, no. We do.

CG: We do?

BL: Yes. When Thiess first says he's a werewolf, the judges ask, "Is this man in his right mind?"

CG: Ah, yes. Right.

BL: What they are actually saying is they've never heard anything like this.

CG: OK, so we have recognition of this as an anomaly, not only through our subjective reaction, but by the actors. . . .

BL: The actors themselves regard it as anomalous.

CG: To explain two anomalies as a reaction to a convergent stimulus, to cultural pressure, meaning something that is widespread, seems to me unpersuasive, which is why I would say explaining *obscurum per obscurius*.

BL: Unconvincing, I understand, but why obscure?

CG: In the case of both anomalies, there is something that is opaque, but your explanation seems to explain something that is anomalous through a very widespread situation, i.e., social and cultural pressure: an explanation which is, in my view, far from self-evident.

BL: Many defendants are accused by courts. Few of them claim to have been in hell, fighting for fertility.

CG: Exactly. On the other hand, I thought your article was a real challenge and that's the reason I tried to answer on a different ground, using a genealogical strategy. So the idea that one could use textual philology in this field is something which emerged from our debate.

BL: Yes. But it's strange, because I take the move to history that you make as very reminiscent of the kinds of method employed by Dumézil, of whom you were sharply critical.[12] I understand that the political and moral distinction remains between you and Dumézil.

CG: Yes, but there is also a major methodological difference: Dumézil's genealogical model was not inspired by textual philology—and therefore did not take into account the possibility of a cultural transmission which implied mistakes or anomalies.

BL: But with regard to method, you're both trying to imagine prehistoric connections at a level of deep antiquity that could explain the morphological resemblances you observe in a moment of relative synchronicity.

CG: Well, you know . . .

BL: And you go even further than Dumézil to imagine a pre-Indo-European, Eurasian shamanism of Lord knows how many millennia back.

CG: Well, I tried to refrain from the use of "prehistoric" as an adjective.

BL: Mm-hmm.

CG: But "Eurasian," I think, is kind of a compressed word that's related to a trajectory that is not linear. Maybe I was not clear enough on this, but I think yours is a somewhat misleading description of my attempt. The synchronous layer I was dealing with in my morphological reconstruction was the outcome of an intellectual experiment: morphological resemblances are, by definition, outside time. The attempt to translate those connections into time, to translate morphology into history, came later—as a conjecture. The title of the last section of my book was "Eurasian Conjectures."

BL: Mm-hmm.

CG: When I try to look at the historical connection, I have to place myself at a stage in which there is diffusion, but not diffusion*ism*, and this takes place in history, not in prehistory. So, the Scythians . . .

BL: If by "prehistory" what we mean is before there are written documents that attest to it, then we are in prehistory.

CG: Well . . .

BL: I don't think you can avoid that.

CG: No, no. I see that. But what I mean is that we are dealing with prehistory even in, say, the sixteenth century, because we are dealing with layers that have only lately been documented. The opposite attitude would be that if you find something that is documented for the first time in the sixteenth-century trials, then the things they are talking about emerged at that time. This seems to me an absurd fallacy. Alternatively, when something is recorded, it may actually have been going on, unrecorded, for—how long?

BL: Well, for the *benandanti*, I don't know. A long time.

CG: Me neither.

BL: A long time. For the werewolves of Livonia, I'm not convinced there ever were any werewolves of Livonia.

CG: But, come on. You remember those texts, Peucer and so on. . . .

BL: Yes.

CG: And Witekind. Those little details pointing to an image of werewolves that was very different from the stereotype. Obviously, I read them, trying to find a context. . . .

BL: Yes, let's talk about that, because it's an important piece of evidence. We have the story in Peucer, who got it from Melanchthon, who got it from Witekind. How do you imagine Witekind . . .

CG: What do you mean?

BL: . . . got this story? Was he an eyewitness? Did he hear a rumor? Was there a hearing of a public nature where he was present? Is this hearsay? I don't know the answer to this.

CG: Yeah.

BL: But I don't think he witnessed anyone who called himself a werewolf cutting a horse in half while chasing a butterfly.

CG: Yes.

BL: I just don't think that happened.

CG: OK. I'm trying to remember who met this werewolf or who said "My master is more powerful. . . ." I'll have to check this.[13]

BL: That's not in Peucer, that's a different testimony.

CG: Yes, this is Witekind recalling his meeting with a werewolf who had been put in jail. . . .

BL: That people were accused of being werewolves and put in jail for it, I have no doubt. That people facing trial sometimes confessed to being werewolves, I have no doubt. That anyone *was* a werewolf, I'm not convinced.

CG: But look . . .

BL: My sense of the Peucer example is that someone was accused of mutilating a horse and in order to defend himself against a serious legal charge, he made up some story. And the story was retold, became exaggerated, and circulated further afield. The story about the butterfly took shape in response to a direct accusation. . . .

CG: And therefore?

BL: The man invented an elaborate fantasy designed to distract the court and save his skin. I think that's much more likely than that his story preserves widespread beliefs from prior millennia.

CG: OK, OK. I think here we have to stop and make a general digression about the nature of evidence.

BL: OK.

CG: Because I was struck by the fact that you said Witekind was not an eyewitness. Now, if I look at all your work as a historian, I think eyewitnesses supply only a tiny minority of the evidence. You are dealing with evidence that refers to long traditions, sometimes in a very indirect way. So if this would be the criterion, you . . .

BL: Most of what we call evidence would be inadmissible.

CG: Exactly. So I was surprised, because this is not a standard you would normally use.

BL: That's not my point. My point is that Witekind was retelling a story he heard others tell. We are in the realm of discourse, not practice.

CG: OK. So, there's a constraint and then somebody is inventing something. Now, I'm really perplexed by this word, not because I don't believe someone is able to invent something, but there are cultural constraints. So maybe we can use—I don't know if you would accept this provisionally as a metaphor—the *langue*-versus-*parole* dichotomy. The idea of using *parole* to articulate a completely new statement should take into account the constraints of *langue*.

BL: Yes.

CG: So, the cultural constraints . . .

BL: The "novel" is not *completely* novel, since it works within a pre-existing system.

CG: Yes. Now, you seem to assume a lot of invention by individuals, dismissing the fact, which seems to me obvious, that they are trying to articulate something that submits to a series of constraints of all kinds, starting with grammar, phonetics. . . .

BL: Yes. But here's my argument—and it's specific to the case of Peucer and Thiess.

CG: Uh-huh.

BL: We have anomalies in both these instances. These two witnesses tell us something we do not encounter elsewhere, which prompts curiosity and calls for explanation. In the case of Peucer, it seems to me we have a peasant accused of werewolfery and violence against an animal. And he gives testimony that says yes, I dismembered this animal, but it was an accident, for I was chasing a witch, who happened to change into a butterfly. The anomaly seems to me best explained by the situation in which he told this story, which others then heard, repeated, and commented upon, being struck by how extraordinary a datum it is.

CG: Yes, I see. I would proceed in a different way, dissecting those statements. So, we have werewolves against witches, witches transforming themselves into animals, witches transforming themselves into butterflies. Now, werewolves against witches, we have at least . . .

BL: We have one other example of this.

CG: Yes. Then, witches transforming themselves into animals. We have a lot of examples.

BL: Many.

CG: And butterflies. I can probably find an example in the *benandanti* trials.[14] Now, one could say . . .

BL: At this point, I think you've established that this is part of *langue*.

CG: Yes.

BL: The elements are present, known to the speaker and his audience. In that moment, he draws on the elements of a shared *langue* to create a novel verbalization at the level of *parole* that has the pragmatic purpose of saving his life.

CG: But, I would say, using the existing elements. Why should we dismiss the commitment of the speaker? Because otherwise, one could say all those . . .

BL: Because I don't think he was chasing a witch or a butterfly, if he was attacking a horse at all.

CG: Yes, but even if those events never took place, the tales about them are there, and they are relevant. Look, we could dismiss all the *benandanti* confessions, because they were extracted under pressure and they were saying something only to save their lives, and what they said did not refer to real events . . .

BL: I'm not suggesting we dismiss this testimony. . . .

CG: But we can't say those people were just *inventing stories* because they were under constraint.

BL: My guess is that in some instances they were. But the great difference between the Livonian case and the *benandanti* is that you have the testimony of so many more people over a much longer period of time, and I'm convinced there was some sort of group. I don't know if it was a cultic association, a kinship association, or what. There were a great many ways these people might have assumed a shared identity in which they called themselves *benandanti*. To me, one of the most striking differences is that in the Friulian case, the accused called themselves by a name very different from anything their accusers had ever heard.

CG: Mm-hmm.

BL: It's a novel datum to the court. In Livonia, the accusation is something that the elite have been saying about certain members of the peasantry for centuries. It's a very well-known category. I see little evidence that any Livonian peasants accepted the identity of werewolf as their own. Under torture, a number of others confessed, but Thiess is the only example of someone who said "Yes, I am a werewolf and I will explain what it means to be a werewolf," which is the most anomalous piece of all this.

CG: OK, this is very similar and I would answer like this: Look at the *benandanti*, because in this case we have their own self-description and self-naming.

BL: Yes, and that persists over decades.

CG: But, there is also the court's pressure, which is documented, trying to turn those *benandanti* into witches.

BL: Yes.

CG: Now, at the moment when they introject this pressure, they were still calling themselves *benandanti*, but the fact is . . .

BL: They start describing themselves through the eyes of their persecutors.

CG: So we can imagine that something similar took place in Livonia as well.

BL: Yes.

CG: In other words, the introjection, but then the resistance. So, the introjection of the name, for instance, but resistance in terms of content.

BL: Yes.

CG: Now, I think there is a general point that should be made about *hapax legomena*.

BL: OK.

CG: Because we are talking about anomalies, and if we take the process of text transmission as a model, we could say "What about *hapax legomena*?" Years ago, I wrote a piece against Hayden White's approach, called "Just One Witness."[15]

BL: Oh, yes.

CG: OK. Now, I take this as a general principle. In other words, as I said in my piece, just because we have only one witness—in that case, the survivor from a collective murder—does not imply we can dismiss this on the principle *unus testis, nullus testis*. As historians, we work on a level of proof that is not identical to that in certain widespread legal traditions. *Unus testis* can be admitted.

BL: It depends.

CG: It depends. We are not compelled to take him or her at face value. . . .

BL: Nor to dismiss the testimony.

CG: So, I was reacting to the fact that you were suggesting that if you have two witnesses, it changes the picture. Maybe two witnesses are better than one, but even *hapax* can be significant.

BL: I think the argument about *langue* and *parole* works extremely well here. Those who give testimony make use of with a vocabulary they share with others . . .

CG: Yes.

BL: . . . and a set of images and assumptions that is well established. But it is also the case they are operating in very specific contexts of personal danger. And they maneuver with considerable skill, although the man described by Peucer, unlike Thiess, failed to save his life.

CG: You know, the idea that something said in a situation of constraint or danger should not be taken at face value seems to me problematic. You see what I mean?

BL: I'm pondering whether anything should be taken at face value.

CG: No, no, no. I agree. So the problem would be to look at each piece of evidence, including evidence delivered in a situation of constraint, because otherwise the historical use of court records would be impossible.

BL: Yes.

CG: Because by definition, all of them were in danger.

(*End of first discussion.*)

The Conversation Continues: Monday, October 2, 2017

CG: Let's begin by talking about "invention." There are comparable situations, and in the case of Thiess, we have an invention. You said that you thought this was not the case with the *benandanti*, because the mass of documents implies that even if there are individual variations . . .

BL: . . . there was a degree of collective and enduring agreement about certain features characteristic of the group.

CG: Yes.

BL: It's not simply an individual product, but something shared by a whole group.

CG: Exactly. But in the case of Thiess, you say "invention." Now, I have two remarks about invention. First of all, if the allegedly invented elements are unexpected—on the one hand, unexpected, but on the other hand, made sense . . .

BL: They're comprehensible.

CG: . . . made sense in a wider context, then I think the claim concerning invention becomes weaker.

BL: I would argue otherwise.

CG: If the elements are unlikely. So, maybe we can start with this, because the other point I want to raise about invention is on a more general level.

BL: All right. I don't think Thiess's "invention" was a radical novelty of such staggering originality as to be utterly unforeseeable and initially incomprehensible by others who participated in the same culture. But it was an invention in that it was a novel assemblage of preexisting elements and structures that produced an intriguing difference that others regarded as surprising, but readily understood.

CG: OK. It's unexpected, but not incomprehensible because it's been constructed with elements that belonged to the cultural context?

BL: Yes.

CG: OK. Now, here we are entering a domain that seems to me difficult to handle, i.e., the question of sincerity.

BL: Mmm.

CG: I have always avoided this term. I remember somebody saying in a different context, only God can judge sincerity. I can see how this metaphor can work—for me it's a metaphor—because we don't know if there was sincerity and this kind of psychological judgment seems to me beyond our reach.

BL: I would differ here and I would modify the proverb you quote and say "Only God can know *with certainty* who is sincere and who is not," but we are obliged to make judgments constantly about the sincerity of those with whom we speak. We understand that we may be mistaken, since you can't access the interiority of another human. But from facial expressions, tone of voice, pauses and hesitation in the way one speaks, there are any number of inferences we use to make a judgment about sincerity.

CG: That's for sure, but when we are dealing with a case like Thiess . . .

BL: With Thiess, it's more difficult than if he were here. . . .

CG: Yes, and you're talking about visual impressions, but I have no idea about Thiess's or the *benandanti's* facial expressions.

BL: No.

CG: But as a matter of fact, in the case of the Inquisition trials, you find remarks that bear on the question of sincerity, but these are framed by our perception of that context. So a Chinese box in which sincerity becomes an issue is certainly understandable to me, but when we use it in terms of our appreciation, that seems to me more difficult. But in any case, this is not my main point, which is again about invention, but at a more general level. When you say "invention," you are talking about something that is etymologically—well, not exactly etymologically, but at least semantically—close to fiction. I'm thinking about the etymology of "fiction."

BL: Like modeling clay.

CG: Yes, exactly. Now, I have been deeply interested in the possible uses of fictional evidence from a historical point of view. Even if the details of an account are invented, there is something about the content that is still rooted in the context in which the invention was created. So, since I started by saying I like to play with the idea of the devil's advocate and I am fascinated by starting with a kind of "as if" reasoning, which seems to me crucial to our discussion and to research in general, let's imagine Thiess was making an invention, as you argued. Would it still be possible to use what he said in a historical perspective?

BL: Oh, absolutely.

CG: In what sense?

BL: Let me develop an argument here. What he said had to be an attempt to persuade the court of certain things, and it had to be couched in a language they would find comprehensible and persuasive. It therefore had to appeal to items of broad cultural currency and others with specific relevance to his case. If it was a fiction, it would have to be recognized by the court as truth, if it were to succeed in its pragmatic purpose. Now, there are other texts we can draw on that are quite close to Thiess's and help us to understand its cultural context. I've brought one for you. This is another werewolf trial, from roughly seventy-five years prior (1617). We have a shorter protocol here, without the complete testimony, and there are about twenty other such trials in which we find materials like this. What you'll see, first of all, is that, as in the case of Thiess, an indigenous defendant, a woman named Aleit, was brought before a noble German court, which was assisted by noble German pastors, and a summary lists eight points the court regarded as proven, largely as a result of her confessions. The text reads as follows:

Trial of the court convened in Fegefeuer [today's Kiviloo] palace, concerning the witchcraft (*Zauberey*) of notorious people on June 20 and 21, 1617, by the noble, most earnest, and manly Junkers: Otto Premcke, Ludolph Strassborg, Meinert Dittmer, Riclauss Bonichausen.

Also in attendance, the worthy and learned Herrn Johannes Popii, pastor at Koskull [today's Kosch], and Gerten Bartholomaei, pastor of St. John's Church.

So that justice could be realized, the peasant elders in attendance are the following: Barne Matz, Gianne Mait, Herria Hein, Giörde Hans, Pauia Tönne, Rokela Laur, Pitque Jacob.

First to appear before the court, a peasant named Serme Hans, who dwells in the village of Fegefeuer, plaintively made known how his deceased wife[16] had made a complaint against a woman named Aleit and thereafter died, after which Aleit, the accused, was imprisoned and questioned about this evil.

1) She immediately confessed to that.
2) Second, she confessed that ten years ago, she ran about as a werewolf and did great harm at that time.
3) She confessed that along with two other sorcerers (*Zauberern*), in the wilds she took down, dismembered, and devoured a pair of oxen and two horses, along with other livestock.
4) When she was asked whether she knew to whom the horses, oxen, sheep, and other animals that she dismembered might have belonged, she answered roguishly and sarcastically: "Does a wolf run through the village and ask to whom the sheep belong before he falls upon them?"

5) She was asked, while she was changed into a wolf, how she could eat the meat. Thereafter, she answered that before she came upon the animal, she laid aside the wolf's form and cooked it according to its type.

6) When she was asked where she had stolen the kettle in which she cooked the meat, she answered roguishly and sarcastically, "Poor people don't go to war for a kettle."

7) She confessed that she strangled Engelbrecht Mecken's calf.

8) When she was asked about her companions, she implicated an old fellow named Matz Lübben, who had previously taught her the evil art.[17]

Almost word for word, these are the same charges and *some* of the same responses. At issue is how wolfish the accused really was—part human and part wolf, or entirely animalistic. And the court begins with the charge: theft of livestock, dismemberment of livestock, illicit consumption of livestock. What we have to bear in mind, I think, is that ownership of large livestock was a prerogative of the German nobility. If the peasantry ate meat, they did so only rarely, on festive occasions, and they didn't own horses. I'm not certain about cattle, but if they did own any, they were few and very precious to them. Where Thiess invents, as I see it, is that he took the implicit structure behind these trials and the related werewolf beliefs, whereby the *Deutsche* were contrasted to the *Undeutsche* along the same lines that the consumption of meat is contrasted to the consumption of vegetable products and, further, as predators are contrasted to prey. The nobility owned livestock, ate livestock, and preyed on others who were weaker. The peasantry ate plants, obeyed the orders given to them by the nobility, deferred to the nobility, and tried to avoid becoming their prey. But if the peasants threatened to become predators—to take, kill, and eat livestock—they would have been acting like nobles, and the elite would have perceived and described this as "acting like wolves." And these are the charges brought against virtually everyone accused of werewolfery in early modern Livonia. Thiess invented by shifting— really, inverting—that whole structure. Initially, he was forced to ac- knowledge that he had eaten some animals, but he went on to say that others had eaten far more, he was not very good at stealing animals, etc. He minimized that side of the charges and shifted the discussion in unexpected but comprehensible ways, when he talked about saving plants, rather than dismembering animals, and about recovering what had been stolen, rather than stealing that which belonged to someone else. And he argued: "I and others like me are not what you think. We are the hounds of God, not the servants of Satan. And just like you, we are at war with the servants of Satan." I think that's a very challenging argument. At a metaphorical level, it offered a stunning analysis of the situation that ought to have been comprehensible to all members of that society, but which was very threatening to the interests of the elite. It mounted a direct challenge at many points, and there are points where the elite didn't understand what he was saying, along with others where they perceived the danger of his argument and, accordingly, *refused* to understand what he was saying. And at the end of the first trial, they threw up their hands and said, "We don't know what to do with this case. It's not like anything we've seen before. It's terribly complicated and we need to appeal to a higher authority." I think that's an indication of their *partial* comprehension of a testimony that radically rearranged elements with which they were familiar.

CG: OK. Now, as you remember, when we started our conversation, I said that in principle I accept your approach, but you are not accepting mine. So, there is a sort of asymmetry and we have to think about this.

BL: Correct.

CG: What you said about the general context seems to me completely acceptable and it's a very insightful reading of this trial. I didn't go in that direction at all; your reading certainly enriches our comprehension of the document. No doubt about that. What I find unconvincing in your argument is the rejection of the symbolic value of a series of elements, which you regard as mere individual inventions. I am also struck by your comparison with Aleit's trial: there is a tiny detail I would like to point out, which is the characterization of her responses as "sarcastic." This is also something that was emphasized by Witekind in his account. Here we have evidence of an actor establishing a certain cultural distance: for a moment, we can see how those accused of being werewolves were making fun of the other side. This is certainly something compatible with the social tensions you are talking about. Now, we have here two documents, not one, and they are not overlapping. But I wonder, if we would start from those documents and if we took two documents at random from the *benandanti* dossier, we would be confronted not with a sort of stereotypical, skeleton-like account, but with a lot of individual variations of the sort I emphasized in my book. So, I was confronted with a phenomenon that certainly was as unexpected to me as it was to the inquisitors, meaning people—men and women—living an experience that is unattainable to us; but the events they were describing were put in terms that were very close to a lived experience, and this was a problem for the inquisitors. If we do not take the *benandanti* descriptions literally, we are confronted with a series of reworking of symbolic structures: may we say this?

BL: Yes.

CG: Which would be compatible with my reading of . . .

BL: Oh, yes. I would have much less difficulty with that argument. Where I found your Bogotá lecture extremely helpful was your notion of "conjunctive anomalies." The Thiess case, for reasons we've discussed, is anomalous in the Livonian context. The *benandanti* are anomalous in Friuli and within the Inquisition more broadly, but less so because there were many *benandanti* and it's a group, rather than an individual or a small number of testimonies. But the two anomalies resemble each other closely. So far, we're in perfect agreement.

CG: OK.

BL: How we account for those morphological resemblances is where we part company.

CG: Yes, because, as you say, they are comparable as anomalies.

BL: Yes.

CG: But only as anomalies insofar as they belong to a category that we label "anomaly."

BL: And which the actors themselves, in their cultural moment, considered anomalous.

CG: As anomalous, they are comparable.

BL: Yes.

CG: But beyond that . . .

BL: They have morphological resemblances to one another that are very strong and very striking. Where I see the strongest similarity is that persons of a subaltern group, accused by a powerful court, respond to the court by affirming their own dignity and benevolence.

CG: OK. I think we are now dealing with different levels of comparison.

BL: Mm-hmm.

CG: And different levels of comparability. So, let us say there is the anomaly, and *also* the tension between the judges or inquisitors and defendants in both cases. Because after all, we are dealing with court records in both cases.

BL: Yes.

CG: Now, there is a further convergence concerning the content . . .

BL: Yes.

CG: . . . of their experiences, in quotation marks. Let's say provisionally "experiences." And at that moment you resist.

BL: I do. Because I think your desire to associate these examples leads you to misread some of the Livonian evidence in order to make it look more like the *benandanti* than it actually does. And I think . . .

CG: Yes, but in what sense?

BL: Let me go just a bit further. I'm inclined to think the pre-Socratic philosopher Empedocles identified the two crucial operations of intellectual activity: analysis and synthesis, i.e., the breaking down of a phenomenon into smaller parts so you can understand its details and workings, and the association of disparate phenomena into larger wholes so that you can see the big picture. One can speak of this via the metaphor of the trees and the forest or in other ways, but the metaphor Empedocles chose was to call what I'm calling "synthesis," "love," and to call what I'm calling "analysis," "strife." For him, love is bringing things together and strife is tearing things apart. He sees these not just as intellectual methods but as cosmic forces responsible for everything that exists. And it's just a wonderful work. But it seems to me the danger here is that love is more attractive than strife. Comparatists regularly wish to bring things together and build larger structures, and it feels both benevolent and productive to assimilate and synthesize, while it feels destructive and hateful and discordant to analyze and tear things apart. Further, since we always know some things better than others, I think we tend to read phenomena that *resemble* the ones we know as being much closer to them than they actually are. And the more examples you consider, the more likely you are to say "Aha, that's just like this other thing I've already studied." Even the best scholars fall victim to that fallacy, and I think there are at least four or five points in Thiess where you've seen more of the *benandanti* in Thiess than the text really permits.

CG: Now, your reading of Empedocles is fascinating. Obviously, for us, that perspective, using those categories—"strife" and "love"— would be utterly misleading, so we can look at that from a distance, but if we go back to "analysis" and "synthesis," I would object to that idea as too simplistic, if you mean that there are two types of scholars. . . .

BL: No, everyone engages in both.

CG: OK. This is not your point.

BL: No.

CG: Because I would insist that in any research, there is an interaction between the analytic moment and the synthetic moment. So, everything is provisional. There is a trajectory, punctuated by uncertainties, in the course of which we shift from a more analytic reading to some sort of generalization. It seems to me if we go beyond what you said—and I completely agree with it—about the comparability of the social context, and I would insist also on the comparability of the source, such as the court record . . .

BL: Yes.

CG: . . . which seems to me something that shapes the evidence.

BL: Yes, absolutely.

CG: If we go beyond that, we are confronted with details, and those details, those little anomalies that I tried to identify as conjunctive anomalies, and I tried to use the model of textual transmission not as a metaphor but as a tool. And if we accept this idea when we are dealing with texts, I think that the shift from a "mistake" to an anomaly is not inacceptable.

BL: I'm not sure I understand here.

CG: OK. I used the model of textual transmission as a tool. So, when considering textual transmission, as you know, when we have two matching anomalies in two manuscripts and those anomalies are not banal, the convergent mistakes imply that they belong to . . .

BL: . . . to the same part of the stemma.

CG: Exactly. It seems to me that if we have two convergent *lectiones difficiliores* that are not banal, inferring a common origin is part of the common tools of a philologist.

BL: Yes.

CG: Now, in my attempt to respond to your criticism, I used that model, because the shift I made from "mistakes" to "anomalies" seems to me acceptable. Now, if we . . .

BL: As a general principle, I would agree.

CG: Ah!

BL: But the question then shifts to the details of the evidence. To the general principle, I have no objection.

CG: OK. So, if we go further, the problem would be to evaluate specific details. Maybe to see if they were really *lectiones difficiliores*. Would this be a possibility?

BL: Yes. And I noted four or five details where I questioned the connections you drew.

CG: Ah.

BL: One is your repeated assertion that Thiess goes, as you put it, "beyond the sea" when he visits hell. In fact, what the text says permits that translation: "*Die wahrwölffe gingen zu fusz dahin in wölffe gestalt, der ohrt wehre an dem ende von der see,*" and this could be translated "beyond the sea," but the text continues, "*von der see, Puer Esser genand, im morast unter Lemburg.*" So it's not the sea, it's the lake named Puer Esser in the swamp just below Lemburg, which in fact is a few kilometers from Thiess's home. It's not an ecstatic journey. . . .

CG: OK. This is a valuable correction, but does it affect my presentation?

BL: Only a little. I think it shows there's an eagerness to assimilate the two cases and to read the . . .

CG: I think I'd like to shift from the psychological level. You may remember that I resisted the idea that you are cautious and I am not, because . . .

BL: You are cautious also.

CG: No, this is not the problem. What I was saying was that you are uncautious also.

BL: That's also true.

CG: OK, but if we go beyond the psychological dimension, which is part of the personality of a scholar, the point is to demonstrate that in that specific case, the psychological drive worked in a certain specific direction.

BL: Fine. Let's just say that Thiess's was not a grand journey but a short journey on land and not over the sea.

CG: But let's see if this affects my argument, because no *benandante* ever mentioned the sea. So this was not a convergent anomaly.

BL: Yes, but it's related to your attempt to insist on ecstasy, which is nowhere attested in the Thiess trial.

CG: OK. Even in the case of the *benandanti*, there are some references to falling asleep and so on, but in many cases, no, they are simply talking about their own experiences, and it is my reading that this should be looked at as a form of ecstatic experience.

BL: I think your interpretation is convincing in the case of the *benandanti*, and the case recounted by Peucer clearly shows ecstasy attested for at least one Baltic werewolf. But for Thiess, it doesn't enter at all. Similarly, the caul does not enter in the Baltic evidence anywhere.

CG: Yes. As you'll remember, I suggested a connection which, I understand it's not the final word on this issue, but in Slavic folklore there is this connection between werewolves and having been born in a caul.

BL: But again, close reading shows that Slavic beliefs about the caul do not refer specifically to werewolves, only to shapeshifters of whatever sort. Those born with the caul there were believed able to transform themselves into any number of animals. It's not specific to werewolves.

CG: And I should say that even in Friuli, there is not the werewolf.

BL: No. The only case of werewolves I know of in Italy is the one Matteo Duni wrote about recently.[18]

CG: Yes. Now, it seems to me that if we are dealing with being born in a caul, and, I must agree, we don't have any evidence of such beliefs in Livonia, but if we agree that being born in a caul implied a kind of mark and the mark was connected to . . .

BL: Yes, and you talk about cases where children born with teeth are treated in similar fashion, for instance. And taking such marks as a sign of miraculous powers is widespread, but again, one finds no evidence of that in the Baltic.

CG: Let's go back to your point, the first point where you corrected my reading. But, as I said, I think this is not relevant to my interpretation.

BL: Individually, these points are not probative. Your argument stands on a great many inferences and—I'll put it more abstractly. If we are studying two phenomena that are anomalous in their own contexts but resemble each other, the more closely they resemble each other in their particularities, the stronger the argument for historic connection between them becomes. If you had two manuscripts that had twelve peculiarities of an identical sort, I would consider that very strong evidence that they descend from a common original. If the features they share were fewer and more general, if it were only one or two spelling errors, I would say, well, people make spelling errors all the time and what we have here is evidence that bad knowledge of orthography is widespread, not proof of a common descent. It seems to me that the more of these details one can adduce, the stronger your argument for a historic explanation of the morphological resemblances becomes.

CG: You know, you started with numbers, and with regard to numbers, I would say that maybe one really strong element would be enough. So, a real lacuna which is not banal, points to a convergence.

BL: A historic connection. Yes, that's possible. But you would grant that two, three, or five lacunae would make an even stronger argument.

CG: Yes, that's for sure. But, what did I—what did we learn from Lévi-Strauss and structuralism more broadly? The fact that when we are dealing with myth, and maybe social phenomena as well, a literal reading would not be enough. So when we are dealing with convergences (and maybe here, there is a difference between convergences and anomalies), the tools provided by textual philology provide only a beginning. There are different kinds of resemblances. So we can start with a literal convergence or a structural, isomorphic orientation. When we are dealing with a structural, isomorphic orientation, we are certainly confronted with a problem; i.e., the cause of those isomorphic, structural orientations and historical connections is not self-evident. So, there is a fine distinction between a structural, isomorphic orientation and something related to details, which are possibly unlikely, and only in the second case could we posit that we are dealing with a historical connection. Here again, maybe I could invoke the *langue*-versus-*parole* distinction. OK, let's play for a moment with a different kind of model, not textual transmission but languages. So, let's say that at a certain structural level two languages are comparable and they may even fit in the same category. This is not enough to conclude that they belong to the same historical family with a real historical connection.

BL: Correct.

CG: So the problem is to see, on the side of languages and also maybe on the side of cultural formations, at which level the convergence becomes sufficiently unlikely to constitute a proof of historical connection. Maybe at the lexical level? In the case of a text about werewolves, there is this idea of the witch turning into a butterfly. This is not only a convergence but also a coincidence with elements present in other parts of Europe, and so on. But I think this makes sense also in a sort of isomorphic structure, in which animal metamorphosis has been inscribed in a trajectory that has been subjected to diabolization, and so on and so forth, so there is a closer and closer contiguity. At which moment—and here, since you quoted Empedocles, I am tempted to quote the sophistic argument about the bald man: if we take off one hair, then another, then another, at which moment are we confronted with a bald man? I think here we are confronted with a real problem and we are back again to ancient Greece on the relationship between continuum and discrete, because language is discrete and our categories tend to be discrete, but the experiences we are talking about—either ecstatic experiences or maybe even individual invention, I'm not sure—are on the side of the continuum. Would you regard this as a problem?

BL: Possibly. I'm still playing with your evocation of Lévi-Strauss and structural linguistics. It seems to me that, when confronted with morphological resemblances of the sort we've discussed, Lévi-Strauss consistently offered the explanation "That's just the way the human mind operates." He appealed to the species at large, treated at a high level of abstraction, and concluded there are always binary oppositions, followed by mediation. Similarly, when Chomsky treats language, he maintains this is just the way language works: there are noun phrases and verb phrases, you can't have language without them, and if anyone is going to say anything comprehensible, those elements will be present. And at that level of abstraction, for phenomena of that sort, I think they're both right, but this isn't terribly useful for the kinds of comparisons we've been pursuing, where the morphological resemblances are of a more specific, precise and culturally contingent sort. To observe "That's just the way defendants defend themselves in court" is not terribly interesting. It seems to me that when confronted with morphological resemblances that are rather precise, rather numerous, and sufficiently anomalous within their cultural setting as to be challenging, you wish to find a historical explanation for that.

CG: *Wish* to find, I don't know. . . .

BL: You imagine that's the likeliest hypothesis, while granting there are other hypotheses.

CG: OK. So, you reread Thiess's case in a perspective that was obviously very different from Höfler's and from my own. But you were obviously aware of both perspectives and you debated them.

BL: Yes, of course.

CG: Now, the fact that you were aware that the dossier concerning the *benandanti* had emerged could have implied a different attitude toward this case.

BL: Yes.

CG: Why? Because the idea of inverting a negative stereotype is something we find in the Friuli, but on a massive scale. The fact that we don't have a series of trials against werewolves—is this an argument against the possibility of establishing a comparison? I doubt it.

BL: No, and I would grant that your hypothesis is possible and worth entertaining. I wouldn't insist that the correct explanation of morphological similarities is *always* of a cultural and sociological sort.

Historical connections do occur and are real enough. Runciman's book *The Medieval Manichee*, for instance, makes a convincing case for some very unexpected contacts and continuities in specific instances of dualism.[19] And I suppose it's possible that Siberian shamans transmitted certain ideas and practices via Scythians and others who entered Slavic, north Italian, and Baltic territory. I can't rule that out with absolute certainty. It's possible. But to conclude that this is the likeliest explanation for the similarities, in my opinion would demand very strong evidence. On the principle of Occam's razor, I find it much simpler and thus more convincing to assume that in these cases, similar dynamics produced similar results.

CG: You know, if the principle of Occam's razor is used against an hypothesis . . .

BL: Few hypotheses will stand.

CG: It becomes self-damaging. Here, I think we are confronted with a general problem: the asymmetry between what we would like to know and the evidence we actually have. This is especially problematic when we are dealing with oral cultures, since there was no recording of them until a period in which a certain persecutory attitude developed.

BL: Right.

CG: This is something that cannot be ignored, because if we permitted ourselves to remain strictly within the limits and under the constraints of the existing evidence, this would constitute a sort of belated victory of the persecutors. It may be banal to observe that there were probably a lot of phenomena that simply left no trace. . . .

BL: No, it's not banal. It's heartbreaking.

CG: OK, but does this awareness imply a different attitude toward the existing evidence? Because that's a crucial problem.

BL: I don't know. Maybe. Let's explore that.

CG: Because here, we have to look at the nature of the phenomena we are dealing with.

BL: Yes.

CG: Because the extent of that asymmetry between evidence and unrecorded phenomena is not the same in different times and places.

BL: Yes.

CG: And according to different phenomena. So, I would say any reflection on the historical method should take this into account. The same rules that can be advanced for a certain kind of phenomena do not necessarily travel to other areas. This seems to me a dangerous kind of remark, elicited—I think—by your reference to Occam.

BL: I agree, but not completely. It's obvious, but far from banal, to observe that the vast majority of human experience has gone unrecorded and is lost, probably forever. This is a tragedy, not only for historians but for all humans.

CG: Yes.

BL: And it is not just historians' profession but their ethical commitment to recover as much as possible. So far, I think . . .

CG: We agree.

BL: OK. The real problem emerges where there are slight traces: small pieces of evidence that are suggestive, but not conclusive. . . .

CG: Yes.

BL: How far is one permitted to go with those suggestions? What are the limits of frustration one can suffer? What are the temptations one can yield to, when trying to build an argument about the past that is *largely*, but not entirely, lost, based on the slim hints we happen to find here, there, and elsewhere? At least in this instance, I'm more resigned to frustration, modesty, and a sense of tragic loss than you are, while you're more optimistic about the possibility of working with those traces to recover large, important structures of which we catch only glimpses and hints. And so you treat those hints very seriously and invest great effort and ingenuity in making the most of them, whatever the risks might be.

CG: OK. I haven't mentioned the name of Marc Bloch so far in this discussion. I think what is most remarkable about Bloch . . .

BL: You're thinking of *Les rois thaumaturges*, or other works of his?

CG: I was thinking more about his essay "Pour une histoire comparée des sociétés européennes," which he wrote in 1928 but which is still very much alive after all these years, because it's a sort of unfulfilled promise.[20] Now, at a certain moment, Bloch said that a historian dealing with comparison is like a *sourcier*, which is a very nice pun.

BL: Does he include the -*u*- or no?

CG: You're thinking of *sorcier*, "wizard," suggesting a sort of triple pun. But Bloch said *sourcier*, comparing the historian using a comparative approach to the *rabdomante*—the one who detects hidden waters that are not visible at the surface. . . .

BL: *Dowser* is the English term for that.

CG: OK. In French, the term *sourcier* points to *sources* in both a literal and a metaphorical sense. . . .

BL: Spring, origins of water . . .

CG: And also evidence.

BL: Yes.

CG: So, detecting underground water, but also detecting evidence. In this sense, one could say that comparison is a potential remedy or antidote to the destruction or disappearance of existing evidence and, even more, the great mass of evidence that never existed, since so much went unrecorded. In a way, this is even more striking, because when we are dealing with oral culture, *verba volant*. In that sense, one could say that maybe the same standards of proof cannot be valid for historians working on oral cultures as for those who work where textual evidence is available. Weaker standards for stronger comparisons? You know, I was struck . . .

BL: No, I think weaker standards for more cautious hypotheses about larger issues.

CG: So you would have said "provisional."

BL: I think one can hypothesize and some hypotheses have real plausibility. I think your hypothesis about shamanic transmission is possible. I can't exclude it entirely, but I don't think it's the likeliest hypothesis. The question admits only different levels of probability, precisely because we don't have sufficient evidence to permit proof and certainty of any hypothesis. I began my career doing comparative Indo-European philology and I spent a good fifteen years working in that paradigm. It's one of the areas where one is able to triangulate into the past, based on massive comparison among the attested record of these various languages, and one can establish with real certainty that these languages are related in nontrivial ways, such that one must account for their morphological resemblances by some hypothesis. And I do think the most probable hypothesis is one of common descent, but I also came to understand that it was the model of the Romance languages, where we have evidence they all came from Latin and we can show their relation not only to each other but also to Latin, which lets us prove that this is a language family of a genetically related sort. In contrast, we don't have direct attestation of "Proto-Indo-European" that would demonstrate it played the same role that Latin played for the Romance family. So we hypothesize Proto-Indo-European, which is to say we *imagine* its existence in the past. Starting from Sir William Jones, people did imagine that, and they went on to imagine not just a protolanguage but a protocommunity and a protohomeland and a period of expansion and global conquest and racial superiority and a host of other things that, to their mind, made sense and filled out the hypothesis, but also fulfilled certain desires they had to think of themselves as the world's crowning achievement. And we all know the dangers this led to. Höfler is an excellent example of the same method you're describing, although a very different ideal informed the deep past onto which he projected an *imagined* set of connections.

CG: Yes, but as I said already—and I think we agreed on this— all those steps were not intrinsically connected. In other words, there were bifurcations. So, starting from the connection of the Romance languages, which is a historical fact . . .

BL: Yes.

CG: . . . then going on and on, there are a lot of bifurcations where . . .

BL: . . . at every step, the hypothesis could be wrong. And often was, I think.

CG: And there were alternatives! So, instead of the hypothesis of filiation and common descent, one could hypothesize waves of influence.

BL: Yes, exactly. And since the war, linguists have been at pains to develop alternatives. But it seems to me that at the level of method, there's no way to distinguish what you tried to do in *Ecstasies* from what Höfler tried to do in his book. There's an ethical and political difference, since a different imaginary informs the kinds of comparisons and hypotheses you generated, but a difference isn't present at the level of method.

CG: Let me ask you a different question: What about Benveniste? What do you think about his great book?[21]

BL: I'm a great admirer of Benveniste.

CG: Yes, me too. But would you say that his method is the one you just mentioned? Because obviously . . .

BL: That's a very interesting question. His work is certainly informed by all of those theories.

CG: Yes.

BL: But he worked within them in ways that minimized their danger. One doesn't find him talking about Aryan supremacism or the movement of peoples. Rather, one finds very, very precise analyses of specific lexemes.

CG: I think there is no reference to, let's say, the original homeland of the Indo-Europeans.

BL: I'm not aware of one. I would have to search carefully, but I don't remember any.

CG: So, the idea is to work in a framework that is purely linguistic and see what it's possible to understand from that standpoint. I'm deeply fascinated by Benveniste's work.

BL: He's among the best models for comparative scholarship, yes. Along with Marc Bloch and some others we've mentioned.

CG: I have to think again about the relation between a purely linguistic perspective and what he says about the referential element, because he's talking about semantics.

BL: And he's talking about language as culture. I think one can work within a flawed paradigm, even a dangerous paradigm, and achieve admirable results, but one has to proceed with extraordinary care.

CG: I wonder. But I have to think about this. Would it be possible to say that Benveniste worked within the Saussurean paradigm?

BL: Oh, yes.

CG: In the sense that the distinction between *signifiant* and *signifié* did not imply a reference to an external reality, and so my question would be: What's the meaning of semantics in this perspective?

BL: Well, I think he was much more influenced by Meillet than he was by Saussure. Saussure was there indirectly, mediated by Meillet, but Meillet reintroduced the whole question of historic Indo-European linguistics into Saussure's model of general linguistics.

CG: That's for sure, but I wonder whether Benveniste was not stepping back.

BL: I think not. He was very much Meillet's student. Saussure was there, but the presence of Meillet between the two was very large and influential. At the very beginning of his career, Benveniste collaborated with Meillet to produce the grammar and dictionary of Old Persian and the relation between *signifiant* and *signifié* is very concrete there. They are historic realia that are being reconstructed.

CG: And after all, I assume that although Bourdieu played an important role in convincing Benveniste to collect his notebooks in order to build up the book, I believe the title was either suggested or accepted by Benveniste.

BL: I would assume. I don't know that for a fact, but I would assume he had to.

CG: It's *Le vocabulaire des institutions indo-européennes*.

BL: Yes.

CG: So, we are dealing with institutions.

BL: I think so.

CG: I brought up Benveniste, because within that method you mentioned, we are dealing with a category so large that even Benveniste could be included. It's the connection between the genealogical perspective—may we say so?

BL: Yes.

CG: Because I think this is at the very heart of Benveniste's approach.

BL: Yes.

CG: So, there are linguistic affiliations that are related to historic institutions.

BL: It's a *Stammbaum* model of language.

CG: So we are dealing with a body of evidence and establishing morphological connections and trying to capture . . .

BL: . . . the historical relations of which they are the product. For which they are also the evidence.

CG: Yes.

BL: And it seems to me this is what Höfler was doing.

CG: Yes.

BL: The *comparanda* he assembled were very different, and the vision he produced was congruent with his ideals, which we find abhorrent.

CG: Yes, but obviously one can say that if a method is effective, it can also be misused. Because otherwise, it would be innocuous.

BL: Yes, I suppose that's true.

CG: So, the misuse is not in itself an argument against the method. A method can be a bad method. . . .

BL: It is an argument for caution in use of the method, however.

CG: Yes, for sure. But innocuous methods are uninteresting.

BL: Yes, agreed. Like innocuous results.

CG: If they are too safe, they're uninteresting.

BL: Yes. I don't think we've reached agreement, but I do think we've reached an interesting juncture in the discussion.

CG: This is true. We've put our divergences in a sharper focus.

BL: Yes. And ultimately we came to a point where we each regard the possibilities privileged by the other as possible, but less likely than those we ourselves privilege. I can't rule out your hypothesis and I don't think you can rule out mine.

CG: No, surely not.

BL: And the evidence does not permit certainty.

CG: But again, if we could start from certainty . . .

BL: . . . there would be little work to do. I think the question remains open. Some things about Thiess are clear, but his connection to others—and more importantly, the question of which others one can legitimately connect him to and how one can best account for the specific resemblances that might hint at such connections—will probably remain open forever.

CG: Yes. Going back to invention for a moment, in my view, the relation between Thiess's case and such evidence as we have about attitudes toward werewolves at that moment in that area reduces the possibility of a singular invention, because there is a contextual quality that cannot be denied, including the element that seems to me crucial, that at least in one other case, werewolves are regarded as enemies of witches. So this is not a *hapax*.

BL: It's a *dupax*.

CG: I would start from the idea that even a *hapax* can exist, and that (as I said before) the principle of *unus testis, nullus testis* does not work for historians.

BL: Also, given what we were saying earlier about the vast quantity of human experience that has been lost, *hapax* simply means this is the sole example that happens to gain documentation and survive.

CG: Exactly. As for Thiess being an anomaly, the anomaly is reduced when we start to dissect the case. For instance, there are some references to specific places (like Thiess's reference to the swamp) in the *benandanti*'s trials, suggesting a sort of porosity between everyday life and ecstatic experiences.

BL: I would frame it differently, although this may not be precisely the point you're making, but there's always a geography of the imagination that interacts with the physical terrain one happens to inhabit.

CG: Yes.

BL: And that's a human universal. Like noun phrase and verb phrase, it's found everywhere, but the particularities vary with the local geography and the traditions that are in play.

CG: So, we are back to the question of the imaginary and what it's possible to imagine in different circumstances.

BL: Mmm.

CG: Because I mentioned the relation to everyday life and you mentioned the area of geography. Apparently, we are both deeply committed to understanding what is imaginary, fictional, or whatever. And we are committed to the idea that it's possible. . . .

BL: And the way it is both informed by and informs lived experience.

CG: Exactly.

BL: Where we depart most consistently can be summarized, I think, in your settling on the term "invention" as problematic. In that, I infer, you take me to be rendering Thiess more anomalous, more original, and more individual than strikes you as proper.

CG: Yes.

BL: In contrast to which, I resist your attempts to connect him to a long, deep tradition of pre-Christian, agrarian religiosity that he draws on in his moment before the court. You want to see him rooted in a community with its integrity, traditions, and a set of beliefs that have been there for a long time, but which have been hidden from us.

CG: This would be a sort of provisional conclusion, but I'm actually more interested in what is in between. So, for instance, I was impressed and dissatisfied with the way Michel Foucault read Pierre Rivière's case.[22]

BL: Yes.

CG: Because this was a reading that emphasized the absolute anomaly of the case and was not interested in what emerged from those documents about Pierre Rivière's culture, his readings, and so on.

BL: I would never want to depict Thiess, or anyone else, as radically individual, isolated, unique, and without connections. That seems to me a parodic exaggeration of the bourgeois ideal of the "creative individual." All human subjects are embedded in culture and society, in a web of human relations, an upbringing that familiarizes them with all manner of discourses and constructs that they draw on throughout their lives. Thiess is an indigenous Livonian, who knows his people's folkways, as he draws on them and lives by them. And aspects of the tradition and identity in which he participates lead him into conflict with the local elite, at which point he defends himself in an unexpected way, for which we don't have clear precedents in the surviving evidence. We have a few *comparanda,* such as Aleit, who spoke sarcastically to the court, saying some things similar to what Thiess later said. There must have been other defendants who engaged in skillful defensive maneuver, but about whom we know nothing, because no records survive. What I think is unusual—I won't say unique—about Thiess is that he happens to find himself in front of a court just a few years after torture has been abolished. In contrast to all preceding defendants in cases of werewolfery, he thus knew he would not be tortured, and that gave him a freedom to speak to the court in unexpected ways. "Invention" may be too strong a term to describe what he did with that freedom.

CG: The most likely procedure would have been to deny everything. That would have been much easier.

BL: Yes, except there were many people present who were prepared to say otherwise and he certainly knew that. That's introduced to the court at the outset, when the witness on the stand says "I see Old Thiess here, and everyone knows he's a werewolf. How can he take this oath?" That doesn't come from the court, but from one of his fellow peasants.

CG: What struck me when I first read your essay is that you have been keen in looking at the relation of this man and the community to which he belonged on a sociological level, but much less about his symbolic world.

BL: That's true.

CG: And this is surprising, given your background and professional commitments, don't you think so?

BL: Ah, I suppose so. It's the move I've consistently tried to make: to force historians of religion not to focus exclusively on religion, but to look at society and politics and culture and other things. And yes, I probably lean further and further in that direction as time goes by.

CG: I see. You said "not exclusively": this I understand. But you are also saying that possibly you are moving further in the other direction.

BL: Well, it's a gradual shift of emphasis, I suppose.

CG: I see. But would you be able to interpret this—are you looking for something that would be less hypothetical? Because this case would be an interesting anomaly in your own trajectory, if you see what I mean.

BL: I suppose. In part, I don't know what to do with the discourse of "werewolf." I'm not persuaded there was a cultic group or an indigenous imaginary, i.e., a set of myths and beliefs about werewolves outside of the accusations the elite leveled against the peasantry. I'm not certain what to make of the story that describes how a fellow gave me a drink and said some words over it and after that I could turn into a werewolf. This is a story they've all heard and they all tell. Were there really people who felt this happened to them? I honestly don't know.

CG: Yes.

BL: I find those questions unanswerable, in contrast to other questions about what happened in that courtroom, which I find relatively easy to answer, if you only look hard enough.

CG: Yes, but we have a learned discourse about werewolves that provides a long, continuous trajectory.

BL: Yes, that is clear.

CG: On the other hand, we also have evidence from a different side. Obviously, the connection between the two sides is very difficult to understand, but the likelihood of the one side having introjected elements from the stereotype is certainly more than a possibility, since we have other examples.

BL: Yes.

CG: And I think the *benandanti* case is particularly interesting because we can see this trajectory in its making. In the case of the witches, this has been already something that was part of a cultural legacy, not biological. I am surprised, however, that you are not more interested in the possibility of this introjection of a negative stereotype, which is part of social manipulation.

BL: You do find evidence of that process in the confessions extracted under torture. Under torture, people assent and tell their accusers, "Yes, I'm all those things you say," but that's a very particular form of introjection. I'm not sure it would have happened without the fact of torture. I'm reasonably certain there were Latvian and Estonian peasants who stole livestock from the estates of the local gentry and ate them. Did they think of themselves as behaving like wolves in that moment? I would love to know.

CG: Yes.

BL: I think it's entirely possible. They certainly thought something and had stories they told and jokes they shared and beliefs that informed their practice. Did they put on wolf pelts when they went out to do this? I have no idea, but I think it's possible. . . .

CG: Obviously, we have to make a sharp distinction between the ritual level and the mythical level. In most cases Höfler missed the distinction, reading everything at the ritual level—and this is unacceptable.

BL: Right.

CG: We have really scanty evidence on this. But as far as the mythical level is concerned, this possibility seems to me undeniable. Now, in some way you seem not so much interested in it. But from your point of view, it would be possible to use Thiess's case, because, as you rightly pointed out, since torture had been abolished, this provides a sort of ideal experiment. So, what will a man accused of being a werewolf say when torture is not a threat? Was he inventing something, instead of denying? Why? The *lectio facilior* would be to deny everything.

BL: If he thought he could get away with it, yes.

CG: We don't know what he thought.

BL: But for me, a subtextual analogue and unspoken *comparandum* is the behavior of African American defendants in American courts, who are subjected to all manner of negative stereotypes and accusations rooted in the prejudice not only of the judge but of the institutions and dominant culture the judge represents. Their behavior varies widely. Some deny everything, some turn contrite and confess much more than they have ever done, some plead extenuating circumstances or argue details of the evidence, but occasionally there are some who embrace the negative stereotypes and invert them, saying, "Yes, I am a *bad motherfucker* [or worse], but that's not what you think it is. It's the name you folks give to someone who defends his people against forces like you."

CG: Yes.

BL: And there are folktales and a mythology about a number of legendary heroes who incarnate that kind of attitude, and some defendants identify with that powerfully and eloquently. It's not the most common behavior, but it happens, and I suppose at some level that informed my understanding of what Thiess was up to.

CG: This is a really enlightening comparison and I can understand your attitude better. In both cases, the comparison implies a negative stereotype.

BL: Yes, and asymmetric power relations.

CG: Indeed. But the starting point in the cases we have been discussing is the presumption that those people were innocent, which is not always the case. . . .

BL: That raises the question: innocent under whose laws and constructions of morality and legality?

CG: Yes, but in terms of likelihood, it seems to me that Thiess's obvious strategy should have been just to deny everything. So, here you are confronted with something that is doubly unexpected. Not only is his content anomalous, but even the fact that he did not deny is anomalous.

BL: His age is also probably relevant. He's a man of eighty-something, he's nearing the end of his life. He's been given an opportunity to take a stand of an unusual sort. Most people would probably not behave as he does . . .

CG: I understand that.

BL: . . . but I can imagine some individuals thinking in those circumstances, "I've always wanted to speak truth to power, now is my moment."

CG: Yes, but the problem is: which truth? It could be his inner truth.

BL: Yes.

CG: His inner truth. This is also a possibility. Perhaps also a mythic truth. I am holding open the possibility that, in addition to this reading, which seems to me absolutely perfect in terms of the sociological context and so on, maybe the possibility that he was also saying something related to some inner experience should not be dismissed. Why? Because there was not the threat of torture, and there are elements that point to a larger context, starting from Livonia, the attitude to witches, and so on. So this possibility might be open.

BL: I think you might make an even stronger point. It's not just an inner experience, but a shared, communal experience. That possibility also cannot be dismissed and is worth consideration.

CG: This is possible. But when we are dealing with something like stealing animals, that is different from, let's say, the inner experience, which would be different from the negative stereotype, probably, but still something that is present in other contexts.

BL: Here's what I would entertain: Thiess may well have stolen animals in the company of others, who thought of themselves as forces of (cosmic) good, in opposition to forces of (cosmic) oppression. That seems to me entirely possible.

CG: Ah, that's an interesting reworking and reversal of Höfler's reading, because in a way you are also stressing the possibility of a ritual component.

BL: I wouldn't call it ritual, but . . .

CG: Let me tell you in what sense. Obviously, you are not talking about an army or a military ritual, but something more like an organized group of thieves, who use theft as a gesture of social aggression. So, in that sense, the ritual element . . . I said ritual because . . . well, think about it.

BL: I would connect it more to something like Hobsbawm's notion of social banditry.

CG: OK, but as you know, social banditry implies a lot of rites.

BL: Yes.

CG: I take ritual . . .

BL: . . . in a broad sense.

CG: Yes. I wrote a little piece on the Chinese rites dispute, arguing that this dispute was ultimately about the adverb *rite*, "according to rule."

BL: Ah!

CG: And it's as simple as that. Jesuit missionaries like Matteo Ricci were thinking in Latin: an adverb like *rite*, meaning "according to the rule," allowed them the possibility of adopting an open and flexible attitude toward those Chinese who had recently converted to Christianity, by including in the same category the cult of ancestors and etiquette formalities.[23]

BL: Fascinating.

CG: So, in that sense, you cannot deny that in your interpretation, social banditry would include some ritual element.

BL: And to continue, where my notion is similar to Höfler is acknowledging the possibility of collective action and collective consciousness. Where it's antithetical to Höfler is that he saw in such werewolfish groups the origins of the state.

CG: Absolutely.

BL: Whereas I'm arguing that to the extent such groups may have existed, they took action in opposition to a very well-established state, whose interests were antithetical to their own and whose legitimacy they rejected.

CG: Yes. So this is why I said it's a reworking and also a reversal of aspects of his argument.

BL: Yes.

CG: But then there's the possibility that all of this could have coexisted with some inner image, maybe shared, because what seems to me so striking in the case of the *benandanti* is that we're dealing with individual people, but they were also talking about this: so the everyday life side, the nonecstatic experiences, also fueled the ecstatic world.

BL: If we had the wealth of evidence for the Livonian werewolves that we have for the *benandanti*, we would know much more about them and we could pursue the comparison with more subtlety. We would have a better idea how unusual a figure Thiess was and how many others like him there may have been. But, it's impossible to know. You're probably right that in speaking of "invention," I grant him more originality and strangeness than is appropriate. I think he's unusual and the court certainly thinks he's unusual . . .

CG: Sure.

BL: . . . but given how small a body of evidence survives and how many Livonian peasants there were over the centuries, it's unlikely he was *radically* different from everyone else.

CG: Yes, but this sentence can be read in different ways. Unlikely, but in what sense?

BL: We don't know. I'd think it's most probable there were others who resembled him in significant ways and with whom he perhaps had communications, but we don't know. The record won't permit us to do more than speculate.

CG: Yes. And if we assume, and I think we're in agreement on this, that given the asymmetry between the evidence available to us and the unrecorded series of phenomena in a lot of areas of history, the idea of using Occam's razor to cut hypotheses is counterproductive.

BL: If by "cut," you mean eliminate completely, I agree. If by "cut," we simply mean to identify as more and less likely, then I would defend the principle.

CG: I agree. I remember once jokingly suggesting that we should mark the level of proofs like winds at sea, you know, like "Wind, force 8." The level of proof could in principle be marked in some nonbinary way: it's not yes or no, but with a lot of shades. I think this also implies that since we reject the black-and-white, yes-or-no dichotomy, then hypothesis should play a role in our presentations.

BL: It must. There's no alternative to hypothesis, save acceptance of ignorance with no further inquiry. But in the same measure, conclusive proof and definitive resolution of the question are very unlikely. We simply don't have enough direct evidence of a past that deep.

CG: So, the problem would be how it's possible to pave the way for further research. It seems to me that some sort of hypothesis for which, for the time being there is no answer, could do that—and this would be my cautious defense of the lack of cautiousness.

BL: If I had infinite resources available, not just money, but talent, I would think you could assemble an army of researchers, each one looking at every case and every example that you assembled in *Storia notturna*, getting at the intimate details of every datum, after which you could reorganize the dossier. Some examples would acquire new importance as a result of that reconsideration, others you would now decide to throw out, some commonalities having proven much more extensive than you imagined and others more superficial. Then you rethink the whole business.

CG: So, in a way we are back to a theme that has been at the very center of our discussion: the relation between case studies and comparison.

BL: Yes. You could undertake the same kind of reconsideration for Frazer, Lévi-Strauss, or others, but money and talent are rare. Time, too, perhaps rarest and most precious of all. This has been a real pleasure, Carlo.

CG: Yes, really it's been a great joy, Bruce. Many thanks.

BL: And to you.

Appendix A

Commonalities between Thiess's Testimony and Descriptions of Livonian Werewolves in Learned Literature

Theme and source	Quotation
Transformation into wolf form	
Olaus Magnus, 1555	This reason for his transformation, which is most contrary to his nature, is that someone skilled in this kind of magic has handed him a mug of beer [which he accepts], over which he has spoken certain words.[a]
Paul Einhorn, 1627	The transformation results from drinking together. Thus, when one takes up a drink, *Vi istorum verborum* ("By the power of these words"), through those words that the other person has spoken over the drink, one becomes a werewolf.[b]
Christian Kortholt, 1677	One day around Christmastime, he was led to an inn by some Germans, and as he was a newly arrived fellow countryman, they wanted to honor him with a welcoming drink. But on one side of this pub, there was a table with common peasants seated all around, from which one stood up, took a mug in his hand, and walked over to the German table and, as is common when one man brings something to another, he speaks in his own language: *Pasz Guntzing!* (in German): "That's for you, mein Herr!" And the peasant did this bowing low and with a friendly face and showing deference to
	(continued)

Theme and source	Quotation
Christian Kortholt, 1677 (*continued*)	him. Although his language was still not understood, he addressed him with these words: *Pus do dad man güntzig* (in German): "It will be for you, as for me, mein Herr!" As he truly did not understand what was said, he might readily have taken the drink that the peasant brought to him, thinking he had blessed the drink for him in German. His countrymen, however, were sitting beside him and they quickly pulled his hand away from his mouth, and all the other Germans who were present forbade him to drink, saying that he had not blessed it for him and only bowed as if he were blessing. And as he did not know what was happening, they jumped up from the table, fell on the peasant, beat the poor fellow, dragged him around the inn until they saw blood, and drove him out with many threats and insults. After that, he asked why they had beaten the good fellow who had been so friendly to him, without any reason to do so? They answered that if that man had charmed that drink for him, by evening he surely would turn into a werewolf, and he should certainly believe this, for the same temptation and cruel deception had already led astray many Germans unacquainted with the vernacular language.[c]
Thiess trial, 1692	Q: What advantage did he gain from becoming a werewolf, since in most obvious ways he was a poor man and thoroughly powerless? A: None. Rather, a scoundrel from Marienburg did this to him by a drink of something he brought and thus from that time on he had to conduct himself like the other werewolves.[d] Q: In what way will he impart this to another? A: He will do as happened to him and one is permitted only once to drink and to breathe into the tankard three times, and to say the words "It will be for you as it was for me," and if the recipient receives and accepts the tankard, the witness will then be freed from it.[e]

Ritual timing of werewolf assemblies

Olaus Magnus, 1555	At night on the feast of Christ's Nativity, a horde of wolves assembles, who have changed from men that dwell in different places.[f]

Theme and source	Quotation
Philip Melanchthon, 1558	Every year he was made to be a wolf for twelve days after the day of our Lord's Nativity.[g]
Kaspar Peucer, 1560	We have learned from the reliable testimony of trustworthy witnesses what happened each year in Livonia and neighboring regions during the twelve days after Christmas.[h]
	In the days that follow the birthday of our Lord, a limping child goes about and he calls together those who are the devil's slaves.[i]
	They never are brought together in a single horde, except in the days as stated.[j]
Thiess trial, 1692	Q: When do such things take place?
	A: On St. Lucia's Eve before Christmas.
	Q: How often in the year do you go into hell together?
	A: Ordinarily thrice: Pentecost Eve, St. John's Eve, and St. Lucia's Eve.[k]

Size of the werewolf bands

Olaus Magnus, 1555	A horde of wolves assembles, who have changed from men that dwell in different places.[l]
Philip Melanchthon, 1558	He ran with many other wolves.[m]
Kaspar Peucer, 1560	[Their] number is shockingly large.[n]
	Some thousands of them come together.[o]
Thiess trial, 1692	Twenty or thirty of them often came together.[p]

Violence against livestock in wolf form

Olaus Magnus, 1555	In Prussia, Livonia, and Lithuania, nearly all year long the inhabitants suffer great damage from the rapacity of wolves, because a huge number of their animals are torn to pieces and eaten if they stray only a small distance from the herd in the woods. However, this loss is not reckoned by them to be so great as those they must suffer from men who have turned into wolves.[q]
	He attacked the flock of sheep with great force and, having carried one of them into the wood, he tore it into pieces.[r]
Philip Melanchthon, 1558	[They] tore apart livestock.[s]

(*continued*)

Theme and source	Quotation
Kaspar Peucer, 1560	In the appearance of wolves, they wander fields to attack herds of sheep and cattle. Tearing those they encounter into pieces, they either carry some off or they roam about burial places.[t]
	They attack any livestock they meet on the way, and those they capture they tear apart with their teeth. They carry off what they can and inflict other damage.[u]
Paul Einhorn, 1627	[They] run about, doing injury to both people and livestock.[v]
Christian Kortholt, 1677	Witches and sorcerous fiends change themselves into wolves. By night they run about to harm people, animals, and fruit of the fields, and to cause great damage.[w]
Thiess trial, 1692	They ran about as wolves and seized whatever horses and livestock fell to them.[x]

[a] Olaus Magnus, *Historia de Gentibus Septentrionalibus* 18.46: "Hanc mutandi rationem, ipsi naturæ maxime contrariam, a quodam huius veneficii perito, per poculum cervisiæ propinando (dummodo is, qui huic illicito consortio applicatur, illud acceptat) certis verbis adhibitis consequitur."

[b] Paul Einhorn, *Wiederlegunge der Abgötteren*, chap. 6: "Die Transmutatio und verwandelunge sollen sie einander zutrincken, also, deß derselbe so den trunck bekompt, alßbald, Vi istorum verborum, durch dieselben Worte so der ander im zutrincken ihm zugesprochen, ein Waerwolff werde."

[c] Christian Kortholt, under the pseudonym Theophilus Sincerus, *Nord-Schwedische Hexerey, oder Simia Dei, Gottes Affe* (1677), 31–32: "Er von etlichen Teutschen eines Tages umb weyhnachtliche Zeit in einem Krug (dann so werden allda die gemeine Gast- oder Wirths-Häuser genennet) geführet wurde, welche ihm als einen Lands-Mann und neuem Ankömmling mit einen Willkommens-Trunck beehren wolten. Es ware aber in solcher Gast-Stube einer Seits besonders ein Tisch von gemeinen Land-Bauren rings-umher besesztet, aus denen einer nach geraumen darinnen seyn, von dem Tisch aussgestanden, das bey sich stehende Trinck-Geschirr zur Hand genommen, vor der Teutschen Zech-Tisch getreten, und da es sonsten gebräuchlich, dasz, wann einer dem andern eines zu bringet, man der Land-Sprach nach zu sagen pflege: Pasz Guntzing! (zu Teutsch;) es gilt dir mein Herr! als habe selbiger Bauer mit besondern Bücken und Reigen, auch freundlichem Gesichte und geneigten Geberten ihme (der Sprach noch unbekanten) es mit diesen Worten zubebracht; Pus do dad man güntzig (zu Teutsch) es gilt dir, wie mir mein Herr! Er, ob er zwar nicht wuste was dieses gesagt wäre, doch leichtlich aus den Geberden abnehmen kunte, dasz ihme der Bauer eines zugebracht, wolte ihme auff Teutsch den Trunck gesegnen, allein es wurde so balden von seinem an der Seiten sitzenden Landsmann ihme die hand auff das Maul gelegen, und so wol denselbigen als auch allen andern anwesenden Teutschen, verboten, er solte es ihme ja nicht gesegnen, auch sich nicht neigen als ob ers ihme gesegnett, weil er nicht wüste was es auff sich habe, darauff sie von den Tische auffgesprungen, den Bauren überfallen, erbärmlich geschlagen, und so lange in der Stube herum gezogen bisz dasz sie Blut sahen, alsdann sie ihm mit noch vielen Bedrohen und aller Beschimpffung zum Haus hinaus gestossen. Nach diesem habe er gefragt, warum sie den guten Kerls so unverschuldet geschlagen hätten, der es doch ihme so freundlich zugebracht habe? Darauff sie zur Antwort gegeben, wann er ihme hätte den

Trunck gesegnet, wäre er des Abends gewisz zu einem Währ-Wolff, jener aber dessen erlediger worden, und solte er es sicher glauben, dann dergleichen Verführung und böse Anführung seye schon vielen der Sprach unkündigen Teutschen wiederfahren."

[d] Thiess trial, paragraph 23, von Bruiningk, 208: "Q: Was er dan vor nutzen davon gehabt, dasz er ein wahrwolff geworden, weil ja kundbahrer weise er ein bettler und ganz unvermögend sey? R: Keinen, sondern es hätte ihm ein schelm aus Marjenburgk durch zutrincken solches zugebracht und also hätte er von der zeit ab einem andern wahrwolffe gleich sich verhalten müszen."

[e] Thiess trial, paragraph 26, von Bruiningk, 208-9: "Q: Auff was art er es einem andern beybringen wolle? R: Er wolle es so machen, wie ihm geschehen wäre, und dürffe nur einem ein mahl zutrincken und 3 mahl in die kannen hauchen und die worte sagen: Es werde dir so wie mir,—und wenn dann der jenige die kanne entgegen nähme, so hätte er es weg und referent würde dann frey davon."

[f] Magnus, *Historia* 18.45: "In festo enim Nativitatis CHRISTI sub noctem, statuto in loco quem inter se determinatum habent, tanta luporum ex hominibus diversis in locis habitantibus conversorum copia congregatur."

[g] Philip Melanchthon, *Publicas Lectiones* CXXXI: "Se quotannis factum esse lupum per dies duodecim, post natalem diem Domini."

[h] Kaspar Peucer, *Commentarius de præcipuis generibus divinationum*, 141r: "De certis & exploratis indicationibus testium ἀξιοπίστων comperimus, qui accidere tale aliquid proximis a die natali duodecim diebus annuatim per Liuoniam & uicinas regiones."

[i] Peucer, *Commentarius*, 141r: "Ineuntibus diebus, qui proximi natalem Domini sequentur, circumit puer altero pede claudus, qui illa diaboli mancipia."

[j] Peucer, *Commentarius*, 142r: "Uideantur fieri lupi, nunquam tamen in unum colleguntur agmen, nisi iis diebus quibus dixi."

[k] Thiess trial, paragraph 13, von Bruiningk, 206: "Q: Wenn dann solches geschehen? R: In Lucien nacht vohr Weynachten. Q: Wie offt sie des jahrs in der hölles zusammen kommen? R: Ordinarie dreymahl: die Pfingst nacht, Johannis nacht und Lucien nacht."

[l] Magnus, *Historia* 18.45: "Tanta luporum ex hominibus diversis in locis habitantibus conversorum copia congregatur."

[m] Melanchthon, *Publicas Lectiones* CXXXI: "Concurrisse multos alios lupos."

[n] Peucer, *Commentarius*, 141r: "Quorum ingens est numerus."

[o] Peucer, *Commentarius*, 142v: "Conveniunt aliquot millia."

[p] Thiess trial, paragraph 6, von Bruiningk, 205: "Weil ihrer oft 20 à 30 zusammen giengen."

[q] Magnus, *Historia* 18.45: "In Prussia, Livonia, atque Lithuania, quam vis luporum rapacitatem per totum pene annum incolæ haud exiguo cum damno experiuntur, quia eorum pecora ingenti multitudine passim in sylvis, dummodo exiguo intervallo a grege aberrant, dilaniantur, ac consumuntur: tamen hoc dispendium non adeo magnum ab illis reputatur, quam quod ab hominibus in lupos conversos sustinere coguntur."

[r] Magnus, *Historia* 18.47: "Postea in ovium gregem haud aliter quam magno impetu irruit, & unam ex eis retro in sylvam fugiendo diripuit."

[s] Melanchthon, *Publicas Lectiones* CXXXI: "Lacerasse pecudes."

[t] Peucer, *Commentarius*, 141v–141r: "Luporum specie pererratis campis grassari in greges pecorum & armenta, obviam quæuis dilaniando; vel rapere aliquid, vel vagari circum sepulchra."

(*continued*)

ᵘ Peucer, *Commentarius*, 142v: "Educti in obvia pecora irrunt mordicus, & apprehensa dilacerant: rapiunt quæ possunt: dant et alia damna."

ᵛ Einhorn, *Wiederlegunge*, chap. 6: "Und alßbald herumb lauffe, daß er Menschen und Viehe schaden zufüge."

ʷ Kortholt, *Nord-Schwedische* Hexerey, 31: "Die Hexen und zauberischen Unholden in Wölffe verwandeln, bey Nacht-Zeit herum lauffen die Leute, Vieh und Feld-Früchten jämmerlich beschädigen, und grossen Schaden verursachen."

ˣ Thiess trial, paragraph 6, von Bruiningk, 204: "Lieffen dann als wülffe herumb und zerriszen, was ihnen an pferden und vieh vorkähme."

Appendix B

A Livonian Narrative Featuring the Opposition of Werewolves and Witches

Kaspar Peucer, 1560[a]	Hermann Witekind, 1586[b]
There is a true story about a certain rustic werewolf who dined with his prefect, not far from the city of Riga.	Shortly before it happened in the same place that a peasant came into the prefect's house to eat there that night.
Drunk, he finally fell asleep and tumbled back from his chair onto the floor, in front of other worthies.	After he had eaten and drunk well, he suddenly fell backward off the bench, as if he'd been struck silly.
The prefect was a wise man, who immediately recognized this man to be a werewolf.	The prefect, who understood what this meant,
He bade his servants to go, after putting him to bed.	let him lie undisturbed, as if this servant had fallen asleep.
The next day, a horse was found in the field cut apart down the middle.	The next day, on the meadow outside the city, people found a dead horse that had been cut down the middle into two pieces with a scythe, which lay nearby.
The prefect's guess laid blame on the man who collapsed the previous night and revived that morning.	The prefect had the peasant, his guest, taken in.

(*continued*)

Kaspar Peucer, 1560[a]	Hermann Witekind, 1586[b]
He was therefore led into prison, and once interrogated, he quickly confessed to the deed.	He confessed that he had done it.
He asserted that he was pursuing a witch in the form of a fiery butterfly that was circling about	There was a witch that had flown over as a bright flame.
(for werewolves boast that they are hired to ward off witches)	Werewolves are enemies of these
in order to defend against danger.	and he had to chase it, after which he hacked at it with the scythe.
By chance, the witch had hidden herself there under the horse.	But it hid itself under the horse as it went out to graze,
Sneaking up with a sickle, he struck powerfully, but she narrowly escaped his intended blow, and as a result of this unexpected turn of events, he accidentally cut the horse in two.	and his blow cut through the horse.
	Thus this man confessed that he had done nothing; rather, he had dreamed it. . . .
	This fellow lay in the chamber all night, body and soul; therefore he could not have been out in the field in which these events took place.
In this way, demons play among themselves for the ruin of people.	The devil did it and put him so powerfully in a deep sleep and dream that he believed and confessed it was his work.
	For that, he was burnt.

[a] Kaspar Peucer, *Commentarius de præcipuis generibus divinationum*, 145v: "Vera narratio est de quodam Lycaone rustico, qui cum apud præfectum suum non procul ab urbe Rigensi cœnasset, tandem inebriatus sub somni tempus subito e sella decidit supinus in pavimentum cœterus spectantibus. Præfectus homo sapiens, quod Lycaonem esse statim agnosceret, iubet familiam hoc relicto cubitum ire. Postridie reperitur in agro equus per medium diffectus. coniectura præfecti culpa confertur in eum, qui pridie exanimatus sub noctem, mane revixerat. Ducitur is ergo in carcerem et interrogatus mox confitetur factum, Ait se veneficam ignei papilionis specie circumvolitantem persequutum esse (gloriantur enim Lycanthropi, quod ad arcendas veneficas conducantur) hanc, ut declinaret periculum, sub equo forte ibi pascente se abscondisse; ibi se arrepta falce, dum petit validius veneficam intentatum ictum arte eludentem, ex improviso imprudenter discidisse equum. Ad hunc modum ludunt inter se diaboli de hominum pernicie."

[b] Hermann Witekind, writing under the pseudonym Augustin Lercheimer von Steinfelden, *Christlich bedencken und erinnerung von zauberey* (1586), text from Birlinger, *Augustin Lercheimer und seine Schrift wider den Hexenwahn*, op. cit., 58: "Kurtz zuvor wars geschehen am selbigen ort, dasz ein bawr ins vogts hausz kam, asz da zu nacht. Nachdem er wol gessen und getruncken, fellt er plötzlich von der banck hindersich, alsz wann in der tropff schlüge. Der Vogt, der dasz ding, wie er meynte, verstund, liesz in also ligen unangerürt, hiesz d[a]sz gesind schlaffen gehn. Morgens fand man vor der statt auff der weyde ein todt pferd, war mit einter sänsen mitten von einander gehawen, die lag dabey. Der Vogt liesz den bawren, seinen gast, eynziehen. Der bekennt, er habs gethan. Es sey ein Hexe da umher geflogen, wie ein liechtflamm, welchen die wehrwölffe feind sind, und müssen sie verfolgen, nach der habe er gehawen mit der sänsen: da sie aber unders pferd sich verbarg, das gieng und grasete, sey der haw durchs pferd gangen. Also hat der mensch bekannt, dasz er nicht gethan, sondern das im geträumet hatte . . . Dieser lag mit leib und seel die gantze nacht in der stuben, darumm konte er nicht draussen auff dem felde seyn, das er die that begienge. Der teufel hats gethan, und es im so starck im tieffen schlaff und traum eyngebildet, dasz er gemeynt und bekent, es sey sein werck. Ist darauff verbrennt worden."

Acknowledgments

For permission to translate and adapt selected pages from Otto Höfler's *Kultische Geheimbünde der Germanen* (1934), we thank Verlag Traugott Bautz GmbH; excerpts from John Tedeschi and Anne C. Tedeschi's English translation of Carlo Ginzburg's *The Night Battles: Witchcraft and Agrarian Cults in the Sixteenth and Seventeenth Centuries* (pp. 28–32, with minor modifications), English translation © 1983 Routledge and Kegan Paul plc., edition with new preface © 2013 The Johns Hopkins University Press, are reprinted with permission of Johns Hopkins University Press; excerpts from Ginzburg's *Clues, Myths, and the Historical Method* (1984/1986), again, in the Tedeschis' English translation (with minor modifications), © Carlo Ginzburg; excerpts from Raymond Rosenthal's English translation of Ginzburg's *Ecstasies: Deciphering the Witches' Sabbath*, English translation © 1991 by Random House, Inc., University of Chicago Press edition 1989 © Carlo Ginzburg.

Notes

Introduction

1. Elmar Lorey, "Werwolfprozesse in der Frühen Neuzeit," available at https://www.elmar-lorey.de/Prozesse.htm (last consulted January 16, 2018). Cf. Willem de Blécourt, "The Differentiated Werewolf: An Introduction to Cluster Methodology," in de Blécourt, ed., *Werewolf Histories* (New York: Palgrave Macmillan, 2015), 1–24 (esp. 7–10). The specialized studies in this volume and its predecessor, Willem de Blécourt and Christa Agnes Tuczay, eds., *Tierverwandlungen: Codierungen und Diskurse* (Tübingen: Francke, 2011), probably constitute the best contemporary research on the werewolf, which is now more focused on specific studies than on broad theory and generalization. Popular literature on the topic is vast and constantly growing, but there is little reliable scholarship. The earlier literature begins with Wilhelm Hertz, *Der Werwolf. Beitrag zur Sagengeschichte* (Stuttgart: A. Kröner, 1862) and includes Sabine Baring-Gould, *The Book of Were-Wolves* (London: Smith, Elder, 1865), Montague Summers, *The Werewolf* (London: Routledge, 1933), and Robert Eisler, *Man into Wolf* (London: Routledge and Kegan Paul, 1951), all of which have been frequently reprinted.

2. Following Karlis Straubergs, *Latviešu buŗamie vārdi: I. Magija un buŗamo vārdu tematika* ("Latvian Blessing Spells: I. Magic and the Thematics of Blessing Spells") (Riga: Latviešu Folkloras Krātuves Izdevums ar

Kulturas Fonda Pabalstu, 1939), 98, behind the Germanized form *Thiess* that appears in the court record, one can perceive Latvian *Tīss*, short for *Matīss* ("Matthew").

3. Among the most dramatic moments in the transcript is the passage that describes Thiess as having obstinately rejected the pastor's reproaches and intemperately told the court that he understood these things better than the Herr Pastor, who was just a young man. Transcript of the Thiess trial, paragraph 63: "Je mehr nun der Hr. Pastor ihm seinen irthumb und die teufelische verblendung vorhielte, auch sich bemühete ihn davon abzuleiten und auff den weg der erkäntnüs zu bringen, auch zur busze zu bewehgen, je verstokter erwiese sich der Thiess und wolte durchausz nicht davon hören, dasz es böse werke wehren, so er betrieben, sagete, er verstünde es beszer als der Hr. Pastor, der noch jung wehre."

4. Transcript of the Thiess trial, paragraph 78: "Ob man auch zwahr folgig bey der session zu Wenden die acta vornahm, kondte und wolte man sich dennoch über einen so schwehren und miszlichen casum zu keinem definitiven auszspruch entschlieszen."

5. Transcript of the Thiess trial, paragraphs 78–79: The court announces its intention to have the case considered again upon arrival of the new District Court Judge von Palmberg (*des neuen Hrn. Landrichters von Palmbergs*). When von Palmberg was delayed, as reported in paragraph 79, Judge von Trautvetter served "in place of the absent District Court Judge" (*in stelle des abwehsenden Hrn. Landrichters*). In that capacity, von Trautvetter presided over the review and issued the final decision, subject to ratification by the Royal Court of Dorpat.

6. Hermann von Bruiningk, "Der Werwolf in Livland und das letzte im Wendenschen Landgericht und Dörptschen Hofgericht i. J. 1692 deshalb stattgehabte Strafverfahren," *Mitteilungen aus der livländischen Geschichte* 22 (1924–28): 163–220, based on his study of werewolf trials from 1630 to 1710, preserved in the archives of the High Court of Dorpat. The Thiess transcript, which von Bruiningk reproduced verbatim as an appendix (203–20), represents Kriminalakte number 30 of 1692 from this archive. The article's title page announces that a shorter form of this paper was presented at the Gesellschaft für Geschichte und Altertumskunde in Riga (April 9, 1924).

7. Von Bruiningk was the son of Baron Ludolf August von Bruiningk (1809–91) and Princess Marie Lieven (1818–53). After studying law in Tartu, he devoted himself to historic research, serving as director of the archives of the Noble Corporation (*Ritterschaft*) of Livonia from 1899 to 1920, after which he shifted his activities to the state archives of the newly independent Latvian nation. From 1890 to 1902, he was president of the Society for

History and Ancient Studies in Riga, and he received an honorary doctorate from the University of Leipzig in 1919.

8. On the strongly stereotyped association of Livonia with werewolfery, see, inter alia, Karlis Straubergs, "Om Varulvarna i Baltikum," in Sigurd Erixon, ed., *Liv och Folkkultur* (Stockholm: Samfundet för Svensk Folklivs-forskning, 1955), 107–29; Tiina Vähi, "The Image of Werewolf in Folk Religion," in Manfried L.G. Dietrich and Tarmo Kulmar, eds., *The Significance of Base Texts for the Religious Identity / Die Bedeutung von Grundtexten für die religiöse Identität* (Münster: Ugarit, 2006), 213–37; and Stefan Donecker, "The Werewolves of Livonia: Lycanthropy and Shape-Changing in Scholarly Texts, 1550–1720," in *Preternature: Critical and Historical Studies on the Preternatural* 2 (2012): 289–322.

9. Von Bruiningk, "Der Werwolf in Livland," 168: "In der christlichen Zeit, wo man die Existenz der heidnischen Götter zugab, um sie für Teufel erklären zu können, wurde der heidnische Cultus zum Greuel der Teufelsan-betung, die Diener der Götter zu Teufelsdienern, und hier entstand mit dem Hexenglauben die Vorstellung von Menschen, die sich mit Hilfe des Satans aus reiner Mordlust zu Wölfen verwandelten."

10. Von Bruiningk asserted the "Aryan" origins of werewolf beliefs (167), following Hertz, *Der Werwolf* (133), and repeating the latter, word for word, without proper citation:

We find the characteristic development of the werewolf saga to have been primarily concentrated among a specific group of people, the Aryan tribes of Greeks, Romans, Celts, Germans, and Slavs who migrated westward from their original home in Central Asia.

Die eigentümliche Entwicklung der Werwolfsagen finden wir vorzugs-weise auf eine bestimmte Völkergruppe concentriert, auf die aus der mittelasiatischen Urheimat westwärts gewanderten arischen Stämme der Griechen, Römer, Kelten, Germanen und Slaven.

Von Bruiningk did differ with Hertz on one intriguing point, the identity of the Neuroi, who figure in the earliest attestation of werewolfery (Herodo-tus, *The Histories*, 4.105.2), where the father of history reported:

Among the Scythians and the Greeks dwelling in Scythia, they say that once every year, each of the Neuroi becomes a wolf for a few days and then is restored to himself. I am not persuaded of these things, although they tell them no less and those who do the telling swear.

λέγονται γὰρ ὑπὸ Σκυθέων καὶ Ἑλλήνων τῶν ἐν τῇ Σκυθικῇ κατοικημένων, ὡς ἔτεος ἑκάστου ἅπαξ τῶν Νευρῶν ἕκαστος λύκος γίνεται ὀλίγας ἡμέρας καὶ αὖτις ὀπίσω ἐς τὠυτὸ ἀποκατίσταται. Ἐμὲ μέν νῦν ταῦτα λέγοντες οὐ πείθουσι. λέγουσι δὲ οὐδὲν ἧσσον καὶ ὀμνῦσι δὲ λέγοντες.

Where Hertz took the Neuroi to be Slavs (133), von Bruiningk preferred to think they were Livonians (168–69).

11. Von Bruiningk, 166: "Wir müssen uns vorhalten, wie viel inniger sich das Verhältnis der Naturvölker zu der sie umgebenden Natur und ganz besonders zur Tierwelt gestalten musste, als in unserer Umwelt, ja dass der "Rangunterschied" zwischen Mensch und Tier" wie Hertz es ausdrückt, eigentlich erst unserem Geschlechte klar zum Bewusstsein gekommen ist. Hatte der Mensch im Kampfe ums Dasein jahrtausendelang erfahren müssen, wie ihm so manches Tier an Kraft, Gewandtheit, Schlauheit, ja sogar an Fleiss und allerhand Fertigkeiten, überlegen sei, so konnte es nicht fehlen, dass sein Empfinden und Vorstellungsvermögen an der Vermensch-lichung des Tieres und umgekehrt keinen Anstoss nahm, dass die Tierfabel und das Tiersymbol in üppigster Ausgestaltung sich bis zur Vergöttlichung des Tieres verirrten, dass die nimmer ruhende Phantasie des Menschen sich nicht mit der natürlichen Tierwelt begnügte, sondern allerhand fabelhafte Tiergestalten, wie Greif, Drache, Vampir usw. hinzutat." The passage in Hertz to which von Bruiningk here alludes is *Der Werwolf* (11), the wording and argument of which he followed closely.

12. Von Bruiningk, 186–87.

13. Von Bruiningk was effusive regarding the unique nature of the Thiess transcript, which had

> such outstanding documentary value and such great folkloric interest that not only all the archives and libraries of the former Baltic provinces could not have produced something similar, but it might be assumed that even in the far-flung areas to which the werewolf saga was distributed, there are not many sources of comparable value (164).

> wir es hier mit einer Quelle zur Kenntnis des Werwolfwahnes von so hervorragendem dokumentarischem Werte und von so grossem volkskundlichem Interesse zu tun haben, wie nicht nur die sämtlichen Archive und Bibliotheken der ehemaligen Ostseeprovinzen ähnliches kaum aufzuweisen haben dürften, sondern weil angenommen werden darf, dass es sogar in den weitausgedehnten auswärtigen Verbreitungge-bieten der Werwolfsage wohl nicht viele gleichwertige Quellen gibt.

14. On the way nationalism informed and helped shape scholarship on werewolf and witchcraft trials in the Baltic after von Bruiningk, see Andrejs Plakans, "Witches and Werewolves in Early Modern Livonia: An Unfinished Project," in Lars M. Andersson, Anna Jansdotter, Badil E. B. Persson, and

Charlotte Tornbjer, eds., *Rätten: En Festskrift till Bengt Ankarloo* (Lund: Nordic Academic Press, 2000), 255–71. We regret that we have been unable to make use of the scholarly literature in Latvian and Estonian, which includes Walter Anderson, "Uus töö Balti libahundiprotsesside kohta" ("New research on Baltic Werewolf trials"), *Ajalooline Ajakiri* 3 (1924): 151–54; Karlis Straubergs, "Vilkaču ideoloģija Latvijā" ("Werewolf ideology in Latvia") and "Raganu prāvas idejiskie pamati Latvija 17. gadu simtenī" ("The intellectual basis of witchcraft trials in seventeenth-century Latvia"), in Margers Stepermanis, ed, *Latviešu vēsurnieku veltijums Profesoram Robertam Viperam* (Riga: Gulbis, 1939), 98–114, and *Latvijas Vēstures Institūta žurnāls* 3 (1939): 213–40, respectively; Tālivaldis Zemzaris, "Vilkaču prāvas Vidzemē" ("Werewolf Trials in Vidzeme"), in Stepermanis, ed., *Latviešu vēsurnieku* (115–41); and Maia Madar, "Nõiaprotsessid Eestis XVI sajandist XIX sajandini" ("Witch trials from Estonia from the sixteenth to the nineteenth century"), in Juhan Kahk, ed., *Religiooni ja ateismi ajaloost Eestis III* (Tallinn: Eesti Raamat, 1987), 124–45.

15. Otto Höfler, *Kultische Geheimbünde der Germanen* (Frankfurt am Main: Moritz Diesterweg, 1934). It is probably worth noting that the Diesterweg publishing house, founded in 1873 to produce school books and pedagogical materials, moved to support National Socialism when it came to power in 1933, expanding its list to include such titles as Kurt Schwedtke, *Adolf Hitlers Gedanken zur Erziehung und zum Unterricht* (1933); Rudolf Ibel and Ernst von Salomon, *Das Reich im werden: Arbeitshefte in Dienste politischer Erziehung* (1933); Adolf Krüper, *Essays on Race* (1934) and *Die veränderte Nation: Zeugnisse des neuen Nationalismus* (1934), Wilhelm Voss and Adolf Hitler, *Die lebengesetzlichen Grundlagen des Nationalsozialismus* (1934); and Rudolf Hennesthal, *Deutschland untern Hakenkreuz: Dichtungen gesammelt zu Feiern in Schule und Jugendbund* (1934), as well as Höfler's volume.

16. Höfler (25) citing Hertz, *Der Werwolf* (88, 109–10, et pass.).

17. Hertz, *Der Werwolf* (88): "Noch muß hier einer Werwolfsart gedacht werden, welche in ein anderes, weit unheimlicheres Sagengebiet hinüberweist, nämlich des gespenstigen Werwolfs, der mit dem Vampyr von einem Geschlecht ist. Der Werwolf ist hier nicht ein verwandelter lebender Mensch, sondern ein dem Grabe in Wolfsgestalt entstiegener Leichnam."

18. Höfler, *Kultische Geheimbünde* (343–57). Höfler reproduced paragraphs 1–32 of the trial transcript, while omitting paragraphs 33–79 and the Royal High Court's verdict.

19. On the cult of dead comrades in the Nazi paramilitaries, see, inter alia, Jay W. Baird, *To Die for Germany: Heroes in the Nazi Pantheon* (Blooming-

ton: Indiana University Press, 1990); Sabine Behrenbeck, *Der Kult um die toten Helden: Nationalsozialistische Mythen, Riten und Symbole 1923 bis 1945* (Vierow: SH-Verlag, 1996); Monica Vierkant, *Märtyrer und Mythen: Horst Wessel und Rudolf Hess: nationalsozialistische Symbolfiguren und neonazistische Mobilisierung* (Marburg: Tectum, 2008); and Jesús Casquete, "Martyr Construction and the Politics of Death in National Socialism," in *Totalitarian Movements and Political Religions* 10 (2009): 265–83. On Höfler's involvement with the SA and the SS Ahnenerbe, see Olaf Bockhorn, "The Battle for the *Ostmark*: Nazi Folklore in Austria," in James Dow and Hannjost Lixfeld, eds., *The Nazification of an Academic Discipline: Folklore in the Third Reich* (Bloomington: Indiana University Press, 1993), 135–55; Harm-Peer Zimmermann, "Männerbund und Totenkult. Methodologische und ideologische Grundlinien der Volks und Altertumskunde Otto Höflers 1933–1945," *Kieler Blätter zur Volkskunde* 26 (1994): 5–28; and Esther Gajek, "Germanenkunde und Nationalsozialismus. Zur Verflechtung von Wissenschaft und Politik am Beispiel Otto Höfler," in Richard Faber, ed., *Politische Religion, religiöse Politik* (Würzburg: Königshausen & Neumann, 1997), 173–204.

20. Höfler's strong influence is clear in numerous works of these authors, all of whom maintained close personal relations with him throughout their lives. See, inter alia, Stig Wikander, *Der arische Männerbund* (Lund: C. W. K. Gleerup, 1938); Georges Dumézil, *Mythes et dieux des Germains* (Paris: E. Leroux, 1939), *Horace et les Curiaces* (Paris: Gallimard, 1942), and *The Destiny of the Warrior*, trans. Alf Hiltebeitel (Chicago: University of Chicago Press, 1970); Geo Widengren, *Der Feudalismus im alten Iran. Männerbund, Gefolgswesen, Feudalismus in der iranischen Gesellschaft im Hinblick auf die indogermanischen Verhältnis* (Cologne: Westdeutscher Verlag, 1969); and Mircea Eliade, "Dacians and Wolves," in *Zalmoxis: The Vanishing God* (Chicago: University of Chicago Press, 1972), 1–20, and "Some European Secret Cults," in Helmut Birkhan, ed., *Festgabe für Otto Höfler* (Vienna: Wilhelm Braumüller, 1976), 190–204. Höfler's theories continue to influence specialized researches like Richard Ridley, "Wolf and Werewolf in Baltic and Slavic Tradition," *Journal of Indo-European Studies* 4 (1976): 321–32; Hans-Peter Hassenfratz, "Der indogermanische 'Männerbund.' Anmerkungen zur religiösen und sozialen Bedeutung des Jugendalters," *Zeitschrift für Religions- und Geistesgeschichte* 34 (1982): 148–63; Kim McCone, "Hund, Wolf, und Krieger bei den Indogermanen," in Wolfgang Meid, ed., *Studien zum indogermanischen Wortschatz* (Innsbruck: Institut für Sprachwissenschaft der Universität Innsbruck, 1987), 101–54; Daniel Gershenson, *Apollo the Wolf-God* (Washington: Institute for the Study of Man, 1991); Arnold H. Price, *The Germanic Warrior Clubs. An Inquiry into the Dynamics of the Era of*

Migrations and into the Antecedents of Medieval Society (Lück: VGT, 1994); Priscilla K. Kershaw, *The One-Eyed God: Odin and the (Indo-)Germanic Männerbünde* (Washington: Journal of Indo-European Studies, 2000); and Michael Speidel, "Berserks: A History of Indo-European 'Mad Warriors,'" *Journal of World History* 13 (2002): 253–90, idem, *Ancient Germanic Warriors: Warrior Styles from Trajan's Column to Icelandic Sagas* (New York: Routledge, 2004).

21. Reading Ginzburg's fierce critique of Höfler and Dumézil, "Germanic Mythology and Nazism," in *Clues, Myths, and the Historical Method*, trans. John Tedeschi and Anne C. Tedeschi (Baltimore: Johns Hopkins University Press, 1989), 114–31 (Italian original, 1984), alongside Arnaldo Momigliano's earlier article, "Introduction to a Discussion of Georges Dumézil," in Momigliano, *Studies in Modern Scholarship*, G. W. Bowersock, ed. (Berkeley: University of California Press, 1994), 286–301 (Italian original, 1983), was among the major influences that pressed Lincoln to rethink his earlier positive evaluation of their work and the paradigm of "Indo-European studies" that had been a centerpiece of his academic training.

Introduction, a Postscript

1. Marcel Mauss, "Essai sur les variations saisonnières des sociétés eskimos: Étude de morphologie sociale," in *Sociologie et anthropologie*, 3rd ed. (Paris: Presses Universitaires de France, 1966), 389–477 (English trans., *Seasonal Variations of the Eskimo: A Study in Social Morphology*, trans. James J. Fox [London: Routledge and Kegan Paul, 1979], 20).

2. The distinction implies Edoardo Grendi's oxymoron *"eccezionale normale"* (normally exceptional); see his essay "Micro-analisi e storia sociale," *Quaderni storici* 35 (1977), 506–20.

3. Thomas Kuhn, *The Structure of Scientific Revolutions* (Chicago: University of Chicago Press, 1962).

4. Willem de Blécourt, "A Journey to Hell: Reconsidering the Livonian 'Werewolf,'" *Magic, Ritual, and Witchcraft* 2 (2007), 49–67 (esp. 66–67).

5. Carlo Ginzburg, "Our Words, and Theirs: A Reflection on the Historian's Craft, Today," in Susanna Fellman and Marjatta Rahikainen, eds., *Historical Knowledge: In Quest of Theory, Method and Evidence* (Newcastle upon Tyne: Cambridge Scholars, 2012), 97–119.

6. Gervase of Tilbury, *Otia Imperialia. Recreation for an Emperor*, ed. and trans. S. E. Banks and James W. Binns (Oxford: Clarendon Press, 2002), 86–89 (I, 15): "Vidimus enim frequenter in Anglia per lunationes homines in lupos mutari, quod hominum genus 'gerulfos' Galli nominant, Angli vero *werewolf* dicunt; *were* enim Anglice virum sonat, *wolf* lupum."

7. "We ought confidently to judge to be false the stories of men turned into wolves and restored back to themselves or, alternatively, to believe all the things we have ascertained to be fabulous over the course of so many centuries. However, the fact that one has the term *Versipellis* as an insult in vulgar speech will indicate that this rumor is deeply implanted among the masses." (Homines in lupos verti rursusque restitui sibi falsum esse confidenter existimare debemus aut credere omnia quae fabulosa tot saeculis conperimus. Unde tamen ista vulgo infixa sit fama in tantum, ut in maledictis *versipelles* habeat, indicabitur.) Cf. Stefan Donecker, "The Werewolves of Livonia: Lycanthropy and Shape-Changing in Scholarly Texts, 1550–1720," *Preternature: Critical and Historical Studies on the Preternatural* 1 (2012), 289–322 (esp. 313).

8. Heinrich von Ulenbrock, *Encomion urbis Rigae Livoniae emporii celeberrimi* (n.p.: Rostochi Pedanus, 1615): "O vanitatem vanissimam! O caecitatem deplorandam! Quid enim quaerat rusticos Livonos olim tanta profanitate dementata fuisse, cum hodie dum eandem insaniam insaniant, et in tanta Evangelii luce specioso quoque titulo suam diabolicam societatem etiamnum indigitare ausint. Vocant enim Dei amicitiam seu etiam Deo familiaritatem, et seipsos Dei amicos."

9. Donecker, "The Werewolves of Livonia," 308–9, 321n89.

10. Pierre de Lancre, *Tableau de l'inconstance des mauvais anges et demons, où il est amplement traicté des sorciers et de la sorcellerie* (Paris: Chez Nicolas Buon, 1613), 307; Simone Maioli, *Dies caniculares . . . hoc est colloquia phisica nova et admiranda* (Moguntiae: Joannis Theobaldi Schönwetteri, 1615), l. III, c. III ("De sagis"), 644.

11. De Lancre fondly quoted passages from Dante, Ariosto, and Tasso (*Tableau de l'inconstance*, 12, 53).

12. Kaspar Peucer, *Commentarius de praecipuis generibus divinationum* (Frankfurt: A. Wecheli, 1593), cc. 133v–134r: "Ait se veneficam ignei papilionis specie circumvolitante, persecutum esse (gloriantur enim lycanthropi quod ad arcendas veneficas conducantur)."

13. De Lancre, *Tableau de l'inconstance*, 309 (see also 255 ff., 289 ff.). A different version ("Il était un peu hébété") can be found in de Lancre, *Tableau de l'inconstance des mauvais anges et démons où il est amplement traité des socrciers et de la sorcellerie*, ed. N. Jacques-Chaquin (Paris: Aubier, 1982), 229; followed by C. Oates, "Démonologues et lycanthropes: les théories de la métamorphose au XVIe siècle," in Laurence Harf-Lancner, ed., *Métamorphose et bestiaire fantastique au Moyen Âge* (Paris: École normale supérieure de jeunes filles, 1985), 71–105 (esp. 91, "un enfant idiot"; see also 91–97).

14. "Il me confessa ingenuement qu'il avoit esté loup-garou, et qu'en cette qualité il avoit couru les champs par commandement de Monsieur de la

Forest, ce qu'il confessa librement à tout le monde, et ne le nioit à personne, croyant elider tout reproche et infamie de cet accident, en disant qu'il ne l'estoit plus" (de Lancre, *Tableau de l'inconstance*, 309).

15. "Il s'est trouvé autrefois que c'estoit ce Monsieur de la Forest qui va à la chasse des sorciers et sorcieres, et leur donne la chasse par les bois et par les champs, iusques à les tirer du cercueil aprez leur decez, pour avoir le plaisir de les tourmenter, et les faire courir, voire apres la mort" (de Lancre, *Tableau de l'inconstance*, 313).

16. "Il [Jean Grenier] n'a non plus inventé ce tiltre de Monsieur de la Forest, dont il nomme le malin esprit" (de Lancre, *Tableau de l'inconstance*, 294).

17. Eva Pócs, "Nature and Culture—'The Raw and the Cooked': Shape-Shifting and Double Beings in Central and Eastern European Folklore," in Willem de Blécourt and Christa Agnes Tuczay, eds., *Tierverwandlungen: Codierung und Diskurse* (Tübingen: Francke, 2011), 99–134.

Chapter One

1. *Segensprecher* can have a condescending, pejorative connotation, describing a conjuror and charlatan. The pastor enters just after Thiess has been describing his healing practice and consistently sees himself as obtaining blessings (*segen*) for others, so an ambiguity here is probably intentional.

2. Translated from the trial transcript published by von Bruiningk, "Der Werwolf in Livland," 219–20.

3. An official who administers corporal punishment and also serves as executioner.

Chapter Two

1. Law provides us with many analogies where important influences of Germanic mythology on the local religions (*Volksreligionen*) east of the Baltic are evident. For the cults described here, it is important to state explicitly that Germans also participated. And in fact, the North Estonian terms for the werewolf, *inimesehunt* ("human wolf") and *koduhunt* ("house wolf") are Germanic loanwords. Cf. Oskar Loorits, *Estnische Volksdichtung und Mythologie* (Tartu: Akadeemiline Kooperativ, 1932), 73.

2. Olaus Magnus, *Historia de gentibus septentrionalibus*, book 18, chaps. 45 and 46.

3. As this work was being printed, I learned of a Livonian trial transcript that confirms the evidence offered here in striking ways. I am reproducing the most important part of this transcript as an appendix to this volume.

4. See H. F. Feilberg, *Bidrag til en Ordbog over Jyske Almuesmål*, 4 vols. (Copenhagen: Thieles Bogtrykkeri, 1886–1914) 2:731 ff.

5. See in particular, Lily Weiser, *Altgermanische Junglingsweihen und Männerbünde* (Baden: Konkordia, 1927), 58 ff., and Karl Meuli, "Bettelumzüge im Totenkultus, Opferritual und Volksbrauch," *Schweizerisches Archiv für Volkskunde* 28 (1928): 7 ff. and 10 ff.

6. H. Ellekilde, *Fynsk Hjemstavn* 4 (1931): 19 ff.

7. See, for example, Paul Zaunert, *Westfälische Sagen* (Jena: Eugen Diederich, 1927), 48.

8. Cf. Wilhelm Hertz, *Der Werwolf: Beitrag zur Sagengeschichte* (Stuttgart: A. Kröner, 1862), 88, 109 ff., et al.

9. *Ethnographische Parallelen und Vergleiche* (Stuttgart: J. Maier, 1878), 65n3.

10. Cf. Albrecht Dieterich, *Kleine Schriften* (Leipzig: B. Teubner, 1911), 420: "If previously in our country people went about in animal mummery during the twelve bright nights, they should be understood as the dead, who wander the upper world at that time."

11. Leopold Rütimeyer, *Ur-Ethnographie der Schweiz* (Basel: Schweizerische Gesellschaft für Volkskunde, 1924), 357 ff.; Rütimeyer, "Über Masken und Maskengebräuche im Lötschental (Kanton Wallis)," *Globus* 91 (1907): 201 ff.; and Weiser, *Altgermanische Junglingsweihen*, 57 ff.

12. One must emphasize that the different sorts of mummery with animal skins are not always strongly distinguished. In the Alps, the youths mostly make use of sheep or goat pelts in their masquerades. If the wolf impersonators appear with wolves' heads, as appear in the *Schembartlauf* of Nuremburg, or if they always have true wolf pelts at their disposal as part of their attire, is unknown to me. In my opinion, in discussions of the Roman Lupercalia, people have drawn much too far-reaching conclusions that the participants actually wore goat skins. In the North, bear and wolf skins were occasionally confused (cf. Andreas Faye, *Norske Folke-Sagn* [Christiana: Guldberg & Dzwonkowki, 1844], 78). Already in the Old Norse period *berserkir* and *úlfheðnar* were mixed up at times. Thus, the warriors of the elite squadron on Harald Hairfair's royal ship were sometimes referred to as *berserkir* (*Egilssaga*, chap. 9.3), and sometimes as *úlfheðnar* (*Vatnsdœlasaga*, chap. 9.1). In the *Vatnsdœlasaga*, it says "The *berserkirs* ['the bear-shirted ones'], who were called *úlfheðnar* ['the wolf-headed ones'] had wolf pelts for armor" (... *þeir berserkir, er úlfheðnar váru kallaðir; þeir hǫfðu vargstakka fyrir bryniur* ...). In the ninth century, Thorbjorn Hornklofi was described thus:

> ... grenioðo berserkir
> guðr var þeim a sinom
> emiaðo úlfheðnar
> ok isarn glumdo.

Haraldskvæði, stanza 8, lines 5–8; see Finnur Jónsson, ed., *Den norsk-islandske Skjaldedigtning* (Copenhagen: Gyldendal, 1912–15), 1:25 ff.

In later time, pelt-like mummeries are often artistically reproduced (see, for example, H. Moesch, "Das Klausen in Urnäsch," *Schweizerisches Archiv für Volkskunde* 10 [1906]:263) and people are not so precise concerning the type of pelt depicted. In contrast, the theriomorphic skin covering was strongly traditional.

13. Rütimeyer, 364.

14. Rütimeyer, 364.

15. J. J. Hanush, "Die Wer-wölfe oder Vlko-dlaci," *Zeitschrift für deutsche Mythologie und Sittenkunde* 4 (1859): 196.

16. Hertz, *Der Werwolf*, 120. It should be pointed out that the Russian word denotes the wolf pelt as well as the demonic werewolf itself. Cf. Oskar Loorits, *Estnische Volksdichtung und Mythologie* (Tartu: Akadeemiline, 1932), 73 ff. Directly comparable are Old Norse *úlfheðinn* and *-hamr*.

17. Herodotus 4.105.

18. Hertz, *Der Werwolf*, 120 ff.

19. Johannes Praetorius, *Saturnalia, das ist, Eine Compagnie Weihnachts-Fratzen, oder Centner-Lügen und possierliche Positiones* (Leipzig: Wittigau, 1663), 65 ff.

20. David Franck, *Des Alt- und Neuen Mecklenburgs, Erstes Buch von Mecklenburgs Heydenthum* (Leipzig: Fritze, 1753), 55.

21. Ernst Johann Friedrich Mantzel, *Bützowsche Ruhestunden: gesucht in Mecklenburgschen* (np: Fritze Bützow, 1761), 21, 23.

22. Karl Bartsch, *Sagen, Märchen und Gebräuche aus Mecklenburg: 2. Gebräuche und Aberglaube* (Vienna: Braunmüller, 1880), 246. People in northern Germany also fear the wolf's rage against the herds particularly at holidays, just as werewolves attack the herds in the Baltic.

23. "Se quotannis jactum esse lupum per dies duodecim, post natalem diem Domini vidisse se parvam speciem pueri, qui diceret, ut converteretur in lupum, postea cum non faceret, venisse speciem terribilem cum flagello, et ita conversum esse in lupum, postea concurrisse multos alios lupos, et cucurrisse per sylvas, lacerasse pecudes, hominibus tamen non potuisse nocere, praeeunte illo spectaculo cum flagello pavisse eos in flumine, et illa facta esse quotannis per dies duodecim, postea recepisse speciem hominis." *Corpus reformatorum*, vol. 20, 552; quoted by O. Clemen, *Zeitschrift für Volkskunde* (1922): 141.

24. See above. A further striking confirmation is imparted by the Livonian court transcript reproduced as an appendix to this volume.

25. For further evidence regarding Baltic werewolfery, see Hertz, *Der Werwolf*, 114n2. Kaspar Peucer, author of a *Commentarius de praecipuis*

divinationum generibus (1591), was certain that the story of Baltic werewolves was long no more than a fable, until accounts by merchants who traveled much in Livonia took them for truth.

26. Paul Drechsler, in F. Vogt, ed., *Schlesiens volkstümliche Überlieferungen*, 6 vols. (Leipzig: B. G. Teubner, 1901–13) 2/1, 17.

27. Hermann von Bruiningk, "Der Werwolf in Livland und das letzte im Wendenschen Landgericht und Dörpfschen Hofgericht i. J. 1692 deshalb stattgehabte Strafverfahren," *Mitteilungen aus der livländischen Geschichte* 22 (1924–28): 163 ff. (esp. 203 ff.).

28. He does, however, admit this without evasion! Nevertheless, he repeatedly emphasizes: "Everything (!) the werewolves do profits people best" (para. 19: *alles was sie, die wahrwölffe, thäten, gereichte den menschen zum besten*). It is remarkable that, in spite of this, he made no attempt to lie about the raids.

29. See H. F. Feilberg, *Jul. Vol. 2: Julmørkets löndom, Juletro, Juleskik* (Copenhagen: Det Schubotheske Forlag, 1904), 53 ff., and 334 (a harmless form is the procession of the *Lussi-gossarne*, i.e., the Youths of St. Lucy, in Sweden, ibid. 2:248 and 375). On the Norwegian *lussiføerd*, cf. Nils Lid, *Joleband og vegetasjonsguddom* (Oslo: J. Dybwad, 1928), 62 ff. and 114, Edvard Hammarstedt, "Lussi," in *Meddelanden från Nordiska Museet 1898* (Stockholm, 1900): 13 and 29, Hilding Celander, *Nordisk Jul* (Stockholm: H. Geber, 1928), 32 ff.

30. Hammarstedt, "Lussi," 8 ff.

31. Hammarstedt, "Lussi," esp. 11; see also 18n44, 32n98.

32. On the occasion of the recovery of the seed corn, Thiess had his nose broken (trial transcript paragraph 2), and he complained about this in court: it thus appears that this was no common injury.

33. Cf. Wilhelm Mannhardt, *Mythologische Forschungen* (= *Quellen und Forschungen zur Sprach- und Kulturgeschichte der germanischen Völker* 51 [1884]), 208 ff.

34. This is especially transparent in the struggles between Count May and Count Winter and the corresponding games in winter (after the solstice). Cf. Nils Lid, *Jolesveinar og grøderikdomsgudar* (Oslo: J. Dybwad, 1933), 104 ff., et al.

35. See Hammarstedt, "Lussi," esp. 8 ff., 32, and 37 ff.

36. Hammarstedt, "Lussi," 36.

37. As depicted in Celander, *Nordisk Jul*, 39.

38. Mannhardt, *Mythologische Forschungen*, esp. 227 ff., 232, and 234 ff.

39. Thiess trial, paragraph 5. In Sweden, *Helvete* ("hell") is frequently attested as a place name, particularly well in the Middle Ages (see L. Carls-

son, *Namn och Bygd* 21 [1933]: 138 ff.). These places consistently lie in the northern part of the relevant area (144). Should this alone—without any particular "mythological" support, i.e., without any taboos set on the places—have led to this unusual name? Has the memory that the realm of the dead lies in the (Far!) North itself been sufficient to name villages located in the North "hell"?—It is, however, reported that folk traditions repeatedly state that the *Wilde Heer* proceeds on its regular route, always from north to south (see Axel Olrik, "Odinsjægeren i Jylland," *Dania* 8 [1901]:145; Hans Plischke, *Die Sage vom wilden Heere im deutschen Volke* [Ellenburg: Offenhauer, 1914], 63n10; Zaunert, *Hessen-Nassauische Sagen* [Jena: Eugen Diederich, 1929], 12). Nature mythology cannot account for these legends. It must be left to local research to explore whether the points of departure for the ghostly processions—which are often precisely identified by the legend—correspond with ancient cult places.

40. Breads of this sort also play an important role in the feasts of Santa Lucia in the North: they were named "cats of the devil" (*Teufelskatzen*, cf. Hammarstedt, "Lussi," 24 ff.) and point to a connection with "hell."

41. See Hugo Rabe, *Scholia in Lucianum* (Leipzig: B. G. Teubner, 1906), 275 ff. Cf. Sir James George Frazer, *Pausanias' Description of Greece*, vol. V (London: Macmillan, 1908), 29 (to Pausanias 9.8.1), and *The Golden Bough*, vol. VIII (London: Macmillan, 1911), 16 ff.

42. Cf. Mannhardt, *Mythologische Forschungen*, 248 ff., 251 ff., 264 ff.

43. See Levi Johansson, "Lucia och de underjordiske i norrländisk folksägen," *Fataburen* (1906), 193 ff. (esp. 195).

44. See Scholium 80 to Lucian in Rabe, *Scholia in Lucianum*, 276.

45. Compare also the designation of the dead as δημήτρειοι ("those of Demeter"), as well as the role of the Norse Freyja as Queen of the Dead.

46. Thiess trial transcript, paragraph 17.

47. This sort of demonic clothing is securely attested. After he first mentioned this, Thiess evaded the more penetrating questions about his comrades in the werewolf band, altering his testimony that the transformation took place simply by casting off one's clothes. He also consistently avoided naming any of those comrades, with the exception of the son of his enemy (Thiess trial transcript, para. 14).

48. This will be treated in volume II of this work [which was announced here, but never published].

49. Olaus Magnus, *Historia de Gentibus Septentrionalibus*, 18.46.

50. Most deserving of thanks is research that permits one to establish the influence of one group on another, e.g., by using linguistic analysis to show that certain mythological terminology enters as a loanword. On the

influence of Norse mythology on Baltic, see most recently Lid, *Jolesveinar och grøderikdomsgudar*, 153 ff.

51. *Historia de Gentibus Septentrionalibus*, 18.46.

52. Examples will be given in volume II [again, this was never published]. One also notes the irreversible and virtually magical character the recruitment drink has even in contemporary times, as used for reception into a military unit. Whoever empties the fateful recruitment goblet is taken up and bound to the troop. This fully irrational significance of the drink, which is decisive for the rest of one's life—often enough described in literature with some horror—must stem from an older tradition.

53. Thiess trial transcript paragraph 11. That the goad was iron, as Thiess maintained, is also reported by Olaus Magnus, Melancththon's informant, and Peucer.

54. Thus, the transformation by shedding of clothes (trial transcript, para. 6); the meals of sorcerers in "hell," to which werewolves were not admitted (para. 11; people in Greece also believe that in the grotto of Kore, a portion of the food brought there by the dragon who guarded the cave was eaten; see Scholium 80 to Lucian in Rabe, *Scholia in Lucianum*); the blooming of seeds in the underworld (para. 15; he obviously invented this fairy tale to avoid the uncomfortable question of the judges); the account of the Russian werewolves (para. 19), clearly a piece of "pious fraud" "intended to bring the reputation of the werewolves, the importance and necessity of the fertility magic, into a sharper light. In the case of other motifs, like the destruction of livestock, the inquisitors made no such favorable assumptions!

55. Trial transcript, paragraphs 19 and 44: "The devil has nothing to do with him. Rather, he—namely the witness—was God's hound and he stole from the devil that which the sorcerers brought to him. Therefore, the devil was an enemy to him." Similarly, paragraph 62: "They were God's friends and hunting dogs."

56. Jacob Grimm, *Deutsche Mythologie*, vol. 4 (Gütersloh: Bertelsmann, 1877), 557.

57. See the entry for 1639, 19 October in Boëtius Murenius' *Acta visitatoria 1637–1666*, ed. Kaarlo Österbladh (Borgå: Tryckeri- & Tidningsaktiebolaget, 1908), 18.

Chapter Three

1. Carlo Ginzburg, from *The Night Battles: Witchcraft and Agrarian Cults in the Sixteenth and Seventeenth Centuries*, trans. John Tedeschi and Anne C. Tedeschi (London: Routledge & Kegan Paul and Baltimore: Johns Hopkins

University Press, 1980), 28–32. Originally published as *I benandanti: Stregoneria e culti agrari tra Cinquecento e Seicento* (Turin: Einaudi, 1966).

2. See H. von Bruiningk, "Der Werwolf in Livland und das letzte im Wendenschen Landgericht und Dörptschen Hofgericht i. J 1692 deshalb stattgehabte Strafverfahren," *Mitteilungen aus der livländischen Geschichte* 22 (1924): 163–220. The credit for having brought this document, appearing in such an out-of-the-way organ, into the light of day, belongs to Otto Höfler who reprinted it in part, with commentary, in the appendix to *Kultische Geheimbünde der Germanen* (Frankfurt am Main: Moritz Diesterweg, 1934), 345–57.

3. Höfler, *Kultische Geheimbünde*, 352, in addition to recalling, a propos this trial, the ritual battles between Winter and Spring, inserts the beliefs documented there into the mythical-cultic complex of Balder—Attis—Demeter—Persephone—Adonis. For the interpretation in an archetypal key of the "ritual battles" between Summer and Winter, see Mircea Eliade, *Patterns in Comparative Religion* (Cleveland & New York: World Publishers, 1970), 319 ff., who accepts the conclusions of Waldemar Liungman, *Der Kampf zwischen Sommer und Winter* (Helsinki: Academia Scientiarum fennica, 1941) in this regard.

4. The observation is by von Bruiningk, in the introduction to the document, p. 190. He observes that the details in the account of the old man appear in no other source known to him. "Der Werwolf in Livland," 190–91.

5. Kaspar Peucer, *Commentarius de praecipuis generibus divinationum* (Wittenberg: Johannes Crato, 1560), folios 133v–134r (these pages are missing in the first edition, printed in 1553). This passage had already been cited by von Bruiningk. One should note that Peucer introduces his discussion of the problem of the werewolves in a section devoted to "ecstatics."

6. Carlo Ginzburg, "Germanic Mythology and Nazism: Thoughts on an Old Book by Georges Dumézil," in *Clues, Myths, and the Historical Method*, 122–27. Originally published as "Mitologia Germanica e Nazismo: Su un vecchio libro di Georges Dumézil," *Quaderni Storici* 57 (1984): 857–82.

7. Heinrich Schurtz, Altersklassen und Männerbünde: Eine Darstellung der Grundformen der Gesellschaft (Berlin: Georg Reimer, 1902); Hermann Usener, "Ueber vergleichende Sitten und Rechtsgeschichte," in *Verhandlungen der 42. Versammlung deutscher Philologen und Schulmänner in Wien* (1893).

8. Lily Weiser, *Altgermanische Jünglingsweihen und Männerbünde* (Baden: Konkordia, 1927), which also cites Moritz Zeller, *Die Knabenweihen: Eine ethnologische Studie* (Bern: Haupt, 1923), a comprehensive survey in which Reik's contribution had already received ample attention: see 120 ff.

9. See Will-Erich Peuckert and Otto Lauffer, *Volkskunde: Quellen und Forschungen seit 1930* (Bern: Francke, 1951), 118, where a distinction is made between Weiser's *bündisch* inspiration and Otto Höfler's and Robert Stumpfl's, "influenced by the political events" (read: Nazism). Wolfgang Emmerich, *Germanistische Volkstumsideologie: Genese und Kritik der Volksforschung im Dritten Reich* (Tübingen: Tübinger Vereinigung für Volkskunde, 1968), 202, generically groups the positions of the three schools under the label of the school of Much.

10. See Walter Laqueur, *Young Germany: A History of the German Youth Movement* (London: Routledge & Kegan Paul, 1962).

11. Weiser, *Altgermanische Jünglingsweihen*, 24.

12. Ibid., 51.

13. Ibid., 48. Weiser returned to this subject in an important essay, "Zur Geschichte der altgermanischen Todesstrafe und Friedlosigkeit," *Archiv für Religionswissenschaft* 30 (1933): 209–27.

14. Otto Höfler, *Kultische Geheimbünde der Germanen* (Frankfurt am Main: Moritz Diesterweg, 1934). Robert Stumpfl, *Kultspiele der Germanen als Ursprung des mittelalterlichen Dramas* (Berlin: Junker und Dünnhaupt, 1936), p. x, mentioned the existence of a second volume and said that he had used it. Höfler noted in the introduction to *Kultische Geheimbünde* (p. xi, n. 1) that the book, which originally was to be entitled *Totenheer-Kultbund-Fastnachtspiel*, was already basically completed in January 1932.

15. Note that chap. 6 ("Les Guerriers-Fauves") of Dumézil's *Mythes et dieux des Germains* (Paris: E. Leroux, 1939), heavily based on Höfler's work, is taken up again in part in Dumézil's *The Destiny of the Warrior* (Chicago: University of Chicago Press, 1970). See also Höfler's introduction to the German translation of Dumézil, *Loki* (Darmstadt: Wissenschaftliche Buchgesellschaft, 1959) and Dumézil's contribution to the *Festgabe* for Höfler's seventy-fifth birthday (Vienna, 1976), which contained essays by Mircea Eliade, Siegfried Gutenbrunner, and others. Geo Widengren, *Der Feudalismus im alten Iran* (Cologne and Opladen: Westdeutscher Verlag, 1969), 45 ff., suggests that the work of Höfler and Weiser-Aall should be used with caution. By Weiser-Aall, see also *Volkskunde und Psychologie. Eine Einführung* (Berlin and Leipzig: Walter de Gruyter, 1937), 105–6; by Stig Wikander, *Der arische Männerbund: Studien zur indo-iranischen Sprach- und Religionsgeschichte* (Lund: C. W. K. Gleerup, 1938), 64 ff. See the very favorable review of Karl Meuli in *Schweizerisches Archiv für Volkskunde* 34 (1935): 77 and Meuli's considerably more critical opinion in "Schweizer Masken und Maskenbrauche" (1943), now in Meuli's *Gesammelte Schriften*, ed. Thomas Gelzer (Basel and Stuttgart: Schwabe, 1975), 273n3. It should be

noted that, beginning in 1938, Meuli took a publicly anti-Nazi position; see the biographical appendix by F. Jung, ibid., 1166–67. On Höfler's work (and critical reactions to it), see also Alois Closs, "Iranistik und Völkerkunde," in *Monumentum H.S. Nyberg* (Leiden, Teheran, and Liège: E. J. Brill, 1975) 1:157 ff.

16. Höfler, *Kultische Geheimbünde*, 205–6.

17. Ibid., 277–78. See Emmerich, *Germanistische Volkstumsideologie*, 202 ff. for discussions within the orbit of Nazi folklore studies between supporters of the primacy of rite and supporters of the primacy of myth.

18. See Norman Cohn, *Europe's Inner Demons: An Enquiry Inspired by the Great Witch-Hunt* (London: Heinemann, 1975), 107 ff.

19. Friedrich Ranke, "Der Wilde Heer und die Kultbünde der Germanen: Eine Auseinandersetzung mit Otto Höfler" (1940), now in his *Kleinere Schriften*, ed. Heinz Rupp and Eduard Studer (Bern: Franke, 1971), 380–408. (Ranke was the only German folklorist to emigrate because he was anti-Nazi: See Emmerich, *Germanistische Volkstumsideologie*, 59). Höfler replied many years later, restating his old theses, without substantial changes or additions in the documentation: see his *Verwandlungskulte, Volkssagen, und Mythen*, Oesterreichische Akademie der Wissenschaften, Phil. -hist. Klasse, Sitzungsberichte 279, Band 2 Abhandl. (Vienna, 1973).

20. Weiser, *Altgermanische Jünglingsweihen*, 55, 77, 82. I intend to return to these themes in a later work.

21. Höfler, *Kultische Geheimbünde*, 341. On ecstasy, 262n337a is illuminating apropos Rudolf Otto, *Gottheit und Gottheiten der Arier* (Giessen: Alfred Töpelmann, 1932). On fertility themes, see 87 ff., 386 ff.

22. Thus, Höfler in polemic against Friedrich von der Leyen in *Zeitschrift für deutschen Altertum*, n.s. 73 (1936): 109–15, esp. 110. But in the same vein, see also *Kultische Geheimbünde*, 15. For some appropriate critical observations, see Alois Closs, "Die Religion des Semnonenstammes," *Wiener Beiträge zur Kulturgeschichte und Linguistik* 4 (1936): 665 ff.

23. See Karl Meuli, "Die deutschen Masken" (1933), now in his *Gesammelte Schriften*, 160, where the ritual interpretation later developed by Höfler was already being proposed. The proceedings of the werewolf trial were originally published in *Mitteilungen aus der livländischen Geschichte* 22 (1924): 203–20.

24. Höfler, *Kultische Geheimbünde*, 345 ff. In a penetrating review, Willy Krogmann, *Archiv für das Studium der neueren Sprache* n.s. 68, Band 90 (1935): esp. 98–100, has noted that Höfler's thesis as a whole was clearly contradicted by this document. I have proposed a completely different interpretation for it in *The Night Battles*, 26 ff.

25. Höfler, *Kultische Geheimbünde*, 357. A similar passage is cited in Hermann Bausinger's brilliant article, "Volksideologie und Volksforschung: Zur nationalsozialistischen Volksforschung," *Zeitschrift für Volkskunde* 2 (1965): 177–204, esp. 189. Höfler reiterated his ideas in a still more explicitly pro-Nazi direction in *Die politische Leistung der Völkerwanderungszeit* (Neumünster: Wachholz, 1939); see especially his concluding pages.

26. The phrase is cited by George L. Mosse, *The Crisis of German Ideology: Intellectual Origins of the Third Reich* (New York: Grosset & Dunlap, 1964), 216.

27. See Laqueur, *Young Germany*, 109, 193–95. Krebs, chief of the Nazi party in Hamburg, was expelled from the party in 1933.

28. H. Spehr, "Waren die Germanen 'Ekstatiker'?," *Rasse* 3 (1936): 394–400.

29. Carlo Ginzburg, *Clues, Myths, and the Historical Method*, translated by John and Anne C. Tedeschi (Baltimore: Johns Hopkins University Press, 1989), 132–40 from the Italian original, *Miti, emblemi, spie: Morfologia e storia* (Torino: Giulio Einaudi, 1986).

30. Sigmund Freud, *Collected Papers*, trans. Alix and James Strachey, The International Psycho-Analytical Library, no. 9 (London: 1950), 3:471–605.

31. Ibid., 498–99. Freud had already published the dream in his essay "The Occurrence in Dreams of Material from Fairy Tales," ibid., 4:236–43.

32. Carlo Ginzburg, *The Night Battles. Witchcraft and Agrarian Cults in the Sixteenth & Seventeenth Centuries* (London: Routledge & Kegan Paul and Baltimore: Johns Hopkins University Press, 1980; reprint ed. 2013).

33. Ibid., 28.

34. Roman Jakobson and Marc Szeftel, "The Vseslav Epos," *Memoirs of the American Folklore Society* 42 (1947): 13–86.

35. See Carlo Ginzburg, "Présomptions sur le sabbat," *Annales: E.S.C.* 39 (1984): 341–54. The connection of the second and third elements with Slavic beliefs in werewolves has already been noted by Nicole Belmont, *Les signes de la naissance. Études des représentations symboliques associées aux naissances singulières* (Paris: Plon, 1971), 108 ff., in a study of symbolic representations of persons born with the caul that reaches conclusions very different from those presented here.

36. Freud, *Collected Papers*, 3:506, 580.

37. Ibid., 536.

38. See Franco Venturi, ed., *Antiche fiabe russe*, raccolte da A.N. Afanasjev (Torino: Giulio Einaudi, 1955), 95–96.

39. See Ginzburg, *The Night Battles*, 11.

40. Gabor Klaniczay, "Shamanistic Elements in Central European

Witchcraft," in Mihály Hoppal and Vilmos Diószegi, *Shamanism in Eurasia* (Göttingen: Edition Herodot, 1984), 404–22.

41. See Ruth Mack, Muriel Gardiner, et al., eds. *The Wolf-Man by the Wolf-Man* (New York: Basic Books, 1971) and Harold P. Blum, "The Borderline Childhood of the Wolf-Man," in Jules Glenn and Mark Kanzer, eds., *Freud and His Patients* (New York and London: Jason Aronson, 1980), 341–58.

42. Freud, *Collected Papers*, 3:501.

43. Sigmund Freud and D. E. Oppenheim, *Dreams in Folklore* (New York: International Universities Press, 1958). This essay, found miraculously, was published posthumously first in 1953.

44. Freud, *Collected Papers*, 3:580–81.

45. *The Complete Letters of Sigmund Freud to Wilhelm Fliess, 1887–1904,* trans. and ed. Jeffrey Moussaieff Masson (Cambridge, MA: Belknap Press, 1985), 238–42.

46. A point often made. See, for example, Marianne Krüll, *Freud and his Father* (New York: W.W. Norton, 1986).

47. Letters of Freud to Fliess, 224, 227.

48. Ibid., 225.

49. Ibid., 264 (letter dated September 21, 1897).

50. Ibid., 227 (letter dated January 24, 1897). On this and the preceding letter, see also Jeffrey Moussaieff Masson, *The Assault on Truth: Freud's Suppression of the Seduction Theory* (New York: Farrar, Straus, & Giroux 1984), 105 ff.

51. It appeared in 1925; see Freud, *Collected Papers*, 5:181–85.

52. Freud, *Collected Papers*, 3:577. On this point see also the perceptive remarks by Peter Brooks, "Fictions of the Wolf-Man: Freud and Narrative Understanding" in *Reading for the Plot* (Oxford: Clarendon Press, 1984), 264–85.

53. Freud, *Collected Papers*, 3:575.

54. Ibid., 1:299.

55. See Masson, *The Assault on Truth*, esp. chap. 4 (cf., however, Krüll, *Freud and His Father*, 68 ff. et passim). The analytical side of Masson's book is much more convincing than its conclusions. Nevertheless, it is a serious piece of research (as well as a rich repository of unpublished documents) that the international psychoanalytic community has wrongly attempted to portray as scandalous libel.

56. See Ginzburg, "Présomptions sur le sabbat."

57. See Freud, *Collected Papers*, 3:596. In general, see Aaron H. Esman, "The Primal Scene: A Review and a Reconsideration," *Psychoanalytic Study*

of the Child 28 (1973): 49–81, and more specifically, Mark Kanzer, "Further Comments on the Wolf-Man: The Search for a Primal Scene," in Kanzer and Glenn, *Freud and His Patients*, 358 ff., esp. 363–64. On Freud's Lamarckism, see Ernest Jones, *The Life and Work of Sigmund Freud*, 3 vols. (New York: Basic Books, 1953–57), *ad indicem*.

58. Freud, *Collected Papers*, 3:577–78, 603.

59. Géza Róheim, "Hungarian Shamanism," *Psychoanalysis and the Social Sciences* 3 (1951): 131–69.

60. *The Freud–Jung Letters: The Correspondence between Sigmund Freud and C.G. Jung*, ed. William McGuire, trans. Ralph Manheim and R. F. C. Hull (Princeton: Princeton University Press, 1974), 260.

61. The passage that follows is taken from Carlo Ginzburg, *Ecstasies: Deciphering the Witches' Sabbath*, trans. Raymond Rosenthal (New York: Pantheon Books, 1991), 153–68, first published in Italian as *Storia Notturna. Una decifrazione del sabba* (Torino: Giulio Einaudi, 1989).

62. The trial records have been published by Hermann von Bruiningk, "Der Werwolf in Livland und das letzte im Wendenschen Landgericht und Dörptschen Hofgericht i. J. 1692 deshalb stattgehabte Strafverfahren," *Mitteilungen aus der livländischen Geschichte* 22 (1924): 163–220. I develop here the interpretation sketched in *The Night Battles*, 28–32. I had missed the declarations (irrelevant) of Josef Hanika, "Kultische Vorstufen des Pflanzen-anbaues," *Zeitschrift für Volkskunde* 50 (1953): 49–65, and Hermann Kügler, "Zum 'Livländischen Fruchtbarkeitskult'," ibid. 52 (1955): 279–81. An earlier testimony on Baltic werewolves occurs in Helmut Birkhan, "Altgermanische Miszellen . . ." in *Festgabe für Otto Höfler* (Vienna: W. Braumüller, 1976), 36–37. For some folkloric connections, cf. Andrejs Johansons, "Kultverbände und Verwandlungskulte," *Arv* 29–30 (1973–74): 149–57 (courteously pointed out to me by Erik af Edholm, whom I thank here).

63. See especially Otto Höfler, *Kultische Geheimbünde der Germanen* (Frankfurt am Main: Moritz Diesterweg, 1934). On the ideological matrix (Nazi) and the widespread fortune of this book among scholars such as Stig Wikander, Karl Meuli (who subsequently took a more critical attitude) and Georges Dumézil, see the present author's "Germanic Mythology and Nazism," in *Clues, Myths, and the Historical Method*, 126–45. Against the prevailing tendency to accept or reject Höfler's thesis en bloc, it should be emphasized that in reality it is divided into three points. The sagas and the general evidence on the "wild hunt" (*Wilde Jagd*) or "the army of the dead" (*Totenheer*) had (a) a mythico-religious content; (b) expressed a heroic or bellicose myth, substantially Germanic, (c) must be interpreted as rites practiced by organizations or secret groups of generally masked young

men, pervaded by ecstatic fervor, who felt that they were impersonating the spirits of the dead. In my opinion, only point (a), which goes back at least to Grimm, has good grounds; the objections of an anti-Nazi folklorist like Friedrich Ranke ("Das wilde Heer und die Kultbünde der Germanen" (1940), now in his *Kleine Schriften*, ed. Heinz Rupp and Eduard Studer (Bern: Franke, 1971), 380–408, which considers the testimonies on the "wild hunt" as hallucinations, pure and simple, are completely unacceptable. Point (b), inspired by the philo-Nazi orientation of Höfler, interprets the documentation in unilateral fashion, isolating the bellicose themes from a wider context which also includes themes related to fertility. Point (c) exaggerates, also for obvious ideological reasons, the suggestive hypotheses formulated by Lily Weiser in *Altgermanische Jünglingsweihen* (Baden: Konkordia, 1927), reaching, as pointed out by Willy Krogmann (in *Archiv für das Studium des neueren Sprache* 168, Band 90 [1935], 95–102) completely absurd conclusions, dictated by the preconceived notion of systematically interpreting the descriptions of the processions of the dead and the forays of the werewolves as testimonies of real events. On this current of research, see the timely critical observations of E.A. Philippson, "Die Volkskunde als Hilfswissenschaft der germanischen Religionsgeschichte," *The Germanic Review* 13 (1938): 273–51. Höfler's influence is evident in Franco Cardini, *Alle radici della cavalleria medievale* (Florence: La nuova Italia, 1981).

64. Cf. respectively, Höfler, op. cit., 345 ff.; Will-Erich Peuckert, *Geheimkulte* (Heidelberg: Pfeffer, 1951), Leopold Kretzenbacher, *Kynokephale Dämonen südosteuropäischer Volksdichtung* (Munich: R. Trofenik, 1968), 91–95. In polemic with my essay "Freud, the Wolf-Man and the Werewolves," see Rudolf Schenda, "Ein Benandante, ein Wolf, oder Wer," *Zeitschrift für Volkskunde* 82 (1986): 200–202 (other interventions appear in the same volume).

65. Though from different viewpoints, the interpretation of Thiess's confessions in the ritual key is shared by Hanika, art. cit., and Hellmut Rosenfeld, "Name und Kult der Istrionen (Istwäonen), zugleich Beitrag zu Wodankult und Germanenfrage," *Zeitschrift für deutsches Altertum und deutsche Literatur* 90 (1960–61): 178.

66. Dated, but still useful, is the body of studies by Wilhelm Hertz, *Der Werwolf* (Stuttgart: A. Kröner, 1862); Richard Andree, *Ethnographische Parallelen und Vergleiche* (Stuttgart: J. Maier, 1878), 62–80; Caroline Taylor Stewart, "The Origin of the Werewolf Superstition," *University of Missouri Studies, Social Science Series*, II, 3 (1909). A systematic bibliography that improves on the attempt of George Frazer Black, "A List of Books relating to Lycanthropy," *New York Public Library Bulletin* 23 (1919): 811–15, is lacking.

Studies of specific characters will be cited as we proceed. Among those devoted to extra-European phenomena, see, for example, Birger Lindskog, *African Leopard Men* (Stockholm: Almqvist & Wiksell, 1954).

67. See the book (very erudite but utterly unconvincing) by Robert Eisler, *Man into Wolf* (London: Spring Books, 1951); on the author, cf. the ferocious portrait drawn by Gershom Scholem, *From Berlin to Jerusalem* (New York: Schocken Books, 1980), 126–32. In a perspective analogous to that of Eisler (still substantially Jungian), see also Walter Burkert, *Homo necans* (Berkeley: University of California Press, 1983), 31, 37, 42, etc. (but on 77, Thiess's confessions are understood, as usual, as testimony to ritual behavior).

68. A typographical error in the English translation of this sentence, where the Italian *eccezionale* was rendered as "typical" rather than "atypical," has been corrected here. Cf. *Ecstasies*, 154 and *Storia notturna*, 131.

69. Cf. Laurence Harf-Lancner, "La métamorphose illusoire: des théories chrétiennes de la metamorphose aux images médiévales du loup-garou," *Annales E.S.C.* 40 (1985): 208–26; to the studies on *Bisclavret*, add Will Sayers, "Bisclavret in Marie de France: a Reply," *Cambridge Medieval Celtic Studies* 4 (Winter 1982): 77–82 (with a rich bibliography). According to Harf-Lancner, the contradictory physiognomy of werewolves in medieval texts would seem to be inspired by the attempt to temper a metamorphosis unacceptable to Christian thought: the folklore tradition, by contrast, insisted on the "bestial and inhuman behavior of the werewolf" (art. cit., 200–221). But this same folkloric tradition should be regarded as the result of a historical process, not as an immutable datum.

70. Cf. on all this *The Night Battles*.

71. Cf. the splendid essay by Roman Jakobson and Marc Szeftel, "The Vseslav Epos," *Memoirs of the American Folklore Society* 42 (1947): 13–86, in particular 56–70, to be combined with Jakobson and Gojko Ružičić, "The Serbian Zmaj Ognjeni Vuk and the Russian Vseslav Epos," *Annuaire de l'Institut de philologie et d'histoire orientales et slaves* 10 (1950): 343–55. Both essays are taken into account by the very useful book by Nicole Belmont, *Les signes de la naissance* (Paris: Plon 1971),. 57–60. In Italian see Renato Poggioli, ed., *Cantare della gesta di Igor* (Torino: Giulio Einaudi, 1954) and Bruno Meriggi, ed., *Le byline: Canti popolari russi* (Milan: Accademia, 1974), 41–49 ("Volch Vseslav'evič").

72. Cf. *The Night Battles*, 15; *Le byline*, 16. The custom is also documented in Lapland; cf. T. I. Itkonen, *Heidnische Religion und späterer Aberglaube bei den Finnischen Lappen* (Helsinki: Suomalais-ugrilainen Seura, 1946), 194–95.

73. Ibid., 103.

74. Cf. *Augustin Lercheimer (Professor H. Witekind in Heidelberg) und seine Schrift wider den Hexenwahn*, Carl Binz and Anton Birlinger, eds. (Strassburg: J. H. E. Heitz, 1888), 55 ff. Elsewhere the same person is called Wilken.

75. See *The Night Battles*, 5.

76. See O. Clemen, "Zum Werwolfsglauben in Nordwestrussland," *Zeitschrift des Vereins für Volkskunde* 30–32 (1920–22): 141–44.

77. Cf. Kaspar Peucer, *Commentarius de praecipuis generibus divinationum* (Witteberg: Johannes Crato, 1560), 140v–45r (these pages are missing in the first edition, printed in 1553).

78. Cf. *Corpus Reformatorum*, XX (Brunsvigae, 1854), col. 552. The identification (missed by Binz) of the author of the letter with Witekind is made by Clemen, art. cit. Both this essay and the *Christlich Bedencken* by Lercheimer have been generally neglected by scholars of this subject: among the exceptions are von Bruiningk, art. cit. and Straubergs, "Om Varulvarna i Baltikum,"), op. cit., 107–29, esp. 114–16. But see now, from another point of view, Frank Baron, "The Faust Book's Indebtedness to Augustin Lercheimer and Wittenberg Sources," *Daphnis* 14 (1985): 517–45 (with further bibliography).

79. The detail of the lame child who guides the werewolves, lacking in *Christlich Bedencken*, is also missing in the account of Melanchthon's lesson (cf. *Corpus Reformatorum*, XX, cit.): Peucer will have taken it from Witekind's letter or directly from him in conversation.

80. Besides Herodotus, *Histories* IV.105, cf. Peucer, op. cit., 141r. Jean Bodin affirmed that a letter in his possession from a German to the High Constable of France described similar phenomena: "Posterity has in the meanwhile verified many things written by Herodotus, which appeared incredible to the ancients" (*Demonomania degli stregoni*, Italian trans. by Ercole Cato [Venice: 1597], 176). Marija Gimbutas, *Bronze Age Cultures in Central and Eastern Europe* (The Hague: Mouton, 1965), 443, refers to Herodotus and to linguistic and archaeological evidence not further identified.

81. The passages of Herodotus (IV.105), Pausanias (VIII.2.6) and Pliny (VIII.81) are commented upon in what is to my mind a reductionist perspective by Giulia Piccaluga, *Lykaon: Un tema mitico* (Rome: Ateneo, 1968). On Petronius, cf. the fine essay by Mauritz Schuster, "Der Werwolf und die Hexen. Zwei Schauermärchen bei Petronius," *Wiener Studien* 48 (1930): 149–78, which escaped Ronald M. James, "Two Examples of Latin Legends from the Satyricon," *Arv* 35 (1979): 122–25 (sketchy but useful for its mention of parallel themes in the Scandinavian ambit). For Ireland, cf. Hertz, op. cit., 133, which refers to Giraldus Cambrensis, *Topographia Hibernica* II.19

(*Opera* V, London 1887, ed. J. F. Dimock, 101 ff.) published not later than 1188, in which is related the encounter that took place five or six years before between a priest and a man and woman transformed into wolves; Eisler, op. cit., 138–39n111. For Burchard of Worms, cf. Migne, *Patrologia Latina*, CXL, 971.

82. See respectively Richard Buxton, "Wolves and Werewolves in Greek Thought," in Jan Bremmer, ed., *Interpretations of Greek Mythology* (London: Routledge, 1988) 60–79 and Schuster, art. cit., 153n14 (not mentioned in the preceding essay).

83. On the first point, it seems symptomatic that the discovery of "rites of passage" occurred in the researches of Robert Hertz on double burial. As to the second, it will suffice to consult Vladimir Propp, *Le radici storiche dei racconti di fate*, trans. Clara Coïsson (Torino: Boringheri, 1972).

84. Cf. the fundamental essay of W. H. Roscher, "Das von der 'Kynan-thropie' handelnde Fragment des Marcellus von Side," *Abhandlungen der philologisch-historischen Classe der königlich Sächsischen Gesellschaft der Wissenschaften* 17 (1897): in particular 44–45 and 57; on 4 the overall debt to Rohde's *Psyche* is recognized. The latter relied with an important review, which appeared posthumously in the *Berliner Philologische Wochenschrift* 18 (1898): coll. 270–76 (included in his *Kleine Schriften* [Tübingen and Leipzig: 1901] 2:216–23. Roscher's indications were developed by Louis Gernet, "Dolon le loup," now in *Antropologie de la Grèce antique* (Paris: Maspero, 1968), 154–71. On Hades' head-covering, cf. Salomon Reinach's article on "Galea" in Charles Daremberg and Edmond Saglio, *Dictionnaire des antiquités grecques et romaines*, II, 2 (Paris: Hachette, 1896), 1430; other bibliographic indications can be found in A. Alvino, "L'invisibilità di Ades," *Studi storico-religiosi* 5 (1981): 45–51, which seems, however, to ignore Gernet's essay. There is copious documentation on the link between the wolf (and the dog) and the world of the dead in Freda Kretschmar, *Hundess-tammvater und Kerberos*, 2 vols. (Stuttgart: Strecker & Schröder, 1938).

85. Cf. Will-Erich Peuckert, in *Handwörterbuch des deutschen Aberglau-bens* (Berlin: Walter de Gruyter, 1938–41) 9:783–84 and Höfler, op. cit., 16–18. It should be noted that on the island of Guernsey the *varou* is a nocturnal spirit, identifiable with the dead (*varw* in Breton): cf. Sir Edgar MacCulloch, *Guernsey Folk Lore* (London: E. Stock, 1903), 230–31.

86. See the important essay by Lily Weiser-Aall, "Zur Geschichte der altgermanischen Todesstrafe und Friedlosigkeit," *Archiv für Religionswissen-schaft* 30 (1933): 209–27. Cf. Adalbert Erler, "Friedlosigkeit und Werwolfs-glaube," *Paideuma* 1 (1938–40): 303–17 (strongly influenced by Höfler); Georg Christoph von Unruh, "Wargus, Friedlosigkeit und magisch-kultische

Vorstellungen bei den Germanen," *Zeitschrift für Rechtsgeschichte*, Germ. Abt. 74 (1957): 1–40; Theodor Bühler, "Wargus-friedlos-Wolf," in *Festschrift für Robert Wildhaber* (Basel: G. Krebs, 1973), 43–48. Against this interpretive line, cf. Hinrich Siuts, *Bann und Acht und ihre Grundlagen im Totenglauben* (Berlin: Walter de Gruyter, 1959), 62–67; M. Jacoby, *Wargus, vargr, 'Verbrecher', 'Wolf'. Eine sprach- und rechtsgeschichtliche Untersuchung* (Uppsala: Almqvist & Wiksell, 1974), which seeks, unconvincingly, to demonstrate that the medieval and post-medieval testimonies on werewolves have no link with the folkloric culture because they were heavily influenced by classical and Christian notions; see also the astringent review by James E. Knirk in *Scandinavian Studies* 49 (1977): 100–103. On the roots of the connection between wolves and outlaws in ancient Greece and Roman antiquity, cf. Jan Bremmer, "The 'suodales' of Poplios Valesios,' *Zeitschrift für Papyrologie und Epigraphik* 47 (1982): 133–47; and see now Jan Bremmer and N. M. Horsfall, *Roman Myth and Mythography* (London: University of London, Institute of Classical Studies, 1987), 25 ff.

87. In a penetrating review of Kretzenbacher, op. cit., Ronald Grambo proposes to link the complex beliefs in werewolves "to an ecstatic technique widespread in the Eurasian ambit" (*Fabula* 13 [1972]: 202–4).

88. Olaus Magnus, *Historia de gentibus septentrionalibus* (Rome: J.M. de Viottis, 1555), 442 ff.

89. Cf. E. Strauch, *Discursus physicus lykanthropíam quam nonnulli in Livonia circa Natalem Domini vere fieri narrant, falsissimam esse demonstrans . . . praeses M. Michael Mej Riga Livonus* (Wittenberg: 1640), F. T. Moebius, *De transformatione hominum in bruta . . . sub praesidio J. Thomasii* (Leipzig: 1667). In general, around the middle of the seventeenth century, the theme of werewolves became a great fashion in Germany: this is shown, for example, by *Cyllenes facundus, hoc est problema philosophicum de lycanthropis, an vere illi, ut fama est, luporum et aliarum bestiarum formis induantur? cum aliis quaestionibus hinc emanantibus . . . ?* (Spirae Nemetum: 1647), which contains the titles of the speeches delivered by twelve professors and as many students in the gymnasium of Speier.

90. Thus, e.g., Höfler, Peuckert, and Kretzenbacher, op. cit.

91. See Waldemar Deonna, "Croyances funéraires. La soif des morts . . . ," *Revue de l'histoire des religions* 119 (1939): 53–77.

92. See Ginzburg, *Ecstasies*, 100.

93. Cf. *The Night Battles*, 193, and the isolated mention in Peucer, 134.

94. Cf. the observation of Ludwig Wittgenstein, "Bemerkungen über Frazer's *Golden Bough*," *Synthese* 17 (1967): 233–53: "Historical explanation, explanation as a hypothesis of development is only *one* way of gathering

data—their synopsis. It is equally possible to see the data in their mutual relationships and sum them up in a general image that does not have the form of a chronological development."

95. Cf. for all that follows Maja Bošković-Stulli, "Kresnik-Krsnik, ein Wesen aus der kroatischen und slovenischen Volksüberlieferung," *Fabula* 3 (1959–60): 275–98 (a revised version is now available in Italian translation in *Metodi e ricerche*, n.s. 7 [1988]: 32–50). Knowledge of this excellent essay would have permitted me to treat adequately the juxtaposition *benandanti-kresniki*, which was dealt with too hastily in *The Night Battles*, 142. On the enduring vitality of these phenomena, see P. Del Bello, *Spiegazione della sventura e terapia simbolica. Un caso istriano* (thesis defended at the University of Trieste during the academic year 1986–87; the sponsor, G. P. Gri, kindly sent me the most relevant sections).

96. The text was published for the first time in 1837; here I take account of corrections proposed by Bošković-Stulli (279n11) and, independently, by Giuseppe Trebbi, "La Chiesa e le campagne dell' Istria negli scritti di G.F. Tommasini," *Quaderni giuliani di storia* 1 (1980): 43.

97. Bošković-Stulli maintains that the *kresniki* can be both men and women (art. cit., 278); in fact, all the cases cited except one (281) involve men.

98. See Dagmar Burkhart, "Vampirglaube und Vampirsage auf dem Balkan," *Beiträge zur Südosteuropa-Forschung* ... (1966), 211–52 (a very useful essay, although occasionally flawed by over-insistence on such outdated categories as animism or preanimism).

99. Cf. *The Night Battles*, 59–60.

100. For linguistic reasons, the bibliography in Hungarian has remained inaccessible to me. See, however, on the analogy between *benandanti* and *táltos*, the excellent essay by Gábor Klaniczay, "Shamanistic Elements in Central European Witchcraft" and, more generally), Mihály Hoppál, "Traces of Shamanism in Hungarian Folk Beliefs," in *Shamanism in Eurasia* (Göttingen: Edition Herodot, 1984), 404–22, 430–46—both overlooked by Anne Marie Losonczy, "Le chamane-cheval et la sage-femme ferrée. Chamanisme et metaphore équestre dans la pensée hongroise," *L'Ethnographie* 127 (1986): 51–70. These studies complement the bibliographic review by Jenö Fazekas, "Hungarian Shamanism. Material and History of Research," in *Studies in Shamanism*, Carl-Martin Edsman, ed. (Stockholm: Almqvist & Wiksell, 1967), 97–119. In Italian, cf., besides Mihály Hoppal, "Mitologie uraliche," *Conoscenza religiosa* 4 (1978): 367–95, the booklet by A. Steiner, *Sciamanesimo e folklore* (Parma: 1980). Still fundamental, although contentious in part and outdated are Géza Róheim, "Hungarian Shamanism,"

Psychoanalysis and the Social Sciences 3 (1951): 131–69, and Vilmos Diószegi, "Die Ueberreste des Schamanismus in der ungarischen Volkskultur," *Acta Ethnographica Academiae Scientiarum Hungaricae* 7 (1958): 97–134, which summarizes longer works that appeared in Hungarian in 1926 and 1958, respectively. On the ethnographic researches of Diószegi, see T. Dömötör in *Temenos* 9 (1973), 151–55; Éveline Lot-Falck, in *L'homme* 13 (1973), n. 4, 135–41; J. Kodolányi and M. Varga, in *Shamanism in Eurasia*, xiii–xxi. For other indications, see Michael Sozan, *The History of Hungarian Ethnography* (Washington: University Press of America, 1979), 230–45 (on Róheim), 327–30 (on Diószegi). On the etymology of *táltos*, cf. Béla Gunda, "Totemistische Spuren in der ungarischen "táltos"-Ueberlieferung," in *Glaubenswelt und Folklore der sibirischen Völker*, Vilmos Diószegi, ed. (Budapest: Akadémiai Kladó, 1963), 46, which recalls (in the wake of a study by D. Pais) the Turkish *taltis*-taltus—i.e., "he who hits," "he who clubs until the loss of the senses"—seeing in this an allusion to ecstasy (or perhaps to battles?). Another etymology, from the Finnish *tietaja* (wise man, sorcerer), has been proposed by Róheim, art. cit., 146. On Hungarian witchcraft, one can also consult with profit Valesca Klein, "Der ungarische Hexenglauben," *Zeitschrift für Ethnologie* 66 (1934): 374–402.

101. The passage from the trial has been translated by Gyula Ortutay in *Kleine ungarische Volkskunde* (Budapest: Corvina, 1963), 120–21. Cf. also Tekla Dömötör, "The Problem of the Hungarian Female *Táltos*," in Diószegi, ed., *Shamanism in Eurasia*, 423–29, esp. 425.

102. Dömötör, "The Problem of the Hungarian Female *Táltos*," 427.

103. Cf. Klaniczay, art. cit. It should be noted that Diószegi, art. cit., 125 ff., dwells on the theme of the struggle among the *táltos*, but not on its objectives—the fertility of the fields: cf. instead Róheim, art. cit., 140, 142. Mention, albeit quite insufficient, is made of the military organization that emerges from the Hungarian witchcraft trials in *The Night Battles*, 184n73. The wealth of details on this point has led T. Körner, "Die ungarischen Hexenorganisationen," *Ethnographia* 80 (1969): 211 (a summary of an essay that appeared in Hungarian), to suppose that towards the middle of the sixteenth century Hungarian peasants accused of witchcraft had created a real sect, organized militarily. The hypothesis, which is explicitly counterposed to that of Murray on the survival of a prehistoric religious sect is, however, equally lacking in documentary evidence.

104. The connection between *táltos* and *kresniki* had already been grasped by Róheim, art. cit., 146–47. In Bošković-Stulli's essay a comparison with the Hungarian phenomena is absent—as was pointed out by Tekla Dömötör, "Ungarischer Volksglauben und ungarische Volksbräuche zwischen Ost

und West," in *Europa et Hungaria*, Gyula Ortutay and Tibor Bodrogi, eds. (Budapest: Akadémiai Kládo, 1965), 315 (the same criticism applies to *The Night Battles*).

105. See Julius Klaproth, *Voyage au Mont Caucase et en Géorgie*, 2 vols. (Paris: C. Gosselin, 1823) (on the Ossetians, cf. II, 223 ff.).

106. Cf. H. Hübschmann, "Sage und Glaube der Osseten," *Zeitschrift der deutschen Morgenländischen Gesellschaft* 41 (1887): 533.

107. Cf. Klaproth, op. cit., II, 254–55. This passage is not mentioned in the studies cited in the note that follows.

108. Cf. on all this the research of B. Gatiev (1876) and of V. Miller (1882), already singled out and used by Georges Dumézil, *Le problème des Centaures* (Paris: Paul Geuthner, 1929), 92–93. They have been made accessible to me thanks to the help of Aleksándr Gorfunkel (who supplied me with a copy) and of Marussa Ginzburg (who translated it for me). To both my gratitude.

109. Cf. Evliyâ Celebi, *Seyahâtnâme*, VII (Istanbul: Ikdam Matbaasi, 1928), 733–37. Peter Brown, besides telling me about this testimony, sent me an English translation of it. I thank him warmly.

110. It should be noted that (if one excepts the broom) domestic utensils rarely appear among the vehicles used by European witches to go to the Sabbath. Among the exceptions were the witches who sat astride benches and stools, as described by Giovanni Francesco Pico della Mirandola, *Strix sive de ludificatione daemonum* (Bononiae: Hieronymo de Benedictis, 1523) c. Dvr.

111. See *The Night Battles*, 75 ff.

112. Cf. Georges Dumézil, *Il libro degli Eroi. Leggende sui Narti*, trans. Bianca Candian (Milan: Adelphi, 1979), 107–31. Soslan in the country of the dead (the commentary does not consider the analogy with the ecstasy of the *burkudzäutä*). Cf. also Georges Dumézil, *Légendes sur les Nartes suivies de cinq notes mythologiques* (Paris: Honoré Champion, 1930), 103 ff.

113. Cf. Georges Dumézil, *Storie degli Sciti*, trans. Giuliano Boccali (Milan: Rizzoli, 1980), 12; Joel H. Grisward, "Le motif de l'épée jetée au lac: la mort d'Artur et la mort de Badraz," *Romania* 90 (1969): 289–340, 473–514.

114. On the very brief states of loss of consciousness that precede the vocation and transformation into animals of the *táltos*, cf. Diószegi, art. cit., 122 ff.; of a different opinion is Róheim, 162.

115. Cf. Vincent Foix, "Glossaire de la sorcellerie landaise," *Revue de Gascogne* (1903): 368–69, 450 (I thank Daniel Fabre for having informed me of this essay and sending me a copy).

116. Among the *benandanti*, one (Menichino from Latisana) mentioned only three dates—St. Matthew, Corpus Domini, St. John; cf. *The Night*

Battles, 75. Among the *táltos*, the only precise date indicated is the night of St. George, in the area of Debrecen: see Róheim, art. cit., 120.

117. It is obvious that each of these elements, taken by itself, delimits a much vaster space, unusable, in fact, for the purposes of this research. For confirmation, see Ernst Arbman, *Ecstasy or Religious Trance*, 3 vols. (Stockholm: Bokforlaget, 1963–1970), which, assuming I have perused it accurately, does not even mention the phenomena analyzed here.

118. The reference is to Ludwig Wittgenstein's celebrated pages, *Philosophical Investigations*, para. 65 ff. It is known that the notion of "family resemblance" (p. 47, para. 67) was suggested by an experiment of Francis Galton. I have not seen any acknowledgement (but someone will certainly have made it) of the likely conduit between Wittgenstein and Galton's work, namely, Freud's *Interpretation of Dreams*, where "family resemblances" are introduced in a slightly different sense, to illustrate the phenomena of dream condensation. On the theme in general and its implications, see Rodney Needham's fundamental "Polythetic Classification," *Man* n.s. 10 (1975): 349–69.

119. For all this, see Mircea Eliade, "Some Observations on European Witchcraft," *History of Religions* 14 (1975): 158–59. In general see also Harry A. Senn, *Were-Wolf and Vampire in Rumania* (Boulder, CO: East European Monographs, 1982).

120. See *The Night Battles*, 63.

Chapter Four

1. Earlier versions of this chapter were delivered as the Hayes Robinson Lecture in History, Royal Holloway College, University of London (March 2014), the keynote to a conference on "Resistance and Revolution" at Florida State University (February 2015), and the inaugural lecture of the Société d'histoire des religions de Genève (June 2015). The last of these was published as "Le loup-garou et ses juges: Le drame de la résistance religieuse," *Asdiwal* 10 (2015): 111–36.

2. Olaus Magnus, *Historia de Gentibus Septentrionalibus, earumque Diversis Statibus, Conditionibus, Moribus, Ritibus, Superstitionibus, disciplinis, exercitiis, regimine, victu, bellis, structuris, instrumentis, ac mineris metallicis, & rebus mirabilibus* (Rome: Pont. Max. ne quis ad Decennium imprimat., 1555), book XVIII, chap. 45, "On the Ferocity of People Turned into Wolves" (De ferocia Hominum in Lupos conversorum):

> In Prussia, Livonia, atque Lithuania, quam vis luporum rapacitatem per totum pene annum incolæ haud exiguo cum damno experiuntur,

quia eorum pecora ingenti multitudine passim in sylvis, dummodo
exiguo intervallo a grege aberrant, dilaniantur, ac consumuntur: tamen
hoc dispendium non adeo magnum ab illis reputatur, quam quod
ab hominibus in lupos conversos sustinere coguntur. In festo enim
Nativitatis CHRISTI sub noctem, statuto in loco quem inter se determinatum habent, tanta luporum ex hominibus diversis in locis habitantibus
conversorum copia congregatur, quæ postea eadem nocte mira ferocia
cum in genus humanum, tum in cætera animalia, quæ feram naturam non
habent, sævit, vi maius detrimentum ab his, istius regionis inhabitatores,
quam unquam a veris & naturalibus lupis accipiant. Nam uti compertum
habetur ædificia hominum in sylvis existentium, mira cum atrocitate
oppugnant, ipsasque fores effringere conantur, quod tam homines, quam
reliqua animantia ibidem manentia consumant. Cellaria cervisiarum in-
grediuntur, ac illic aliquot cervisiæ, aut medonis tonnas epotant, ipsaque
vasa vacua in medio cellarii unum super aliud elevando collocant: in quo
a nativis ac genuinis lupis discrepant.

3. Theophilius Sincerus, *Nord-Schwedische Hexerey, oder Simia Dei, Gottes
Affe. Das ist: Auszführliche Beschreibung der schändlichen Verführungen des
leidigen Satans, darinnen zusehen Gottes erschröckliches Straff-Verhängen,
wegen greulicher Sünden-Mengen* (n.p., 1677), 31:

> Nicht unfüglich lässet sich alhier bey dieser Gelegenheit (weilen ich
> ohne dis der Teufflischen Verwandlung gedencke) mit anfügen, das
> gemeine ja leider überhand genommene und eingerissene Land-übel, so
> sich meistens in denen Nordischen Landen, und daselbst angränszenden
> Fürstenthümern absonderlich in Cur- und Lieffland zueräget, dasz sich
> allda die Hexen und zauberischen Unholden in Wölffe verwandeln, bey
> Nacht-Zeit herum lauffen die Leute, Vieh und Feld-Früchten jämmer-
> lich beschädigen, und grossen Schaden verursachen; (dahero sie auch
> Wahr- oder Gefahr- und von etlichen gar Fahr-Wölffe genennet werden),
> des Morgens gegen Tage (wann man es wil beobachten) stehet man
> stehduffig über Feld und nach Haus ihren Dörffern und Wohnungen zu,
> wieder anheim lauffen, da sie dann ihre natürliche menschliche Gestalt
> wieder annehmen, ihre Gewerb und Verrichtungen gleich andern Men-
> schen leisten und üben, essen, trincken, reden, und leben wie verständige
> Menschen zu thun pflegen.

Similar accounts can be found in a great many authors of the period,
including Philip Melanchthon, "Annales Ph. Melanthonis ad annum 1558,
spectantes," in *Philippe Melanchthonis opera quae supersunt omnia*, vol. IX,
ed. Carolus Gottlieb Bretschneider (Halle: Schwetschke, 1842), 717–18,

and "Historiae Quaedam recitatae a Philippo Melanchthone inter Publicas Lectiones CXXXI" (1559), in *Corpus Reformatorum* vol. XX, ed. Henricus Ernestus Bindseil (Braunschweig, 1854), 552; Hermann Witekind, writing under the name Augustin Lercheimer von Steinfelden, *Christlich bedencken und erinnerung von zauberey* (1586), republished by Anton Birlinger, *Augustin Lercheimer und seine Schrift wider den Hexenwahn* (Strassburg: J. H. E. Heitz, 1888), 58; Kaspar Peucer, *Commentarius de præcipuis generibus divinationum* (Wittenberg: I. Crato, 1560), 141–45; Paul Einhorn, *Wiederlegunge der Abgötteren und nichtigen Aberglaubens, so vorzeiten auß der heydnischen Abgötterey in diesem Lande entsprossen und bißhero in gebrauche blieben* (Riga: Gerhard Schröder, 1627), chap. VI, "Concerning Lycanthropy or Werewolves: What to Believe about Them" (Von den Lycanthropia oder Waerwölffen, was von denen zu halten); and Hans Jakob Christoph von Grimmelshausen, *Der abenteuerliche Simplicius Simplicissimus*, ed. Emil Ermatinger (Cologne: 1961; original 1669), 468.

4. I am grateful to Professor Jurgis Skilters, Director of the Center for Cognitive Sciences and Semantics at the University of Latvia; Dr. Kristine Ante; and Dr. Marins Mintaurs for help in identifying the Latvian names now used for the locales the transcript gives in German.

5. The trial transcript was first published by Hermann von Bruiningk, "Der Werwolf in Livland und das letzte im Wendenschen Landgericht und Dörptschen Hofgericht i. J. 1692 deshalb stattgehabte Strafverfahren," *Mitteilungen aus der livländischen Geschichte* 22 (1924): 163–220. The text is in Middle German, with occasional Latin phrases inserted, and at points it clearly represents a paraphrase, not a verbatim record of what was said. Whether Thiess and other witnesses testified in German or in the vernacular is unclear. The text is divided into seventy-nine numbered sections, plus a preamble introducing the court and the judges and a transcript of the verdict. The incident of the witness's smile is described in paragraph 1.

6. Thiess trial, paragraph 1, von Bruiningk, 203: "R: Es wüste ja jederman, dasz er mit dem teuffell umbginge und ein wahrwolff wehre; wie er den schwehren köndte, weil er solches selber nicht leugnen würde und von langen jahren solches getrieben."

7. Thiess trial, paragraph 2.

8. Thiess trial, paragraph 3.

9. For comparison of the testimony to stereotyped accounts found in learned literature, see Appendix A.

10. Thiess trial, paragraphs 6, 8, 9, 10, 11, 13, 14, 15, 20, 31, and 32.

11. There is only one other datum from this region in which werewolves are construed in opposition to sorcerers, witches, and the devil. This is

a story reported as fact by Hermann Witekind (1522–1603), who taught in Riga and maintained an epistolary relation with Philip Melanchthon (1497–1560), his former teacher. Melanchthon relied on Witekind for his knowledge of events in Livonia, occasionally making mention of the latter's reports in his own publications and sharing them with his nephew, Kaspar Peucer (1525–1602), professor of mathematics and sometime rector at the University of Wittenburg. Witekind published this story under the pseudonym Augustin Lercheimer von Steinfelden, in a volume titled *Christlich Bedencken und erinnerung von zauberey* (Strassburg, 1586). Peucer, however, had already published it in his *Commentarius de præcipuis generibus divinationum* (Wittenberg: Johannes Crato, 1560). Both authors take it as an actual occurrence and cite it as evidence that the reported occurrences of werewolfery, being physically impossible, ought be understood as illusions produced by the devil. The item of most immediate interest to us, however, is that the accused describes werewolves as the enemies of witches in response to the charges against him, explaining that he did not mean to harm the horse he killed and dismembered, for he swung his weapon at a witch hiding behind the horse and accidentally struck the latter (see Appendix B). Here, as in the case of Thiess, the werewolf-witch opposition emerges as part of a defensive gambit, whereby the accused sought to clear himself by inverting stereotyped images ("Yes, I am a werewolf, but we werewolves are *good*, being the enemies of witches").

12. Thiess used this image at paragraphs 19, 44, and 62.

13. No translation adequately captures all the nuances of this term (= modern German *Segen*), which figures prominently in Thiess's account. Most literally it is a blessing, and in some passages it has that meaning only (paras. 64, 65, 68. 69, 71, and 72). In most occurrences, however (paras. 13, 15, 19, 30, 32, and 62), it denotes the blessing of prosperity, fertility, abundance, and a good harvest, as well as the divine favor or grace that makes these possible and of which they are the material consequence and expression.

14. Thiess trial, paragraphs 11, 12, 15, 19, 24, 30, 35, 44, 62, and 63.

15. Thiess trial, paragraph 20, von Bruiningk, 207–8: "Q: Ob das nicht böse gethan sey, dasz er seinem nechsten sein vieh nicht nur eigener bekentnis nach raube, sondern vornemblich auch das ebenbild Gottes, worzu er als ein mensch erschaffen, seiner einbildung nach in einen wolff verstelle."

16. Thiess trial, paragraph 32, von Bruiningk, 210: "Wie solches möglich seyn könne . . . dasz es nur eine falsche einbildung und teüffelischer betrug und verblendung sey?" See also paragraphs 27, 31, and 63. Ever since St. Augustine, orthodox theology maintained that metamorphosis from human to

animal state was impossible, since this would nullify God's will as expressed in his creation of the human body after his own image. The putative experience of lycanthropic transformation was thus theorized as an illusion created by the devil, which affected both what was seen by those who reported werewolf attacks and the consciousness of those who in sleep, dream, or hallucination, believed they had passed into a wolf's body. This remained the standard explanation thereafter, although a small number of theologians, most notably Jean Bodin, entertained the possibility of real physical transformation. Einhorn, *Wiederlegunge der Abgötteren*, chap. VI, provides a view of contemporary opinion in Livonia, where some thought the werewolf's soul entered a wolf's body, while others held that his body transformed into that of a wolf. Speaking on behalf of religious and legal authorities, however, Einhorn (who was both a Lutheran pastor and superintendent of the Kurland district), insisted that werewolfery "is nothing other than the devil's work and doing, through which he deludes wretched people" (*Ist aber nicht mehr als bey Teuffels Werck und Getrieb, damit er daß elende Volk bethöre*). On these theories, see Nicole Jacques-Lefèvre, "Such an Impure, Cruel, and Savage Beast: Images of the Werewolf in Demonological Works," in Kathryn A. Edwards, ed., *Werewolves, Witches, and Wandering Spirits: Traditional Belief and Folklore in Early Modern Europe* (Kirksville, MO: Truman State University Press, 2002), 181–97; on their influence in early modern Livonia, see Tiina Vähi, "The Image of Werewolf in Folk Religion and Its Theological and Demonological Interpretations," in Manfried L. G. Dietrich and Tarmo Kulmar, eds., *The Significance of Base Texts for the Religious Identity / Die Bedeutung von Grundtexten für die religiöse Identität* (Münster: Ugarit, 2006), 213–37.

17. *Seegensprecher* (Modern German *Segensprecher*) literally denotes one who pronounces blessings (*Segen*), but it usually has a pejorative connotation, indicating a conjuror and charlatan. The pastor entered the procedings just after Thiess had been describing the magic formulas he recited as part of his healing practice, so it is likely that the pastor meant to play on the term's ambiguity, describing Thiess as one who portrayed himself as a speaker-of-blessings, but whom religous authorities rightly regarded as a misguided poser.

18. Thiess trial, paragraph 60, von Bruiningk, 214: "Weil nun der Hr. Pastor hujus loci Magister Bucholtz mit anhero erbeten ward, dem actui beyzuwohnen, ward er ersucht, diesen selbst geständigen seegensprecher und in des teüffels stricken gefangenen sünder auch zuzusprechen, ihme seine grobe sünde, wozu er sich verführen laszen, und darinnen bishero so lange und viele jahre verharret, zu gemühte zu führen und das gewiszen zu rühren, ob er zu bekehren undt zur busze, auch einer rechtschaffenen reüe

und zur ablassung von dergleichen teüffelischen wesen zu bewegen undt zu bringen stehen möchte."

19. Thiess trial, paragraph 61; cf. paragraph 75.

20. Thiess trial, paragraph 63, von Bruiningk, 215: "Er verstünde es beszer als der Hr. Pastor, der noch jung wehre, und ärgerte sich über des Hrn Pastoris zurehden."

21. Thiess trial, paragraph 62, von Bruiningk, 215: "Ille erwiese sich hierauff gahr verstockt und blieb beständig dabey, dasz solches alles, was er begangen, keine sünde wieder Gott wehre, sondern Gott vielmehr dadurch ein dienst geleistet und deszen willen erfüllet würde, den sie nähmen dem teuffell den seegen, so die zauberer ihm zutrügen, wieder weg und thäten dem ganzen lande dadurch gutes."

22. Thiess trial, paragraph 78, von Bruiningk, 218: "Ob man auch zwahr folgig bey der session zu Wenden die acta vornahm, kondte und wolte man sich dennoch über einen so schwehren und miszlichen casum zu keinem definitiven auszspruch entschlieszen, sondern ward erhehblich erachtet, solches nochmahlsz bisz zu supplirung des collegii durch die ehist gewärtige ankunfft des neuen Hrn. Landrichters von Palmbergs." See also paragraphs 75, 77, and 79.

23. At paragraph 78, the court announces its intention to have the case considered again upon arrival of the new District Court Judge von Palmberg (*des neuen Hrn. Landrichters von Palmbergs*). When von Palmberg was delayed, as reported in paragraph 79, Judge von Trautvetter served "in place of the absent district court judge" (*in stelle des abwehsenden Hrn. Landrichters*). In that capacity, von Trautvetter presided over the review and issued the final decision, subject to ratification by the Royal Court of Dorpat.

24. In an important study of roughly fifty trials of accused Livonian werewolves, Tālivaldis Zemzaris found Thiess's trial and his punishment to be among the most lenient in the set, marking a shift to more tolerant attitudes. Zemzaris, "Vilkaču prāvas Vidzemē" ("Werewolf Trials in Vidzeme"), in Margers Stepermanis, ed, *Latvijas Vēstures Institūta žurnāls* 3 (1939): 115–41.

25. Otto Höfler, *Kultische Geheimbünde der Germanen* (Frankfurt am Main: Moritz Diesterweg, 1934), 345–57.

26. Carlo Ginzburg, *Ecstasies: Deciphering the Witches' Sabbath*, trans. Raymond Rosenthal (New York: Pantheon Books, 1991), first published in Italian as *Storia Notturna. Una decifrazione del sabba* (Turin: Einaudi, 1989).

27. Mircea Eliade, "Some European Secret Cults," in Helmut Birkhan, ed., *Festgabe für Otto Höfler* (Vienna: Wilhelm Braumüller, 1976), 190–204.

28. Hans Peter Duerr, *Traumzeit: Über die Grenze zwischen Wildnis und Zivilisation* (Frankfurt: Syndikat, 1978), 49–50, 60–61, 80, 108, and 237–38.

29. Gábor Klaniczay, *The Uses of Supernatural Power: The Transformation of Popular Religion in Medieval and Early-Modern Europe* (Princeton: Princeton University Press, 1990), 133–37.

30. Éva Pócs, "Hungarian Táltos and his European Parallels," in Mihály Hoppál and Juha Pentikäinen, eds., *Uralic Mythology and Folklore* (Budapest: Ethnographic Institute of the Hungarian Academy of Sciences, 1989), 251–74; Pócs, "Nature and Culture—'The Raw and the Cooked': Shape-Shifting and Double Beings in Central and Eastern European Folklore," in Willem de Blécourt and Christa Agnes Tuczay, eds., *Tierverwandlungen: Codierung und Diskurse* (Tübingen: Francke, 2011), 99–134.

31. For a summary of current thought on the repeated failings and remaining possibilities of comparative research of this type, see the essays collected in Claude Calame and Bruce Lincoln, eds., *Comparer en histoire des religions antiques* (Liège: Presses Universitaires de Liège, 2012). My own thoughts on the topic appear as "Theses on Comparison," 99–101 in that volume, reprinted in *Gods and Demons, Priests and Scholars: Critical Explorations in the History of Religions* (Chicago: University of Chicago Press, 2012), 121–30.

32. Starting with von Bruiningk, op. cit., Baltic scholars have treated the werewolf trials with an eye toward local religion and culture in tension with that of the foreign elite. The rich scholarly literature includes Karlis Straubergs, "Om Varulvarna i Baltikum," in Sigurd Erixon, ed., *Liv och Folkkultur* (Stockholm: Samfundet för Svensk Folklivsforskning, 1955), 107–29; Maia Madar, "Estonia I: Werewolves and Poisoners," in Bengt Ankarloo and Gustav Henningsen, eds., *Early Modern European Witchcraft: Centres and Peripheries* (Oxford: Clarendon Press, 1990), 257–72; Vähi, "The Image of Werewolf"; Tiina Vähi, "Werwölfe—Viehdiebe und Räuber im Wolfspelz? Elemente des archaischen Gewohnheitsrechts in estnischen Werwolfvorstellungen," in de Blécourt and Tuczay, eds., *Tierverwandlungen*, op. cit., 135–56; Andrejs Plakans, "Witches and Werewolves in Early Modern Livonia: An Unfinished Project," in Lars M. Andersson, Anna Jansdotter, Badil E. B. Persson, and Charlotte Tornbjer, eds., *Rätten: En Festskrift till Bengt Ankarloo* (Lund: Nordic Academic Press, 2000), 255–71; Merili Metsvahi, "Werwolfprozesse in Estland und Livland im 17. Jahrhundert. Zusammenstöße zwischen der Realität von Richtern und von Bauern," in Jürgen Beyer and Reet Hiiemäe, eds., *Folklore als Tatsachenbericht* (Tartu: Sektion für Folkloristik des Estnischen Literaturmuseums, 2001), 175–84; Willem de Blécourt, "A Journey to Hell: Reconsidering the Livonian 'Werewolf,'" *Magic, Ritual, and Witchcraft* 2 (2007), 49–67; Stefan Donecker, "The Werewolves of Livonia: Lycanthropy and Shape-Changing in Scholarly Texts,

1550–1720," *Preternature: Critical and Historical Studies on the Preternatural* 1 (2012), 289–322; Donecker, "Livland und seine Werwölfe: Ethnizität und Monstrosität an der europäischen Peripherie, 1550–1700," *Jahrbuch des baltischen Deutschtums* 56 (2009): 83–98; and Donecker, "Werewolves on the Baltic Seashore: Monstrous Frontier of Early Modern Europe, 1550–1700," in Niall Scott, ed., *The Role of the Monster: Myths & Metaphors of Enduring Evil* (Oxford: Inter-Disciplinary Press, 2009), 63–75.

33. According to Astaf von Transehe, "Stadtbürger als Lehnsleute des livländischen Adels. Eine rechtshistorische Studie," *Jahrbuch für Genealogie, Heraldik und Sphragistik of the Kurländischen Gesellschaft für Literatur und Kunst* (1898), 13, the Ackerstaff (or Ackersdorf) family was established in the vicinity of Nitau and Lemburg from the fifteenth century, where they served as vassals of the German nobility. Over multiple generations, they acquired more status and property, including Klingenberg, the estate where they resided from 1498 onward.

34. Thiess trial, paragraph 23, von Bruiningk, 208: "Weil ja kundbahrer weise er ein bettler und ganz unvermögend sey."

35. The sole exception is Marienburg (today's Alūksne), located more than sixty miles west of the others. Since Thiess blamed a "scoundrel from Marienburg" for having first made him a werewolf, it may be that he was deflecting unwelcome questions by describing his powers as having a distant origin.

36. See Madar, "Estonia I: Werewolves and Poisoners" and Metsvahi, "Werwolfprozesse in Estland und Livland im 17. Jahrhundert," op. cit.

37. Stefan Donecker, "The Medieval Frontier and Its Aftermath: Historical Discourses in Early Modern Livonia," in Imbi Sooman and Stefan Donecker, eds., *The "Baltic Frontier" Revisited: Power Structures and Cross-Cutural Interactions in the Baltic Sea Region* (Vienna: n.p., 2009), 41–62; "Konfessionalisierung und religiöse Begegnung im Ostseeraum," in Andrea Komlosy, Hans-Heinrich Nolte, and Imbi Sooman, eds., *Ostsee 700–2000: Gsesellschaft, Wirtschaft, Kultur* (Vienna: Promedia, 2008), 91–109; "Livland und seine Werwölfe, op. cit.; and "Werewolves on the Baltic Seashore," op. cit. See further Vilho Niitemaa, *Die undeutsche Frage in der Politik der livländischen Städte im Mittelalter* (Helsinki: Annales Academiae Scientiarum Fennicae, 1949); Paul Johansen, "Nationale Vorurteile und Minderwertigkeitsgefühle als sozialer Faktor im mittelalterlichen Livland," in *Alteuropa und die Moderne Gesellschaft: Festschrift für Otto Brünner* (Göttingen: Vandenhoeck & Ruprecht, 1963), 88–115; Paul Johansen and Heinz von zur Mühlen, *Deutsch und Undeutsch im mittelalterlichen und frühneuzeitlichen Reval* (Cologne: Böhlau, 1973); Juhan Kahk, "Heidnische Glaubensvor-

stellungen, Zauberei und religiöse Eifer in Estland um 1700," *Zeitschrift für Ostforschung* 34 (1985): 522–35; and Wilhelm Lenz, "*Undeutsch*: Bemerkungen zu einem besonderen Begriff der baltischen Geschichte," in Bernhart Jähnig and Klaus Militzer, eds., *Aus der Geschichte Alt-Livlands: Festschrift für Heinz von zur Mühlen* (Münster: Lit Verlag, 2004), 169–84.

38. Donecker, "The Medieval Frontier and Its Aftermath," 48.

39. Ioanne Georgio Godelmanno, *Disputatio de Magis, Veneficis et Lamiis* (Frankfurt: Christophorus Corvinus, 1584), book II, chap. III, sec. 26: "Quid de Lycanthropis in Liuonia statuendum, authoris vera relatio" (What is established concerning werewolves in Livonia: the author's true account.):

> Diabolus eorum, qui se in lupos credunt transmutatos externos sensus sopit & obcoecat: ita, ut in profundissimum somnum incidant, deinde varias rerum formas in pueris, vel infectandis, vel vorandis, sive iumenta laedendo, aut longe lateque vagando, veteranus hic praestigiator obiicit, quas perturbatis iam eorum humoribus, & animis imprimit tam efficaciter, ut se re ipsa lupos esse & fuisse credant. Talibus praestigiis & lusibus delectatur Diabolus, ut misera illa, & DEI ignara mancipia excruciet, atque in errore ac superstitione confirmet. Sunt enim rustici in Liuonia homines miserrimi, superstitiosi, barbari, mera Dominorum mancipia & qui in omnibus parere coguntur, nam si imperata recusant, aut negligenter officium ipsis commissum praestant virgis castigantur, & duriter tanquam pecudes tractantur. Unde apparet huiusmodi homines ac nationes hoc genere Imperii delectati, aut saltem patienter hoc imperium ferre.

40. Thiess's was one of the last trials for werewolfery. Most of the earlier trials ended with a confession extracted by torture, often to avoid conviction on the more serious charge of witchcraft. See Metsvahi, "Werwolfprozesse in Estland und Livland," op. cit., 176–77; and Vähi, "Hexenprozesse und der Werwolfglaube in Estland," op. cit., 226–27 and 230.

41. Thiess repeatedly cited the Nitau court's indulgent treatment of him as something like a precedent that ought lead the Wenden court to recognize not only his innocence but that of werewolves in general. See trial paragraphs 2, 3, 63, 64, and 72.

42. Thiess trial, paragraph 64, von Bruiningk, 215: "Wen solches sünde wehre, so würden die vorige richter, vor denenen er, und die woll so klug alsz die izzige gewehsen, solches auch woll verstanden, ihn deszen berichtet und nicht dahrüber gelachet haben."

43. Thiess trial, paragraph 3, von Bruiningk, 204: "Der substituirter Hr. Landrichter Bengt Johan Ackerstaff, alsz unter wessen gute er in vorigen zeiten auch einige jahre gelehbett und gedienet, declarirte dasz es ihme an

gesundem verstande nimmer gefehlet, er auch solches sein wehsen nimmer
verleügnet und, nachdehme ihme vor diesem von den damaligen richtern
desfalsz nichts geschehen, desto freyer solches getrieben und von den
bauren gleich einem abgotte gehalten worden."

44. Thiess trial, paragraph 20, von Bruiningk, 208: "Und das gelübde,
so er seinem erlöser Christo in der hl. Tauffe gethan, da er dem teüffel und
allem seinem wesen und wercken entsaget, Gotts vergeszener weise breche
und dergleichen höchst verbotene sünde andern zum abscheü und ärgernis
so beharlich treibe und nicht zu Gottes hause, wo er sonst durch die predigt
und christliche lehrer zu Gottes erkäntnis und dienste gelangen könte, sich
begäbe, sondern lieber der höllen zulauffe" (emphasis added in translation).

45. Thiess trial, paragraph 33, von Bruiningk, 210: "Q: Ob er dann nicht
des vorsatzes sey, vor seinem tode sich zu Gott zu bekehren, von seinem
willen und wesen sich unterrichten zu laszen, von solchem teüffelischen
unwesen abzustehen, seine sünde zu bereüen und seine seele von der ewigen
verdamnis und höllen pein dadurch zu erretten? R: Hierauff wolte er nicht
recht antworten, sagete, wer wüste, wo seine seele bleiben würde; er wäre
nun schon alt, was könte er solche dinge mehr begreiffen."

46. Thiess trial, paragraph 18, von Bruiningk, 207: "Q: Where do the
werewolves go after death? A: They are buried like other people and their
souls come to heaven, but the devil takes the sorcerers' souls for himself.
Q: Is the witness diligent toward the church, does he listen faithfully to the
word of God, does he pray diligently, and does he take the Lord's Supper?
A: No, he does neither the one nor the other." (Q: Wo die wahrwölffe nach
dem tode hinkähmen? R: Sie würden begraben wie andere leüte und ihre
seelen kähmen in den himmel; der zäuberer seelen aber nähme teüffel
zu sich.—Q: Ob referent sich fleiszig zur kirchen halte Gottes wort mit
andacht anhöre, fleiszig bäte und sich zum hl, Nachtmahl halte? R: Negat, er
thue weder eines noch das andere.) Cf. paragraph 62.

47. Thiess trial, paragraph 5, von Bruiningk, 204: "Q: Wie dan referent
nach der höllen gekommen und wo dieselbe gelehgen sey? R: Die wahrwölffe gingen zu fusz dahin in wölffe gestalt, der ohrt wehre an dem ende
von der see, Puer Esser genand, im morast unter Lemburg, etwa 1/2 meyle
von des substituirten Hr. Praesidis hoffe Klingenberg, alda wehren herliche
gemächer und bestellete thürhüter, welche diejenige, so etwas von der von
den zauberern dahin gebrachter korn-blüte und dem korn selber wieder
austragen wolten, dichte abschlügen. Die blüte würde in einem sonderli-
chen kleht verwahret und das korn auch in einem andern." Cf. paragraphs 11,
12, 13, 15, 19, 30, 44, and 62.

48. A fairly deep relation connected the judge and the defendant, as indi-

cated by the trial transcript, paragraph 3, von Bruiningk, 204: "In addition to the others present who knew Thiess well, the substitute Herr District Court Judge Bengt Johan Ackerstaff, who had known him well in previous times when Thiess worked for him for several years, declared that he understood his health never to have failed him, also that he never lied about such things, and that in his opinion, nothing happened in the earlier case with the afore-mentioned judges, so that he was set free and he was idolized by the peas-ants. (Wohrauff nehben dehnen andern anwehsenden, so den Thiessen woll kandten, der substituirter Hr. Landrichter Bengt Johan Ackerstaff, alsz unter wessen gute er in vorigen zeiten auch einige jahre gelehbett und gedienet, declarirte dasz es ihme an gesundem verstande nimmer gefehlet, er auch solches sein wehsen nimmer verleügnet und, nachdehme ihme vor diesem von den damaligen richtern desfalsz nichts geschehen, desto freyer solches getrieben und von den bauren gleich einem abgotte gehalten worden.)

49. On Latvian constructions of the otherworld as close at hand, located in lakes, swamps, and burial grounds, also a realm where the seasons are the reverse of ours, such that fertility resides there in the winter when absent from the earth's surface, see Karlis Straubergs, "Zur Jenseitstopographie," *Arv* 13 (1957); 56–110, esp. 85–90.

50. Thiess trial, paragraph 16, von Bruiningk, 206–7.

51. The sorcerers' feasts with the devil in hell are mentioned at paragraphs 6, 11, and 24.

52. Thiess describes the sorcerers' thefts at paragraphs 5, 12, 13, 15, 19, 44, and 62.

53. Thiess trial, paragraph 24, von Bruiningk, 208: "Q: Did they receive any sign from the devil through which he could know them? A: No, but he branded the sorcerers and was generous with them." (Q: Ob sie kein zeichen von dem teüffel bekähmen, woran er sie erkennen könne? Negat. Die zauberer aber zeichnete er undt dieselbe tractirte.)

54. Thiess trial, paragraph 44, von Bruiningk, 212: "Q: Had he then made so strong a pact with the devil that he cannot withdraw from it? A: The devil has nothing to do with him." (Q: Ob er denn einen so festen bund mit dem teüffel gemachet, dasz er nicht davon ablaszen wolle? R: Der teüffel hätte nichts mit ihm zu thun.)

55. The judges (or pastor) place the devil in antithetical opposition to God at paragraphs 19, 20, 33, 61. They speak of the devil's temptations, lies, and delusions at paragraphs 27, 31, 32, 56, 63, and 75, describing how he leads people into sin at paragraphs 27, 33, 43, 60, and 61 and to damnation at paragraphs 33, 43, and 61.

56. Thiess trial, paragraphs 33–36, von Bruiningk, 210:

Q: Wo er denn das wahrsagen gelernet, weil ja viele leute zu ihm giengen und ihn befrageten, was ihnen begegnen würde? R: Er könte nicht wahrsagen, sondern er wäre ein pferdeartzt, und wann andere sünder jemands pferden leyd angethan hätten, so hiebe er sie wieder auff, und nehme solches wieder von ihnen hinweg, wozu er einige und nur etwa 3 worte gebrauchte, und ihnen salz oder brodt eingebe, welches er mit den worten vorhin gesegnet hätte. Q: Was vor sünder er verstehe, so den pferden leyd anthäten? R: Dieselben teüffelsmacher oder hexen, welche nichts als böses thäten. Q: Was es dann vor worte wären, die er dabey gebrauchte? R: Sonn undt mond gehe übers meer, hole die seele wieder, die der teüffel in die hölle gebracht und gib dem vieh das leben und die gesundheit wieder, so ihm entnommen,—und solches hülffe so woll anderm viehe als den pferden.

Cf. paragraph 52, where sorcerers are also said to cause disease.

57. Thiess trial, paragraphs 5, 12, 13, 15, 19, 44, and 62.

58. Thiess trial, paragraphs 11, 16, and 24.

59. Thiess trial, paragraphs 18 and 19.

60. Thiess trial, paragraphs 5, 12, 13, 15, 19, 39, 44, and 62

61. Thiess trial, paragraph 15, von Bruiningk, 206:

Q: Wie referent sagen könne, dasz sie den diesjährigen seegen bereit verwichene Lucien nacht aus der hölle wieder heraus bekommen, welchen die zauberer dahin gebracht, weil ja die saat undt blühte zeit nun erst bevorstehe und also noch nichts dahin gebracht seyn könne? R: Die zauberer hätten ihre sonderliche zeit und säete der teuffel schon lange voraus. Davon nehmen die zauberer alsdann etwas und brächten es in die hölle und solchen seegen trügen die wahrwölffe wieder aus der hölle, und darnach fiele alsdann der wachsthumb von unserer saat ausz, wie auch von obst bäümen, dergleichen auch bey der höllen viele wären, undt von fischerey; auf Weynachten wäre schon vollkommen grün korn allerhand arth und baum gewächs imgleichen bey der höllen.

Cf. paragraphs 12, 30, 44, 62. Of particular interest is paragraph 19, von Bruiningk, 207, where the devil himself is identified as a thief:

Q: How can the soul of someone who does not serve God, but the devil, and who does not go to church, seldom to confession, and does not take the Lord's Supper, as the witness has admitted of himself, ever come to God?

A: The werewolves do not serve the devil, for they take away from him that which the sorcerers brought him, and for that reason the devil is

so hostile to them that he cannot bear them. . . . Everything the werewolves do profits people best, for if they didn't exist and the devil made
off with the prosperity, robbed or stole it, all the world's prosperity would
depart.

(Q: Wie denn deszen seele zu Gott kommen könne, der nicht Gott
dienet, sondern dem teüffel, auch nicht zur kirchen kommet, weniger
zur beichte und zum hl. Nachtmahl sich hält, wie referent von sich selber
gestehe? R: Die wahrwölffe dieneten dem teüffel nicht, denn sie nehmen
ihme das jenige weg, was die zäüberer ihme zubrächten und deswegen
wäre der teüffel ihnen so feind, dasz er sie nicht leyden könnte . . . alles
was sie, die wahrwölffe, thäten, gereichete dem menschen zum besten,
denn wenn sie nicht wären und dem teüffel den seegen wieder wegstiehlen oder raubeten, so würde aller seegen in der welt weg seyn.)

62. Friedrich von Toll, "Zur Geschichte der Hexenprocesse. Auszug
aus dem Protocoll des Wier- und Jerweschen Manngerichts," *Das Inland*
4 (1839): 258: "Worauf sich der böse Persönlich präsentiret, *in schwartzen
Teutschen Kleidern*" (emphasis added). The significance of this testimony
has been discussed by Donecker, "Livland und seine Werwölfe," 95; and
Donecker, "Werewolves on the Baltic Seashore," 67–68. Much the same
kind of testimony recurs in a 1641 trial in Pärnu, where the accused testified
that the devil appeared to him "as a German" (cited in Madar, "Estonia I:
Werewolves and Poisoners," op. cit., 271).

63. Ülo Valk, "Reflections of Folk Belief and Legends at the Witch
Trials of Estonia," in Eszter Csonka-Takacs, Gabor Klaniczay, and Eva Pócs,
eds., *Witchcraft Mythologies and Persecutions* (Budapest: Central European
University Press, 2008), 269–82; the passage cited appears at 273. See further
Valk, *The Black Gentleman: Manifestations of the Devil in Estonian Folk
Religion*, trans. Ülle Männarti (Helsinki: Suomalainen Tiedeakatemia, 2001),
esp. secs. 1.3.1 and 1.3.2, "The Devil as a Landlord" and "The Demonisation
of the German Noblemen in the 17th and 18th Centuries," 74–85 and 86–92,
respectively.

64. Thiess discussed sorcerers in paragraphs 5, 12, 13, 15, 18, 19, 24, 44,
52, and 62. This notwithstanding, neither the judges nor the pastor showed
much interest in the topic, mentioning sorcerers only once, when they tried
to trip Thiess up in a contradiction (para. 15).

65. Thiess trial, paragraph 19, von Bruiningk, 207: "Everything the
werewolves do profits people best, for if they didn't exist and the devil made
off with the prosperity, robbed or stole it, all the world's prosperity would
depart, and (the witness) confirmed this with an oath." (Alles was sie, die

wahrwölffe, thäten, gereichete dem menschen zum besten, denn wenn sie
nicht wären und dem teüffel den seegen wieder wegstiehlen oder raubeten,
so würde aller seegen in der welt weg seyn, und solches bestätigte er mit
einem eyde.)

66. See Appendix A and Vähi, "Werwölfe—Viehdiebe und Räuber im
Wolfspelz?," op. cit.

67. The judges introduced theft of livestock nine times (paras. 8, 9, 10, 11,
20, 29, 31, and 32, and the verdict), compared to the two times they asked
about grain (paragraphs 15 and 30). Thiess responded to such concerns five
times (paras. 8, 9, 10, 20, and 32) and mentioned seizing animals on three
other occasions (paras. 6, 7, 12). In contrast, he introduced the recovery of
agricultural items from the underworld nine times, usually dwelling on it at
length (paras. 2, 5, 11, 12, 13, 15, 19, 30, 62).

68. Thiess trial, paragraphs 9–10, von Bruiningk, 205: "Q: Weil sie in
wölffe verwandelt wären, warumb sie dann nicht das fleisch rohe, wie wölffe,
verzehreten? R: Das wäre die weise nicht, sondern sie äszen es als menschen
gebraten. Q: Wie sie es handtieren können, weil sie ja wolffes häupter und
pfoten seiner auszage nach haben, womit sie kein meszer halten noch spiesze
bereiten und andere darzu erforderte arbeit verrichten können? R: Meszer
gebrauchten sie nicht darzu, sie zerriszen es mit den zähnen und steckten die
stücker mit den pfoten auf stöcker, wie sie dieselbe nur finden, undt wenn
sie es verzehreten, so wären sie schon wieder als menschen, gebrauchten
aber kein brodt darbey; saltz nähmen sie von den gesindern mit sich, wenn
sie ausgiengen."

69. Thiess trial, paragraph 17, von Bruiningk, 207: "Q: Ob nicht weiber
undt mägde mit unter den wahrwölfen, auch Deutsche sich darunter befin-
den? R: Die weiber wären woll mit unter den wahrwölffen, die mägde aber
würden dazu nicht genommen, sondern die würden zu fliegenden Puicken
oder drachen gebrauchet und so verschicket und nehmen den segen von der
milch und butter weg. Die Deutschen kähmen nicht in ihre gemeinschafft,
sondern hätten eine sonderliche hölle."

70. Thiess's remarks about young women allude to the belief that the
devil could steal the spirit from milk and butter, leaving them insipid and
tasteless. Butter that had suffered such a fate was called "dragon butter"
(Drachen-Butter). A discussion of this is found in Christian Kortholt, under
the pseudonym Theophilius Sincerus, Nord-Schwedische Hexerey, op. cit.,
14–15.

71. Thiess trial, paragraph 19, von Bruiningk, 207 (cf. para. 62): "In the
preceding year, the Russian werewolves came earlier and had recovered
the prosperity of their land. Therefore they had also had good growth in

their land, while that of this land failed, for they had come too late on this side. But this year they came before the Russians and thus it was a fruitful year and good for flax." (Die Ruszischen wahrwölffe wären im vergangenen jahre was früher gekommen und hätten ihres landes seegen davon gebracht. Darumb hätten sie in ihrem lande auch ein gut gewächs gehabt, woran es diesem lande gefehlet, weil sie von dieser seiten obberichteter maaszen zu späte gekommen. Dies jahr aber wären sie den Ruszen zuvor gekommen undt würde also ein fruchtbahr auch ein gut flachs jahr seyn.)

See also paragraph 14 for the assertion that those from different villages belong to different bands (es wären unterschiedliche rotten). Here, Thiess specifies that Skeistan, who broke his nose, belonged to another band of werewolves, although Ginzburg and others regularly misidentify him as having been a sorcerer.

72. Thiess described werewolves' relation to hell as hostile and fleeting, in contrast to that of sorcerers, who were recurrent visitors, welcomed and entertained by the devil. The contrast is drawn most clearly in paragraph 11, von Bruiningk, 205: "The sorcerers eat with the devil in hell. The werewolves were not admitted there with them. Nevertheless, they sometimes quickly run in and snatch something, then run back with it as if fleeing." (Die zauberer aber äszen mit dem teuffel in der hölle, die wahrwölffe würden nicht mit dazu gestattet, sie lieffen dennoch bisweilen eilig hinein undt erschnapten etwas und lieffen denn wieder damit als fliehend hinaus.)

Cf. paragraphs 11, 12, 20, and 24. Paragraph 16, von Bruiningk, 206–7, is particularly significant for its implication that sorcerers "belong" in hell, along with the devil: "Q: Whenever you go to other feasts at that place in hell, do you find such buildings and do the same ones consistently stay there? A: Yes. Q: How is it that the other people who dwell nearby can't also see this? A: It's not on top but under the earth, and the entrance is protected by a gate that no one can find, except someone who belongs inside." (Q: Ob allezeit, wenn sie zu andern mahlen sich an dem gemelten orth der höllen begeben, sie solche gebäüde da fanden und dieselbe beständig allda verbleiben? Affirmat.—Q: Wie es denn andere da herumb wohnende leüte nicht auch sehen können? R: Es sey nicht über, sondern unter der erden, und der eingang mit einer pforten verwahret, welche niemand finden könne, alsz der dahin gehöre.)

73. After Thiess refused to repent (paras. 63 and 64, von Bruiningk, 215), the judges turned their attention back to the thief Pirsen Tönnis, whose trial was interrupted by the revelation of Thiess's werewolfery. This man now was asked about Thiess's history and prior dealings, at which point he implicated Gurrian Steppe (paras. 65 and 66, von Bruiningk, 215–16), whom the tran-

script identifies as both a peasant of Jürgensburg (*der Jürgensburgsche baur*) and an old innkeeper (*der alte wirth*). Gurrian was then called to testify and admitted he had sought and obtained healing and prosperity from Thiess (para. 69, von Bruiningk, 216–17).

74. Thiess trial, paragraph 75, von Bruiningk, 217–18:

Nachdehme nun beydes das kgl. Landgerichte, wie auch der Hr. Pastor hujus loci Magister Buchholz sowoll dem Gurrian alsz dem Thiessen die damit betriebene grobe sünde und teuffelische verführung auch aberglauben und abgötterey ernstlich und bewehglich vorgehalten, so doch der Thiess nicht begreiffen wolte, muste der Gurrian, welcher ohne dem selbst in einem bösen gerüchte, dasz er dem veneficio ergehben sey, stehet, praesente judicio et toto congressu, insonderheit in conspectu aller anwehsenden bauren, umb dehnenselben den wahn, alsz ob dahrinnen einige heyligkeit wehre und dawieder nichts verhenget werden köndte, bey mit ansehen des Thiessen, so dabey ganz bestürzt stand, ein bündichen nach dem andern mit eigener hand in das zu solchem ende angelehgtes feur werffen und nach vorsprache des Hrn. Pastoris loci den wahren Gott dabey umb gnädige verzeihung und vergehbung seiner dahrunter begangener sünde bitten, auch hinführo sich dergleichen höchst verbotener gegangener dinge zu äuszern und zu enthalten, bey vermeydung zeitlicher und ewiger straffe angeloben, so er cum horrore et tremore verrichtete, und ward dabenehben, umb die dadurch der gemeine gegehbene ärgernüsz offentlich zu büszen, folgenden sontages wehrender prehdigt am kirchen-pfost zu stehen und peractis sacris mit 12 paar ruhten durch den hoffes executoren gestrichen zu werden, gerichtlich condemniret, auch der Hr. Pastor loci darbey der ganzen gemeine den greuel und hohe straffalligkeit solches wehsens, seiner dexterität nach, nachdrücklich vorzustellen und einen jeden davon abzumahnen ersuchet.

75. Thiess trial, paragraph 76, von Bruiningk, 218:

Ungeachtet nun der vielfaltigen vermahnung, so an den Thiessen geschehen, andere mehr, so dergleichen mittell bey ihme gesuchet und bekommen, wie auch, was er dafür bekommen hette, namhafft zu machen, wolte derselbe sich doch zu keiner weitern bekänntnüsz lenken lassen, vorwendend, wie köndte er sich daszen so erinnern; er wehre ein alter kerl und köndte kaum mehr gedenken, was gestern geschehen were. Wer hette ihm auch viel gegehben, biszweilen einen, biszweilen zwey, auch 3 schillinge oder sonst etwas, offte gahr nichts, den solches wehre keine kauffmanschafft, wo man geld vor fordern müste, es stünde in eines jeden freyen willen, ob er was gehben wolte oder nicht.

76. Thiess trial, final verdict, von Bruiningk, 219–20:

Demnach ausz inquisiti selbst eigener auszuge erhellet, dasz er von langen jahren hehr alsz wahrwolff sich erwiesen und mit andern herumb gelauffen, auch in der hölle gewehsen, und in solche maasze einen und andern raub an vieh und mehrere dergleichen actus mit begehen helffen, alsz ist er nicht nur desfalsz, ob gleich dieses für eine teufflische verblendung zu achten stehet, weil er gleichwoll solcher meinung so veste auch noch vor gerichte angehangen und wehder durch gerichtliche noch des Jürgensburgschen Hrn. Pastoris bewehgliche zurehde sich davon ableiten laszen wollen, auch seiner dem Hrn. Pastori loci vorhin gethaner angelobung zu wieder nicht davon abgestanden, noch sich zum gehör Göttl. wohrts und gebrauch der hl. Sacramenten selbst gestandener maaszen eingefunden, sondern auch, weiln er wieder höchsten Gottes und weltlicher obrigkeit ernstlichen verboht allerhand wahrsagung und seegen sprechereyen getrieben und dadurch sich schwehrlich versündiget und andere nehben sich zum aberglauben verführet.

77. Thiess trial, final verdict, von Bruiningk, 219–20:

Ihme zur wollverdienten straffe und andern zum merklichen abscheu hiemit zum öffentlichen staupenschlage, idoch in ansehen seines hohen alters, nur mit 20 pahr ruhten durch des scharftrichters hand bey Lemburg vor öffentlicher versamlung der unter solches kirchspiel gehörigen baurschafft, dehnen der Hr. Pastor loci vorhehro den terminum executionis anzudeuten und ihnen dabenehben dieses maleficiantis hartes verbrechen vorzustellen, auch andere von dergleichen ärgerlichen und sträftlichen wandell auch aberglauben abzumahnen selbst gefliszen seyn wird, und nechst solchem zur ewigen landes verweysung.

Chapter Five

1. I developed some implications of this point in my essay "Microhistory and World History," in J. H. Bentley, S. Subrahmanyam, and M. E. Wiesner-Hanks, eds., *The Cambridge World History*, vol. VI, *The Construction of a Global World, 1400–1800 CE*, part 2: *Patterns of Change* (Cambridge: Cambridge University Press, 2015), 447–73.

2. Carlo Ginzburg, *The Night Battles: Witchcraft and Agrarian Cults in the Sixteenth and Seventeenth Centuries*, trans. John Tedeschi and Anne C. Tedeschi (London: Routledge & Kegan Paul and Baltimore: Johns Hopkins

University Press, 1980), 28–32. Originally published as *I benandanti: Stregoneria e culti agrari tra Cinquecento e Seicento* (Turin: Einaudi, 1966).

3. Carlo Ginzburg, "The Inquisitor as Anthropologist," in Ginzburg, *Clues, Myths, and the Historical Method,* trans. John Tedeschi and Anne C. Tedeschi (Baltimore: Johns Hopkins University Press, 1989), 156–64.

4. Marc Bloch, *Les rois thaumaturges: études sur le caractère surnaturel attribué à la puissance royal, particulièrement en France et en Angleterre* (Strasbourg: Librairie Istra, 1924); published in English as *The Royal Touch: Sacred Monarchy and Scrofula in England and France,* trans. J. E. Anderson (London: Routledge & Kegan Paul, 1973).

5. Carlo Ginzburg, "Freud, l'uomo dei lupi e i lupi mannari," in *Clues, Myths, and the Historical Method,* 146–64, at 148.

6. Carlo Ginzburg, *Storia notturna: Una decifrazione del sabba* (Turin: Einaudi, 1989).

7. Bruce Lincoln, "Un loup-garou de Livonie: le drame de la résistance religieuse," *Asdiwal,* 10 (2015), 111–35. For a different version, see "The Werewolf, the Shaman, and the Historian: Rethinking the Case of 'Old Thiess' after Carlo Ginzburg," the 2015 Hayes-Robinson Lecture, Royal Holloway College, University of London (http://backdoorbroadcasting.net/2015/03/bruce-lincoln-the-werewolf-the-shaman-and-the-historian-rethinking-the-case-of-old-thiess-after-carlo-ginzburg). See, moreover, Willem de Blécourt, "The Return of the Sabbat: Mental Archaeologies, Conjectural Histories or Political Mythologies?" in Jonathan Barry and Otto Davies, eds. *Palgrave Advances in Witchcraft Historiography* (Basingstoke and New York: Palgrave MacMillan, 2007), 125–45, especially 128–29; de Blécourt, "A Journey to Hell: Reconsidering the Livonian 'Werewolf,'" *Magic, Ritual, and Witchcraft* 2 (2007): 49–67; de Blécourt, "Spuren einer Volkskultur oder Dämonisierung? Bemerkungen über Ginzburgs *Die Benandanti,*" *Kea. Zeitschrift für Kulturwissenschaften,* 2 (2007): 17–29. I commented on these essays in my essay "Travelling in Spirit: From Friuli to Siberia," in Marjorie Mandelstam Balzer, Jan Bremmer, and Carlo Ginzburg, *Horizons of Shamanism: A Triangular Approach to the History and Anthropology of Ecstatic Techniques,* Peter Jackson, ed. (Stockholm: Stockholm University Press, 2016), 35–51.

8. Lincoln, "Un loup-garou de Livonie," 119 (all translations from this essay are mine).

9. Lincoln, "Un loup-garou de Livonie," 115n5.

10. Lincoln, "Un loup-garou de Livonie," 132.

11. Bruce Lincoln (with C. Grottanelli), "Theses on Comparison," in Lincoln, *Gods and Demons, Priests and Scholars: Critical Explorations in the*

History of Religion (Chicago: University of Chicago Press, 2012), 121–30, particularly 123.

12. Lincoln, "Un loup-garou de Livonie," 114–15n3. See Ginzburg, *Storia notturna*, 130–34 (on Peucer, see Ginzburg, *I benandanti*, 40). Another critic of my approach, Willem de Blécourt (see note 7, above), also failed to notice my discussion of Peucer's text, therefore weakening his argument: this has been noted by Matteo Duni, "'What about Some Good Wether?' Witches and Werewolves in Sixteenth-Century Italy," in de Blécourt, ed., *Werewolf Histories* (New York: Palgrave Macmillan, 2015), 121–41, especially 132–34. Duni, who did not focus on Peucer's remark concerning the werewolves' hostility against the witches, refused to unfold its implications for his valuable analysis, based on some inquisitorial trials held in Modena in the early sixteenth century, arguing that "the specific traits found in each of [the documents] would be diluted" ("What about Some Good Wether?," 135). This self-defeating approach was contradicted in another passage of the same essay that praised Maurizio Bertolotti's demonstration of an "ancient and widespread complex of European folklore, typical of societies based on hunting" (126).

13. Augustin Lercheimer (Hermann Witekind), *Christlich Bedencken und Erinnerung von Zauberey* (Strassburg, 1586).

14. Casper Peucer, *Commentarius de praecipuis generibus divinationum* (Wittenberg: Johannes Crato, 1560), 141v–142r. The description of were-wolves' swoon introduces a comparison with sorcerers (i.e., shamans) from Lapland: a detail which I should have mentioned, as Matteo Duni rightly noted ("What about some Good Wether?," 140n40).

15. Peucer, *Commentarius*, 144v: "Ait se veneficam ignei papilionis specie circumvolitantem persequutum esse (gloriantur enim lycanthropi quod ad arcendas veneficas conducantur)." On werewolves's swoon (that Peucer compared to shamans'), see 141v ff.

16. Carlo Ginzburg, *Ecstasies: Deciphering the Witches' Sabbath*, trans. Raymond Rosenthal (New York: Pantheon Books, 1991), 13; first published in Italian as *Storia Notturna: Una decifrazione del sabba* (Turin: Einaudi, 1989).

17. Lincoln (with Grottanelli), "Theses on Comparison," 123.

18. Claude Lévi-Strauss, "Split Representation in the Art of Asia and America," in *Structural Anthropology*, Harmondsworth: Penguin, and New York: Basic Books, 1963), 245–68, in particular 258 (I quoted this passage in *Ecstasies*, 225n54).

19. Claude Lévi-Strauss, "Une science révolutionnaire: l'ethnographie,"

in *De Montaigne à Montaigne*, ed. Emmanuel Désveaux (Paris: Editions EHESS, 2016), 33–62. In his introduction, Désveaux comments on the "diffusionist moment" of Lévi-Strauss.

20. Petronius, *Satyricon*, 42: "At ille circumminxit vestimenta sua, et subito lupus factus est."

21. Pliny, *Naturalis Historia*, VIII, 34, 80–84.

22. Helen King, "Sacrificial Blood: the Role of Amnion in Greek Gynaecology," *Helios* 13 (1986): 117–26 (many thanks to Maria Luisa Catoni, who pointed out the meaning of *amnion* to me).

23. Ginzburg, *Ecstasies*, 265–66.

24. Carlo Ginzburg, *History, Rhetoric, and Proof* (Hanover, NH: University Press of New England, 1999).

25. Carlo Ginzburg, "Family Resemblances and Family Trees: Two Cognitive Metaphors," *Critical Inquiry* 30 (Spring 2004): 537–56.

26. Carlo Ginzburg, "Das Nachäffen der Natur. Reflexionen über eine mittelalterliche Metapher, in *Fälschungen. Zu Autorschaft und Beweis*," in Anne-Kathrin Reulecke, ed., *Wissenschaft und Künsten* (Frankfurt am Main: Suhrkamp, 2006), 95–122; "Dante's Blind Spot (Inferno XVI–XVII)," in Sara Fortuna, Manuele Gragnolati and Jürgen Trabant, eds., *Dante's Pluringualism. Authority, Knowledge, Subjectivity* (London: Legenda, 2010), 149–63; and "The Artist as Counterfeiter," in Mihaela Irimia and Dragos Ivana, eds., *Imitatio-Inventio: The Rise of "Literature" from Early to Classic Modernity* (Bucharest: Institutul Cultural Român, 2010), 11–32.

27. Sebastiano Timpanaro, *The Genesis of Lachmann's Method*, trans. Glenn Most (Chicago: University of Chicago Press, 2005), 49; and *La genesi del metodo del Lachmann*, new ed. (Turin: UTET, 2003), 19–20.

28. Paul Maas, *Textual Criticism*, trans. Barbara Flower (Oxford: Clarendon Press, 1958), 43. Maas's approach has been strongly criticized by Luciano Canfora, "Il problema delle 'varianti d'autore' come architrave della *Storia della tradizione* di Giorgio Pasquali," *Quaderni di storia* 75 (gennaio-giugno 2012), 1–29. If I am not mistaken, Canfora's forceful argument does not affect the cognitive potential of *errores conjunctivi* (conjunctive errors), an argument that of course had a long history before Paul Maas.

29. Timpanaro, *La genesi del metodo del Lachmann*, 17–18.

30. The second chapter of the second part of my book *Storia notturna* (p. 99 ff.) was entitled "Anomalie" (Anomalies).

31. Maas, *Textual Criticism*, 13. See also 12: "We must distinguish sharply between anomaly and *singularity*. What is unique is not for that reason alone to be regarded with suspicion" (here the author's usual laconicity turns into evasiveness).

32. Gianfranco Contini, *Breviario di ecdotica* (Milan and Naples: Ricciardi, 1986), 71, recalls that Gaston Paris, in his edition of *La vie de Saint Alexis* (Paris: A. Franck, 1872), "soggiungeva addirittura che invece di errore ('faute') si può dire: innovazione ('modification') comune; e a copisti ('scribes') sostituire: rimaneggiatori ('renouveleurs')."

33. Ginzburg, "Family Resemblances," 552.

34. Ginzburg, *Storia notturna*, 28 (*Ecstasies*, 14).

35. Giorgio Pasquali, *Storia della tradizione e critica del testo* (Milan: A. Mondadori 1974; 1st ed. 1934; nuova ed. 1952), 41 ff.

Chapter Six

1. Francis Galton, "Composite Portraits," *Journal of the Anthropological Institute of Great Britain and Ireland* 8 (1878): 134–35. The experiment failed to produce its desired results, however, as Galton noted. Instead of revealing "the special villainous irregularities" of the criminal, it leveled these out such that the composites were "much better looking than those of their components . . . they represent not the criminal, but the man who is liable to fall into crime." Note also the remarks DuCane offered after the conclusion of Galton's lecture (*Journal of the Anthropological Institute of Great Britain and Ireland* 8, 142–43). For Galton's later reflections on this project, see further Galton, *Memories of My Life* (New York: Dutton, 1909; first publ. London: Methuen, 1908), 259–60.

2. Sir Francis Galton and F. A. Mahomed, "An Inquiry into the Physiognomy of Phthisis by the Method of Composite Portraiture," *Guy's Hospital Reports* 25 (February 1882): 475–93.

3. Galton, *Memories of My Life*, 262. Galton also took this experiment to be a failure since "their features (i.e. those of 'lunatics') are apt to be so irregular in different ways that it was impossible to blend them."

4. Sir Francis Galton, "Photographic Composites," *Photographic News* (1885): 243–45. See also a closely related article by a student of Galton's, Joseph Jacobs, "The Jewish Type, and Galton's Composite Photographs," *Photographic News* 29 (April 24, 1885): 268–69, which opens as follows: "Most people can tell a Jew when they see one. There is a certain expression in Jewish faces which causes them to be identified as such in almost every instance" (268).

5. Anon., "A Typical Girl-Portrait by Galton's Method," *Photographic News* 29 (April 24, 1885): 512.

6. Galton, "Composite Portraits," 132 ff.

7. Carlo Ginzburg, "Conjunctive Anomalies—A Reflection on Werewolves," pp. 109–26, above.

8. You will surely note that ecstasy drops out of this diagram, since this trait makes no appearance in Thiess's trial, nor in the Russian texts. It does figure in some of the learned accounts of Livonian werewolves, however, and we can discuss that further, if you like.

9. Most recently on this literature, see Johannes Dillinger, "'Species', 'Phantasia', 'Raison': Werewolves and Shape-Shifters in Demonological Literature," in Willem de Blécourt, ed., *Werewolf Histories* (New York: Palgrave Macmillan, 2015), 142–58. With particular reference to the influence this literature exercised in the Baltic, see Tiina Vähi, "The Image of Werewolf in Folk Religion and Its Theological and Demonological Interpretations," in Manfried L. G. Dietrich and Tarmo Kulmar, eds., *The Significance of Base Texts for the Religious Identity / Die Bedeutung von Grundtexten für die religiöse Identität* (Münster: Ugarit, 2006), 213–37; and Stefan Donecker, "The Werewolves of Livonia: Lycanthropy and Shape-Changing in Scholarly Texts, 1550–1720," *Preternature: Critical and Historical Studies on the Preternatural* 1 (2012), 289–322.

10. Peter Jackson, "Cycles of the Wolf: Unmasking the Young Warrior in Europe's Past" in Peter Haldén and Peter Jackson, eds., *Transforming Warriors: The Ritual Organization of Military Force* (London: Routledge, 2016), 37–38. The similarities Jackson adduces between the stereotypes of Livonian werewolves and the foundation myth of the Roman Lupercalia are intriguing, but better explained through their connection to cattle raiding in very different eras than by an appeal to their common origins in Indo-European antiquity. The latter move is all too similar to Höfler's, albeit without his political motives. See Tiina Vähi, "Werwölfe—Viehdiebe und Räuber im Wolfspelz? Elemente des archaischen Gewohnheitsrechts in estischen Werwolfvorstellungen," in Willem de Blécourt and Christa Agnes Tuczay, eds., *Tierverwandlungen: Codierung und Diskurse* (Tübingen: Francke, 2011), 135–56. The same emphasis on theft and consumption of cattle figures prominently in the werewolf case most spatiotemporally proximate to the *benandanti*, recently discussed by Duni, "'What about Some Good Wether?' Witches and Werewolves in Sixteenth-Century Italy," in Willem de Blécourt, ed., *Werewolf Histories* (New York: Palgrave Macmillan, 2015), 121–41. But you will know more about that case than I do.

11. Here, it should be noted that Thiess began his testimony by focusing on the werewolves' recovery of agricultural products and values (trial transcript paras. 2–5) and sought to keep discussion focused on this point (paras. 12–15, 19, 30, 62) or on the therapeutic care he gave to animals (paras. 34–36, 46–59, 65–69). At a number of points, however, the judges press

questions regarding the theft and consumption of livestock (paras. 6–11, 20, 29, 31–32).

12. Ginzburg, 109–26, above.

13. Caspar Peucer, *Commentarius de præcipuis generibus divinationum* (Wittenberg: Johannes Crato, 1560), 133v–134r; Hermann Willken (later Witekind and Witekindus), writing under the pseudonym Augustin Lercheimer von Steinfelden, *Christlich bedencken und erinnerung von zauberey* (Strassburg, 1586). The latter text is most readily available in Anton Birlinger, *Augustin Lercheimer und seine Schrift wider den Hexenwahn* (Strassburg: J. H. E. Heitz, 1888), 58.

14. The term denotes a figure who oversaw peasant labor on behalf of the lord and was therefore bitterly resented. According to Ineta Polanska, *Zum Einfluss des Lettischen auf das Deutsche im Baltikum* (Bamberg: PhD. dissertation in linguistics, Otto Friedrich Universität, 2002), 303–4, the text's parenthetical gloss—*wagger*—is a loanword from Latvian *vagars* into Baltic German. I am grateful to Stefan Donecker for the reference.

15. Karlis Straubergs, *Latviešu buramie vārdi* (Latvian Blessing Spells), vol. II (Riga: Latviešu Folkloras Krātuves Izdevums, 1941), 495. Almost certainly, the original trial transcript would have been in German, traces of which remain in the parenthetical glosses. Straubergs apparently translated the transcripts into Latvian, perhaps to let the defendant speak in his own language, as an expression of nationalist sentiment:

[1] Vai viņš ir vilkatis, kā rūna?

Esot 20 g. vilkačos skrējis, bet savu vilka ādu tēva brālim atdevis uzdzeŗot.

[2] Kā šis to darījis?

Esot prasījis uzdzeŗot: "Brāli, vai tu gribi amatu, kas man ir?," un kad tas ar "jā" atbildējis, amatu nodevis, un uz jautājumu, kas par to jādod, atteicis: "gabals gaļas," ko pircējs arī iedevis; viņš to atlaidis ar vārdiem: "Eji laimīgs un kalpo savam kungam uzticīgi, kā es to esmu darījis."

[3] Kas tas viņa kungs, un kur viņi sanāk kopā?

Viņu kungs tiem parādījies pie Tukuma uz kāda kalna netālu no hercoga izpriecas pils (Fürsten lusthause) kā muižnieks un mājojis pie sava zemnieka Šenkinga; sanāksmes viņi noturot katros ziemas svētkos, vasaras svētkos un Jāņos, pie kam tos sevišķs vagaris (wagger) pieteicot (angesaget würden); selbigen wohneten auch die hexen bey, kuŗu darbs esot labības ziedus no laukiem zagt un savam kungam pienest, bet šie, vilkači, ņemot tos viņām nost un restituējot īpašniekiem, lai tiem nekāds zaudējums nenotiktu.

[4] Kādā izskatā tiem jāierodas?

Viņiem no kunga esot ziede, ar ko tiem jāieziežas, un tad tie topot pavisam viegli un vilka ādā, ko katrs sev mājās glabājot, fuhren. Tad tos izsūtot kungam cepeti atnest; aitas tie nokožot un nesot kungam, kas tās ar alu un miestiņu apēdot.

[5] Vai arī šis aitas nokodis?

Daudzas, kur tik saticis.

[6] Kur?

Visur ārpus zemes, kur kungs dzīvojis.

[7] Lūgšanas prot, pie sv. vakariņa iet—kāpēc pie dieva neturoties? Jau priekš 8 g. atmetis amatu un vairs neskraidot vilkačos apkārt.

[8] Kam viņš sevišķi ko ļaunu darījis?

Nevienam.

According to Metsvahi, "Werwolfprozesse in Estland und Livland im 17. Jahrhundert. Zusammenstöße zwischen der Realität von Richtern und von Bauern," in Jürgen Beyer and Reet Hiiemäe, eds., *Folklore als Tatsachenbericht* (Tartu: Sektion für Folkloristik des Estnischen Literaturmuseums, 2001), 175–84, at 178, this is the only testimony similar to Thiess's in the surviving records of Livonian werewolf trials.

16. Roman Jakobson and Marc Szeftel, "The Vseslav Epos," *Memoirs of the American Folklore Society* 42 (1947): 13–86, at 69.

17. Jakobson and Szeftel, "The Vseslav Epos," 62–63.

18. Jakobson and Szeftel discussed their reasons for translating *jazva* and *jazv'no* as "caul" at 56–57, arguing against many previous translators who rendered them as "wound." Note, however, that virtually all lexicographical authorities consistently define *jazva* as "wound, abscess," and this meaning is well established throughout the Slavic language family (e.g., Ukranian *jázvá, jázvýna*, "wound; abyss" and Old Bulgarian *jazva*, "hollow, cavity; ulcer"). See, inter alia, I. I. Sreznevsky, *Materialy dlja slovarja drevne-russkago iazyka* (St. Petersburg: Tipografia imperatorskoj Akademij Nauk, 1893–1912), col. 1643; Max Vasmer, *Russisches etymologisches Wörterbuch* (Heidelberg: Carl Winter, 1950–58), 3:484–85; and A. G. Preobrazhensky, *Etymological Dictionary of the Russian Language* (New York: Columbia University Press, 1951), 135–36 of the separately numbered final section. Sreznevsky, col. 1644–45, however, offered "skin, hide" (Russian *koža*) and "film" (*plenka*) as definitions for *jazv'no*, with specific reference to the the *Primary Chronicle*'s account of Vseslav's birth. Jakobson and Szeftel extended this interpretation to cover *jazva* as well, making their broader argument much easier, but with very little philological justification.

19. "Въ лѣто 6552 . . . умьре Брячиславь, сынъ Изяславль, вънукъ

Володимерь, отьць Вьсеславль, и Вьсеславъ, сынъ его, сѣде на
столѣ его. Сего же роди мати отъ вълхвования: матери бо родивъши
его, бысть ему язва на главѣ его; рекоша же вълсви матери его: 'се
язвьно навяжи на нь, да носить е до живота своего,' еже носить
Вьсеславъ и до сего дьне на собѣ; сего ради немилостивъ есть на
кръвопролитне." Donald Ostrowski, ed., *The povešt'vremennykh let: An
Interlinear Collation and Paradosis* (Cambridge: Harvard University Press,
2003).

20. The three passages read:

1. He leapt like a wolf to the Nemiga. On the Nemiga they spread sheaves
of heads, threshed with sharp flails. скочи влъкомъ до Немиги
съ<ду> токъ. На Немизѣ снопы стелютъ головами, молотятъ
чепи харалужными. (line 157)

2. Prince Vseslav judged the people. As prince, he ruled the city, but
at night he roamed by himself like a wolf. Вьсеславъ князь людемъ
судяше, княземъ грады рядяшее, а самъ въ ночь влъкомъ
рыскаше. (line 159)

3. Like a wolf, he crossed the path of Great Xors [a pagan deity].
великому Хръсови влъкомъ путь прерыскаше. (line 159)

A. A. Zaliznjak, *Slovo o Polku Igoreve: Vzgljad Lingvista* (Moscow: Jazyki
Slavjanskoj Kyltury, 2004).

21. Supporting interpretation of these references to wolves as metaphoric
is the fact that other heroes are also compared to wolves, without implication of lycanthropy, as in the following: "When Igor flew like a falcon, then
Ovlur ran like a wolf." (Коли Игорь соколомъ полетѣ, тогда Влуръ
влъкомъ потече; Zaliznjak, *Slovo*, line 191).

22. Thus Vladimir Propp, *L'epos eroico russo*, trans. Salvatore Arcella
(Rome: Newton Comptor, 1978), 82.

23. Volx's birth is narrated in lines 1–11 of his *bylina*. His father is identified as a "fierce serpent" (or dragon: *ljota zmeja*) at lines 5–6. Text from
Jakobson and Szeftel, "The Vseslav Epos," 81.

24. *Bylina* of Volx Vseslav'evič, lines 18–25:

для ради рожденья
молода Вольха Всеславьевич.
рыба пошла в морскую глубину,
птича полетела ысоко в небеса,
туры да олени за горы пошли,
зайци, лисицы по чашицам,

а волки, медведи по ельникам,
соболи, куницы по островам.

25. *Bylina* of Volx Vseslav'evič, lines 43–51, text from Jakobson and Szeftel, "The Vseslav Epos," 82:

А и будет Волх десяти годов
поучися Вольх ко премудростям;
а и первой мудростн учился [Волх]
обвертоваться яасным соколом;
ко другой-то мудрости учился он, Вольх—
обвертоваться серым волком;
ко третей-то мудрости учился он, Вольх—
обвертоваться гнедым туром,
[гнедым туром]—золотыя рога

Jakobson and Szeftel, 28 ff., cite variants on this passage, including one they consider "probably more archaic," presumably because it preserves a structure in which the animal transformations (pike/bird/beast) correspond to cosmic regions (water/air/land), instead of one that begins with the distinction air/land (falcon/others) and subdivides land into predator/prey (wolf/aurochs):

At that time Vol'ja Vseslav'evič
Learned to go as a pike in the free sea.
He learned to fly as a bird in the heavens.
He learned to course as the fierce beast in the plain.

Да втопоры Вольия Всеславьевич
училса-бы в вольнем море щукой ходить
училса-бы по поднебесью птицею летать
училса-бы по полю лютым зверем рыскати.

N. Ončukov, *Pečorskie byliny* (St. Petersburg, 1904), no. 84, lines 46–49.

26. *Bylina* of Volx Vseslav'evič, lines 69–71.

27. *Bylina* of Volx Vseslav'evič, lines 81–83, 109–10, 137–40.

28. *Bylina* of Volx Vseslav'evič, lines 104–7.

29. *Bylina* of Volx Vseslav'evič, lines 129–32.

30. *Bylina* of Volx Vseslav'evič, lines 159–66.

31. Russian also uses the form *vurdalak* to denote a werewolf, but only from the nineteenth century onward. On the relation among these and the forms attested in other Slavic languages, see Francis Butler, "Russian *vurdalak* 'vampire' and Related Forms in Slavic," *Journal of Slavic Linguistics*

13 (2005): 237–50, *pace* Johanna Nichols, "Russian *vurdalak* 'werewolf' and Its Cognates," in Michael Flier and Sin Karlinsky, eds., *Language, Literature, Linguistics: In honor of Francis J. Whitfield* (Berkeley: Berkeley Slavic Specialities, 1987), 165–75.

32. The character's name reflects the common noun *volxv*, "sorcerer, magician," as recognized by Jakobson and Szeftel, "The Vseslav Epos," 14–15; Propp, *L'epos eroico russo*, 79, and others.

33. Jakobson and Szeftel, "The Vseslav Epos," 13 (twice), 18 (twice), 20, 22, 23, 44, 62, 63.

34. Jakobson and Szeftel, "The Vseslav Epos," state, as orienting assumptions of their research: "A common Slavic werewolf tradition may be supposed and, in general outline, even reconstructed" (60), "a wolf cult in the pre-Christian Slavic past is very probable" (68). Further: "If the 'Neuroi' in Herodotus' report are really ancestors of the Slavs [a most unlikely assumption] . . . the legends about their magic ability to change themselves into wolves and about their struggle with serpents give us a glimpse of the distant Slavic past and of its mythology" (68).

35. Jakobson and Szeftel, "The Vseslav Epos," 58–62, where a wide variety of evidence is introduced rather breathlessly and uncritically, including a fair number of non-Slavic examples (Swedish, Norwegian, Icelandic, Turkish, Greek, and German). Further, some of the assertions made with regard to this material are quite erroneous, as when Old Icelandic *eigi einhamr* (literally "not having one form") is said to denote a werewolf, rather than a shapeshifter (62n31) or when the guardian spirit known in Old Icelandic as the *fylgja* is said to have had its seat in the child's chorion or caul (61, citing Sir James George Frazer).

36. Antoni Marcinkowski, *Lud Ukrainski*, II (Wilno: T. Glücksberg, 1857), 95–96.

37. Jakobson and Szeftel, "The Vseslav Epos," 59, erroneously cite Edmund Schneeweis, *Grundriss des Volksglaubens und Volksbrauches der Serbokroaten* (Celje: Sv. Mahorja, 1935), 29, for this point. The relevant discussion is actually at Schneeweis, 19, a passage they oversimplified to support their argument:

> Commonly, outlaws turn into vampires [after death], as do people who died with no candles for them, priests who have performed mass when in a state of mortal sin (island of Hvar), Christians who have converted to Islam (Leskovac), witches and men who had supernatural powers during their lives: the *vjedogonja* (from the root *věd-* "to know"), *zduhač* who come into this world with a caul (*košuljica*) and whose spirit can

leave their sleeping bodies and perform actions characteristic of people with superhuman strength, like uprooting trees. The name *vukodlak* (*vuk* "wolf," *dlaka* "hair") originally applied to a living man who can change himself into a wolf for a time (cf. Indic tigranthropy). From the belief that such a person becomes a vampire after death, the identification followed *vukodlak* = *vampir*.

Gewöhnlich werden aber zu Vampiren, Verbrecher, Menschen, die ohne Sterbekerze gestorben sind, Priester, die mit einer Todsünde belastet, die heilige Messe gelesen haben (Insel Hvar), Christen, die zum Islam übertreten (Leskovac), Hexen und Männer, die bei bebzeiten mit übernatürlichen Kräften begabt waren: der (v)jedogonja (zur W. věd- «wissen»), zduhač, der mit einem Glückshäutchen (košuljica) zur Welt kommt und dessen Geist den schlafenden Körper verlassen und Werke verrichten kann, zu denen übermenschliche Kraft gehört, wie Entwurzeln von Bäumen u.ä. Der Name vukodlak (vuk «Wolf», dlaka «Haar») jinnt ursprünglich einem lebenden Menschen au, der sich zeitweise in einen Wolf verwandeln kann (vgl. die indische Tigranthropie). Aus dem Glauben daß ein solcher Mensch nach dem Tode zum Vampir werde, ergab sich die Gleichstellung vukodlak = vampir.

38. See, inter alia, Alberto Fortis, *Travels into Dalmatia* (London: 1778), 61; Prosper Mérimée, "Sur le vampirisme," in *La Guzla, ou choix de Poésies Illyriques, recueillies dans la Dalmatie, la Bosnie, la Croatie et l'Herzegow-ine* (Strasbourg: F.G. Leveault, 1827), 135–56, Schneeweis, *Grundriss des Volksglaubens*, 266 (where *vukodlak* is translated simply as "vampire"); Edmund Schneeweis, *Serbokratische Volkskunde. Erste Teil: Volksglaube und Volksbrauch* (Berlin: Walter de Gruyter, 1961), 8; Peter Skok, *Etimologijski rjetnik hrvatskoga ul srpskoga jezika* (Zagreb: Jugoslavenska Akademija, 1971–75), 636; Dagmar Burkhart, *Kulturraum Balkan. Studien zur Volkskunde und Literatur Südosteuropas* (Berlin: Dietrich Reimer, 1989), 99; Ana Radin, *Motiv vampira u mitu i književnosti* (Belgrade: Prosveta, 1996), 23; and Pieter Plas, "Wolf Symbolism in Western South Slavic Tradition," *Cosmos* 27 (2011): 1–30, esp. 7–11.

39. Along these lines, it is interesting to note that the *bylina* concludes (lines 202–4) by describing the rich booty Volx distributed to his retinue as a result of his victories.

> He rolled out silver and gold,
> Then he gave herds of horses and cattle
> And to every brother a hundred thousand.

он злата-серебра выкатил,
а и коней-коров табуном делил
а на всякого брата по сту тысячей.

Here, as in countless other sources, taking livestock from one's enemy is a glorious accomplishment when done by a noble, while the Livonian material (and countless others) define it as a heinous crime when done by the lower strata. One could expand the comparison to include Old Thiess and the *benandanti* (as in the following table):

Source	What taken	By whom	From whom	Evaluation
Vseslav epos	Gold, silver, horses, cattle	Warrior-prince	Foreigners	Glorious
Livonian judges	Cattle, pigs, livestock	Werewolves (bestial peasants)	Upper strata	Criminal and diabolical
Old Thiess and *benandanti*	Seeds, crops, prosperity	Peasants	Devil and witches	Righteous

40. Carlo Ginzburg, "Germanic Mythology and Nazism: Thoughts on an Old Book by Georges Dumézil," in *Clues, Myths, and the Historical Method*, 122–27; Bruce Lincoln, "Shaping the Past and Future," review of Georges Dumézil, "L'Oubli de l'homme et l'honneur des dieux," *Times Literary Supplement* (October 3, 1986), 1107–8; Lincoln, "Rewriting the German War-God: Georges Dumézil, Politics and Scholarship in the Late 1930s," *History of Religions* 37 (1998): 187–208; and Lincoln, "Georges Dumézil: Continuing Legacy and Continuing Questions," *Archaeus* 4 (2000): 75–89.

Chapter Seven

1. Franco Moretti, "The Slaughterhouse of Literature, *MLQ: Modern Language Quarterly* 61, no. 1 (March 2000): 207–27; "Conjectures on World Literature," *New Left Review*, New Series 1, January–February (2000): 54–68; and "More Conjectures," *New Left Review* 20: March–April (2003): 73–81.

2. Franco Moretti, *Signs Taken for Wonders: On the Sociology of Literary Forms* (London: Verso, 1983), 130–56.

3. Carlo Ginzburg, "Our Words, and Theirs: A Reflection on the Historian's Craft, Today," in S. Fellman and M. Rahikainen, eds., *Historical Knowledge: In Quest of Theory, Method and Evidence* (Cambridge, Cambridge Scholars Publishing, 2012), 97–119, esp. 112 ff.

4. Bruce Lincoln (with Cristiano Grottanelli), "Theses on Comparison," in Lincoln, *Gods and Demons, Priests and Scholars: Critical Explorations in the History of Religions* (Chicago: University of Chicago Press, 2012), 121–30; Lincoln, *Apples and Oranges: Experiments in, on, and with Comparison* (Chicago: University of Chicago Press, 2017), 25–33.

5. Sir William Jones, "The Third Anniversary Discourse, on the Hindus, delivered 2d of February, 1786," in *Works of Sir William Jones* (London: J. Stockdale and J. Walker, 1807), 3:34–35, on which see Bruce Lincoln, "Mr. Jones's Myth of Origins," in *Theorizing Myth: Narrative, Ideology, and Scholarship* (Chicago: University of Chicago Press, 1999), 76–100.

6. Carlo Ginzburg, "Medaglie e conchiglie: Ancora su morfologia a e storia," in *Storia notturna: Una decifrazione del sabba* (Milan: Adelphi, 2017), 347–77, especially 347 (published in English as "Medals and Shells: On Morphology and History, Once Again," *Critical Inquiry* 45, no. 2 [2019]: 380–95). See Wendy Doniger, "Sympathy for the Devil," *New York Times Book Review*, July 14, 1991 (a review of *Storia notturna*, translated into English as *Ecstasies*).

7. Stig Wikander, *Der arische Männerbund: Studien zur indo-iranischen Sprach- und Religionsgeschichte* (Lund: C. W. K. Gleerup, 1938), 64 ff. Wikander had studied under Höfler, and in this work he extended Höfler's thesis to the eastern end of the Indo-European continuity.

8. Carlo Ginzburg, *The Night Battles: Witchcraft and Agrarian Cults in the Sixteenth and Seventeenth Centuries*, trans. John Tedeschi and Anne C. Tedeschi (London: Routledge & Kegan Paul and Baltimore: Johns Hopkins University Press, 1980), 186n88.

9. Lily Weiser, *Altgermanische Junglingsweihen und Männerbünde* (Baden: Konkordia, 1927).

10. Carlo Ginzburg, "Une machine à penser," *Common Knowledge* 18 (Winter 2012: A Special Issue on the Library and Its Readers): 79–85.

11. Wolfgang Behringer, *Shaman of Oberstdorf: Chonrad Stoeckhlin and the Phantoms of the Night*, trans. H. C. E. Midelfort (Charlottesville: University Press of Virginia, 1998).

12. Carlo Ginzburg, "Mitologia germanica e nazismo: Su un vecchio libro di Georges Dumézil," *Quaderni storici* 19 (1984): 857–82, English trans. in *Clues, Myths, and the Historical Method*, 312–30.

13. Carlo Ginzburg, *Ecstasies: Deciphering the Witches' Sabbath*, trans. Raymond Rosenthal (New York: Pantheon Books, 1991), 156 (text cited from A. Lercheimer [H. Witekind], *Christlich Bedencken und Erinnerung von Zauberey* (Heidelberg, 1585).

14. Ginzburg, *The Night Battles*, 103 (trial of Maria Panzona).

15. Carlo Ginzburg, "Just One Witness," in Ginzburg, *Threads and Traces: True False Fictive* (Berkeley: University of California Press, 2012), 165–79, 293–98.

16. I have not translated the incomprehensible phrase that appears at this point in the transcript: "*sein Weib im Worme Beridt vergeben.*" In all likelihood, it is the result of some corruption in copying the text. If that is the case, it may be that some information was lost in the text's transmission, including other details we might otherwise expect concerning the death of Serme Hans's wife under circumstances that led him to accuse Aleit of her sorcerous murder. I am grateful to Stefan Donecker for this suggestion.

17. "Ein Hexenprozess," *Das Inland* 22 (May 29, 1840): 341–42:

Proceß des gehegten Gerichts im Hoffe Fegefewer uber etzliche mit Zauberey berüchtete Persohnen gepflogen Anno 1617 den 20. undt 21. Juny durch die Edle, Ernueste undt Manhaffte Juncker: Otto Premcke, Ludolph Straßborg, Meinert Dittmer, Riclauß Bonichausen.

In bewehsende der auch Erwürdigen undt Wolgelarten Herrn Johannis Popii Pastorn zu Koskull undt Gerten Bartholomaei Pastorn auf Johanniskirche Liberii Palitz Bastian Bock.

Die Alten Pauren, so das Recht eingebracht, seindt nachfolgende: Barne Matz, Gianne Mait, Herria Hein, Giörde Hans, Pauia Tönne, Rokela Laur, Pitque Jacob.

Erstlich ist vor Recht erschienen ein Pauwer mit nahmen Serme Hans, wohnet im Dorf Fegefewer, hatt kleglig zu erkennen gegeben, wie ein Weib mit nahmen Alit genandt, sein Weib im Worme Beridt vergeben, wie daßelbe Sehlig Weib solches geklaget undt darauf gestorben, darauf angeklagte Persohne Alheit gefengklig eingezogen undt umb die bose dat gefraget worden.

1) Dazu sie sich alse balde bekandt.

2) Zum 2ten Bekant sie, das sie 10 Jahr vor einen Wehr Wolff gelauffen undt in der Zeit großen Schaden gethan.

3) Bekandt das sie nebenst zweien andern Zauberern in der Wiek ein Pahr Otzen undt 2 Pferde nebenst andern Viehe mehr darnieder gerißen undt gefreßen.

4) Alse sie befraget: Ob sie nicht wüste, wem die Pferde, Ochsen, Schaffe undt ander Vieh, so sie zerrißen, mochte gewehsen sein, hatt sie hönisch undt lecherlig darauf geantwortet: so leufft der Wolff zu vohr ins Dorff undt fraget, wem die Schaffe gehören eher ehr sie nieder reist.

5) Ist sie befraget, weiln sie sich in Wolffe verwandelen, wie sie dan das

Fleisch genießen können; darauf sie geantwortet: wor sie was an Vieh bekommen, legen sie die Wolffes Gestalt abe undt kochens dar nach ihrer art.

6) Wie sie befraget worden, wor sie die Keßels herkriegen, darein sie das Fleisch kochen, hatt sie hönisch undt lecherlich geantwortet, so kriegen arme Leute nicht einen Keßell.

7) Bekandt das sie Engelbrecht Mecken seine Kelber erwürget.

8) Alse sie von ihrer gesellschaft gefraget worden, hatt sie bekandt auf einen alten Kerll mit nahmen Matz Lübben, das ehr ihr die bose Kunst gelehret habe.

Along with five others who were named as witches or werewolves in the course of this trial, Aleit was sentenced to death by burning. Interestingly, the court construed itself as having acted at the behest of and on behalf of the indigenous peasantry, not the Crown, Church, or landowners, thereby obviating any hint of class domination in its verdict and proceedings:

Aber diese 6 obernante Persohnen ist *von den Pauren* das Recht einge-bracht das sie wegen ihrer bösen thatt mit fewer vom leben zum Tode sollen gebracht werden. Dies eingebracht Urtheil *der Pauwern* haben die obernannten Richter mit ihrem Ja bekrefftiget, darauf die Execution alse balde erfolget.

These six above-named persons were brought before the court *by the peasants* so that they could be taken from life to death by fire on account of their evil deeds. The judgment rendered *by the peasants* was ratified by the assent of the above-named judges, after which the execution quickly followed.

"Ein Hexenprozess," 344, emphasis added.

18. Duni, "'What about Some Good Wether?' Witches and Werewolves in Sixteenth-Century Italy," in Willem de Blécourt, ed., *Werewolf Histories* (New York: Palgrave Macmillan, 2015), 121–41

19. Steven Runciman, *The Medieval Manichee: A Study of the Christian Dualist Heresy* (Cambridge: Cambridge University Press, 1947).

20. Marc Bloch, "Pour une histoire comparée des sociétés européennes," in Bloch, *Mélanges historiques*, vol. I (Paris: S.E.V.P.E.N., 1963), 16–40, especially 22.

21. Emile Benveniste, *Le vocabulaire des institutions indo-européennes*, 2 vols. (Paris: Editions de Minuit, 1969), translated as *Dictionary of Indo-European Concepts and Society* (Chicago: Hau Books, 2016).

22. Michel Foucault, *I, Pierre Rivière, Having Slaughtered My Mother, My*

Sister, and My Brother . . . A Case of Parricide in the 19th Century, trans. Frank Killinek (New York: Pantheon Books, 1975; French original, 1973).

23. Carlo Ginzburg, "Ancora sui riti cinesi: documenti vecchi e nuovi," in *A dieci anni dall'apertura dell'Archivio della Congregazione per la dottrina della fede: storia e archivi dell'Inquisizione (Roma, 21–23 febbraio 2008)* (Rome, 2011), 131–44.

Suggestions for Further Reading

First Publication of the Old Thiess Case (Including the Full Middle German Transcription)

von Bruiningk, Hermann. 1924–28. "Der Werwolf in Livland und das letzte im Wendenschen Landgericht und Dörptschen Hofgericht i. J. 1692 deshalb stattgehabte Strafverfahren." *Mitteilungen aus der livländischen Geschichte* 22.

Important Studies of Old Thiess

de Blécourt, Willem. 2007. "A Journey to Hell: Reconsidering the Livonian 'Werewolf.'" *Magic, Ritual, and Witchcraft* 2.
Ginzburg, Carlo. 1980. *The Night Battles: Witchcraft and Agrarian Cults in the Sixteenth and Seventeenth Centuries*, trans. John Tedeschi and Anne C. Tedeschi. Baltimore: Johns Hopkins University Press.
———. 1991. *Ecstasies: Deciphering the Witches' Sabbath*, trans. Raymond Rosenthal. New York: Pantheon Books.
Höfler, Otto. 1934. *Kultische Geheimbünde der Germanen*. Frankfurt am Main: Moritz Diesterweg Verlag. Reprint, Nordhausen, Traugott Bautz, 2018.

On Livonian Werewolves

Donecker, Stefan. 2009a. "Werewolves on the Baltic Seashore: Monstrous
Frontier of Early Modern Europe, 1550–1700." In Niall Scott, ed., *The Role
of the Monster: Myths and Metaphors of Enduring Evil*. Oxford: Inter-
Disciplinary Press.

———. 2009b. "Livland und seine Werwölfe: Ethnizität und Monstrosität
an der europäischen Peripherie, 1550–1700." *Jahrbuch des baltischen
Deutschtums* 56.

———. 2012. "The Werewolves of Livonia: Lycanthropy and Shape-
Changing in Scholarly Texts, 1550–1720." *Preternature: Critical and
Historical Studies on the Preternatural* 2.

Madar, Maia. 1990. "Estonia I: Werewolves and Poisoners." In Bengt Ankarloo and Gustav Henningsen, eds., *Early Modern European Witchcraft:
Centres and Peripheries*. Oxford: Clarendon.

Metsvahi, Merili. 2001. "Werwolfprozesse in Estland und Livland im 17.
Jahrhundert. Zusammenstöße zwischen der Realität von Richtern
und von Bauern." In Jürgen Beyer and Reet Hiiemäe, eds., *Folklore als
Tatsachenbericht*. Tartu: Sektion für Folkloristik des Estnischen Literaturmuseums.

Plakans, Andrejs. 2000. "Witches and Werewolves in Early Modern Livonia:
An Unfinished Project." In Lars M. Andersson, Anna Jansdotter, Badil
E. B. Persson, and Charlotte Tornbjer, eds., *Rätten: En Festskrift till Bengt
Ankarloo*. Lund: Nordic Academic Press.

Vähi, Tiina. 2006. "The Image of Werewolf in Folk Religion." In Manfried
L. G. Dietrich and Tarmo Kulmar, eds., *The Significance of Base Texts for
the Religious Identity / Die Bedeutung von Grundtexten für die religiöse
Identität*. Münster: Ugarit.

———. 2011. "Werwölfe—Viehdiebe und Räuber im Wolfspelz? Elemente
des archaischen Gewohnheitsrechts in estischen Werwolfvorstellungen."
In Willem de Blécourt and Christa Tuczay, eds., *Tierverwandlungen:
Codierungen und Diskurse*. Tübingen: Francke.

Recent Scholarship on Werewolves in General

Bernhardt-House, Phillip A. 2010. *Werewolves, Magical Hounds, and Dog-
Headed Men in Celtic Literature: A Typological Study of Shape-Shifting*.
Lewiston: Edwin Mellen.

de Blécourt, Willem. 2007. "'I Would Have Eaten You Too': Werewolf
Legends in the Flemish, Dutch and German Area." *Folklore* 118.

———. 2009. "The Werewolf, the Witch, and the Warlock: Aspects of Gender in the Early Modern Period." In Allison Rowlands, ed., *Witchcraft and Masculinities in Early Modern Europe*. New York: Palgrave Macmillan.

de Blécourt, Willem, ed. 2015. *Werewolf Histories*. New York: Palgrave Macmillan.

de Blécourt, Willem, and Christa Tuczay, eds. 2011. *Tierverwandlungen: Codierungen und Diskurse*. Tübingen: Francke.

Buxton, Richard. 1988. "Wolves and Werewolves in Greek Thought." In Jan Bremmer, ed., *Interpretations of Greek Mythology*. London: Routledge.

Bynum, Caroline Walker. 2001. *Metamorphosis and Identity*. New York: Zone Books.

Guðmundsdóttir, Aðalheiður. 2007. "The Werewolf in Medieval Icelandic Literature." *Journal of English and German Philology* 106.

Harf-Lancner, Laurence. 1985. *Métamorphose et bestiaire fantastique au Moyen Âge*. Paris: École Normale Supérieure de Jeunes Filles.

Jacques-Lefèvre, Nicole. 2002. "Such an Impure, Cruel, and Savage Beast: Images of the Werewolf in Demonological Works." In Kathryn A. Edwards, ed., *Werewolves, Witches, and Wandering Spirits: Traditional Belief and Folklore in Early Modern Europe*. Kirksville, MO: Truman State University Press.

Jakobson, Roman, and Marc Szeftel. 1947. "The Vseslav Epos." *Memoirs of the American Folklore Society* 42.

Sconduto, Leslie. 2008. *Metamorphoses of the Werewolf: A Literary Study from Antiquity through the Renaissance*. Jefferson, NC: McFarland.

Index